Cosmopolitan Justice and its Discontents

Cosmopolitan Justice and its Discontents pursues a reflection upon the institutional orders designed to ensure respect for the rule of law, human rights, and social justice. The majority of literature on cosmopolitanism tends to be oriented in sociology, political science or philosophy, and is largely positive. This book fills the lacuna with respect to critical and legal perspectives in this field. In particular, it highlights the importance of international economic law and its institutions when evaluating the evolution of cosmopolitan norms. In addition, it provides critical and multidisciplinary perspectives on Cosmopolitan Justice and Sovereignty; Institutions, Civil Society and Accountability; and Social Exclusion, Migration and Global Markets. This book will be of considerable interest to academics and students concerned with international public and private law, international criminal law, international economic law, human rights, migration, criminology, political science, and philosophy.

Cecilia M. Bailliet is Professor Dr. jur., Deputy Director of the Institute of International and Public Law, and Director of the Masters Programme in Public International Law at the University of Oslo, Norway. Her publications and teaching address International Law, Human Rights and Refugee Law. Her most recent publication is *Security: A Multi-Disciplinary Normative Approach* (Brill, 2009).

Katja Franko Aas is Professor of Criminology at the University of Oslo. She is author of *Globalization and Crime* (SAGE, 2007) and *Sentencing in the Age of Information* (Routledge-Cavendish, 2005) and is currently researching migration and crime control.

Cosmopolitan Justice and its Discontents

Edited by
Cecilia M. Bailliet and
Katja Franko Aas

Routledge
Taylor & Francis Group
a GlassHouse book

First published 2011
by Routledge
2 Park Square, Milton Park, Abingdon, Oxon, OX14 4RN

Simultaneously published in the USA and Canada
by Routledge
711 Third Avenue, New York, NY 10017

A GlassHouse book

Routledge is an imprint of the Taylor & Francis Group, an informa business

British Library Cataloguing in Publication Data
A catalogue record for this book is available from the British Library

Library of Congress Cataloging in Publication Data
Cosmopolitan justice and its discontents/edited by Cecilia M. Bailliet and Katja Franko Aas.
p. cm.
ISBN 978–0–415–59343–4 (hardback) — ISBN 978–0–203–81918–0 (e-book) 1. Cosmopolitanism. 2. Social justice. 3. International organization. 4. Rule of law. 5. Sovereignty. I. Bailliet, Cecilia. II. Aas, Katja Franko.
JZ1308.C667 2011
320.01'1—dc22 2010042392

ISBN: 978–0–415–59343–4 (hbk)
ISBN: 978–0–203–81918–0 (ebk)

Typeset in Times New Roman
by RefineCatch Limited, Bungay, Suffolk
Printed and bound in Great Britain by
CPI Antony Rowe, Chippenham, Wiltshire

For Christophe, who at the age of five declared that he wanted to be a cook, so that he could fly to Africa and feed hungry children (noting that they would teach him how to make proper African recipes).

C.M.B.

For Per Christian in the spirit of achieving a happy ending to his cosmopolitan journeys.

K.F.A.

Contents

Contributors

Cecilia M. Bailliet is Professor, Deputy Director of the Institute of International and Public Law, and Director of the Masters Programme in Public International Law at the University of Oslo, Norway. She received her doctorate at the University of Oslo for her dissertation entitled 'Between Conflict and Consensus: Conciliating Land Disputes in Guatemala, A Study in Preventing and Resolving Internal Displacement'. Her publications and teaching address International Law, Human Rights and Refugee Law. Her most recent publication is *Security: A Multi-Disciplinary Normative Approach* (Brill, 2009).

Katja Franko Aas is Professor at the Institute of Criminology and Sociology of Law, University of Oslo. She has written extensively on issues of globalization, surveillance and uses of information and communication technologies in contemporary penal systems. Her recent publications include *Technologies of Insecurity* (co-edited with H. M. Lomell and H. O. Gundhus) (Routledge-Cavendish, 2009), *Globalization and Crime* (SAGE, 2007) and *Sentencing in the Age of Information: From Faust to Macintosh* (Routledge-Cavendish, 2005).

Sam Adelman teaches Legal Theory and Comparative Human Rights at undergraduate level and several modules in the LLM in International Development Law and Human Rights. He has degrees from the University of the Witwatersrand, Harvard University and Warwick University. He was banned, detained and exiled during the struggle against apartheid. His writings cover legal theory, development and human rights, and he is currently completing a book on sovereignty.

Chrisje Brants is Professor of Criminal Law and Criminal Process at the Willem Pompe Institute for Criminal Law and Criminology, University of Utrecht. She is also a member of the Académie Internationale de Droit Comparé and the Association for International Criminal Justice.

Andreas Føllesdal (PhD Philosophy Harvard University) Professor of Political Philosophy and Director of Research at the Norwegian Centre for Human

Rights at the University of Oslo. He is a member of the Council on Ethics of the Norwegian Government Pension Fund.

Barbara Hudson (BSc, MA, PhD) is Professor (Emeritus) at Lancashire Law School, University of Central Lancashire. Recent publications include *Justice in the Risk Society* (Sage, 2003), 'Punishing Monsters, Judging Aliens: Justice at the Borders of Community', *Australian and New Zealand Journal of Criminology* (2006) and 'Justice in a Time of Terror', *British Journal of Criminology* (2009).

Thomas Hylland Eriksen is Professor of Social Anthropology at the University of Oslo and the author on many books in English and Norwegian on globalisation, identity politics, nationalism, cultural change and other aspects of anthropology, as well as literary essays and polemical writings on a variety of issues. Among his books in English are *Small Places, Large Issues* (3rd edition 2010), *Ethnicity and Nationalism* (3rd edition 2010) and *A World of Insecurity* (ed. with E. Bal and O. Salemink, 2010). His latest book in Norwegian is entitled, simply, *Samfunn* ('Society', 2010).

Malcolm Langford is a Research Fellow at the Norwegian Centre for Human Rights and Director of the Socio-Economic Rights Programme. He has published widely in the field of human rights and development and is an advisor to different UN bodies, governments and NGOs, including organisations intervening in international investment arbitration.

Ronald Tinnevelt is Associate Professor of Legal Philosophy at the Faculty of Law of the Radboud University Nijmegen. He is co-editor of *Between Cosmopolitan Ideals and State Sovereignty* (Palgrave, 2006), *Does Truth Matter?* (Springer, 2008), *Nationalism and Global Justice* (Routledge, 2010) and *Global Democracy and Exclusion* (Blackwell, 2010).

Dr Kyriaki Topidi is a Lecturer and Senior Researcher at the School of Law, University of Lucerne. She teaches, researches and has published in the areas of Comparative and European Law.

Robert Wai is Associate Professor at Osgoode Hall Law School, York University, Toronto. He completed his MPhil in international relations at Oxford and his S.J.D. in international law at Harvard Law School. His current research focuses on the role of private law in transnational economic governance.

Acknowledgements

This book is based on papers submitted to a conference entitled 'Cosmopolitan Justice and its Discontents', held at the University of Oslo on 15–16 October 2009. We wish to express our warm thanks to all the conference participants for their helpful comments during the conference and preparation of this book. We also extend our appreciation to the KULTRANS programme and the Law Faculty at the University of Oslo, for financing the conference. Finally, we are grateful to the editors at Routledge for their patience and, not least, our families for their support.

Introduction

Cecilia M. Bailliet and Katja Franko Aas

At present we are witnessing a state of flux in international law, economics and politics. Unstable financial markets, failed states, forced and clandestine migration, increased regional, cultural, and religious polarization, as well as the phenomenon of transnational organized crime all present formidable challenges. This book is based on the recognition that there is a need for research reflecting upon institutional orders designed to ensure respect for the rule of law, human rights, and social justice. Cosmopolitanism is attributed as having had a direct impact on the evolution of international law, specifically in the arena of human rights, migration, labour rights, international criminal law, security, trade and the protection of the environment. It denotes a philosophical, ethical and scientific world view which aims to transcend national boundaries and a nationalist, state-centred outlook on society and justice. Although the idea has long historic antecedents, most notably in Kant's writing on cosmopolitanism and natural law, theories of cosmopolitan justice have acquired a particular momentum in the past two decades with the acceleration of global interconnectedness. The chapters in this volume present different perceptions of cosmopolitanism, including legal, moral, institutional, identity, and commercial. We have noted that the majority of literature on cosmopolitanism tends to be oriented in sociology, political science or philosophy, and is largely positive. There is a lacuna with respect to legal literature in this field. This book seeks to fill this void by contributing legal perspectives, in particular highlighting the importance of international economic law and its institutions when evaluating the evolution of cosmopolitan norms. The contributions in this collection seek to explore discontents within the cosmopolitan imaginary, examine criticisms against its classic conceptions, and develop innovative theoretical and empirical interpretations and applications.

The book presents the discontents in various manifestations, such as the tension between justice 'from above' (the notion of a world state, or the example of the International Criminal Court), as well as 'from below' (protests against the EU, multilateral investment regimes, and the use of military force). Moreover, we examine cosmopolitanism against the background of globalization. Cosmopolitanism can be seen as a form of globalism, i.e. globalization turned into poltical action (Beck, 2000). And although globalization has led to increased interconnectedness and interdependence among peoples, it has also resulted in a deepening of unequal power relations. The emergence of security and financial crises has prompted cries for re-evaluation of existing forms of governance and institutional orders. Cosmopolitanism can be thereby seen both as a globalizing force of its own and an attempt to amend some of the ills produced by neo-liberalism. Herein also lies the inherent duality of cosmopolitan and other universal projects, their democratic potential and hegemonic undertones. As Tsing (2005: 76) points out: 'Universalism is implicated in *both* imperial schemes to control the world and libratory mobilizations for justice and empowerment. Universalism inspires expansion – for both the powerful and the powerless.'

Paraphrasing Tsing, a question can be asked: how does the universality of a concept such as global justice or humanity operate in a 'world of friction', a world marked by inequality on multiple levels? Generally speaking, ideas of cosmopolitan justice are marked by attempts to develop a more just global order and achieve some form of 'planetary conviviality' (Mignolo, 2000). Although covering a variety of theoretical and normative perspectives, they advocate for a more inclusive social imaginary recognizing our 'common humanity' (Appiah, 2006) and include a variety of normative and political choices, which in various degrees aspire towards ethical universalism, global governance and, ultimately, a shared world citizenship. Their aim is not just to expand the concepts and institutions of justice beyond national borders, but also creating principles for 'global justice' (Pogge, 2001) and norms of universal justice which would acknowledge every human being as a rights-deserving subject. One of the main preoccupations of cosmopolitan thinkers has been to develop new forms of political community which would move beyond state-centred models of citizenship (Benhabib, 2004) and new models of 'global democracy' which override the primacy traditionally given to the nation-state (Archibugi, 2003, 2008). Other central objectives include: to promote and develop new principles for tolerance and inter-cultural dialogue (Kymlicka, 1996; Delanty, 2009); acceptance of difference, hospitality and forgiveness (Derrida, 2001; Benhabib, 2004); strengthen global ethical responsibility regarding issues such as warfare, respond to atrocities and crimes against humanity, and address poverty and the security realities of an emerging 'world risk society' (Pogge, 2001; Beck, 2009).

Although aiming at ethical universality, the concept of cosmopolitanism has been fraught with controversy and open to several critiques directed particularly at the undemocratic nature of existing international institutions and the importance of preserving national democracy, belonging and state sovereignty (Calhoun, 2007). Several observers have pointed to the inability of cosmopolitanism to acknowledge global inequalities and global power relations, particularly evident in the recent international patterns of humanitarian interventions (Douzinas, 2007). Although covering a variety of institutional and social practices (Nowicka and Rovisco, 2009), cosmopolitanism has been portrayed by skeptical voices as NGO evangelism, imperialism, or simply just as a more banal reflection of Western middle-class lifestyles. Calhoun (2001) thus argues that cosmopolitanism is not only a moral and political philosophy, but is also too often 'the class consciousness of frequent travellers', and suggests that much cosmopolitanism 'misrecognizes its own social foundations, assuming these to be universal when in fact they are representative of particular social locations'.

Consequently, there have been several attempts to reclaim the cosmopolitan idea from non-Western or subaltern positions, so to speak 'from below' (Sousa Santos and Rodriguez-Garavito, 2005; Mignolo, 2000). Instead of cosmopolitanism managed 'from above', these perspectives seek to reinvent cosmopolitanism by insisting on its 'unconditional inclusiveness' of marginalized voices, aiming to empower people within communities and traditions, not in spite of them. These perspectives have often stemmed from post-colonial critiques and have stressed the centrality of Southern epistemologies with the focus on cosmopolitan pluralism rather than universalism (Sousa Santos, 2007). Mignolo thus proposes 'critical cosmopolitanism' which can provide a critical perspective on what he terms global designs as well as Eurocentric humanitarianism:

> Instead of cosmopolitanism managed from above (that is, global designs), I am proposing cosmopolitanism, critical and dialogic, emerging from the various spatial and historical locations of the colonial difference.
>
> (Mignolo 2000: 741)

Rather than immediately judging the merits of these characterizations, the chapters within this collection bring together a number of pros and cons to paint a complex and intricate picture of contemporary attempts to create justice in a globalizing world. They address legal, philosophical, theoretical, and empirical aspects of cosmopolitan justice. There is examinination of the changing form of sovereignty and civil society as well as the transnational functions of poltical and legal institutions in times of flux. We review the role of individuals, and the relationship and boundaries between classic civic duties and modern allegiance towards global institutions and norms. Query is made as to whether cosmopolitan federalism is the same as international law. Most innovatively, our authors explain the relevance and challenges of commercial cosmopolitanism. How do we regulate markets and corporations when governments seem to be increasingly unable to do so? As a whole, the chapters ponder whether we need cosmopolitan principles to underscore international law and its institutions in order to produce cosmopolitan justice. Some solutions may be found in smaller scale initiatives rather than formal, grand 'global designs', for example the Council of Ethics of the Norwegian Pension Fund (presented in Føllesdahl's chapter), and the notion of everyday cosmopolitanism discussed in the epilogue by Hylland Eriksen.

Part I contains two chapters presenting juxtaposed approaches to sovereignty and governance. Adelman explores whether it is possible to protect both sovereignty and human rights. He traces neo-conservative developments, such as the application of pre-emptive self-defense and regime change, noting that 'transnational institutions are rendered more supine in the "teeth of sovereign rationality".' He queries whether human rights are 'outside' of sovereignty. He believes that human rights must evolve to address non-state actors, that they should place socio-economic rights on the same level as civil and political rights, and that they should address collective rights, not only individual rights. Pragmatically, he asserts that 'Despite assertions of global citizenship, human entitlements remain overwhelmingly determined by the accident of birth or sovereign prerogative. The biggest unsolved political problem of modernity, sovereignty is also the largest impediment to the cosmopolitan vision.'

Tinnevelt assumes a more optimistic persepective when discussing the viability of a world state. He notes that 'the leap from Walzer's third degree global pluralism or Habermas' proposal for a world domestic politics without a world state, to a subsidiary and federal world republic isn't that far.' The analysis seeks to present arguments against the world state and discusses whether they have any power of persuasion against two possible forms of the world state: (a) a unified global state and (b) a minimal world state. Nevertheless, he warns that principles of subsidiarity and all-affectedness contain a tendency to hierarchical centralization, and there remain tensions between the contradictory demands for centralization and decentralization.

Part II contains two chapters which address varied approaches to accountability, institutions, and the role of civil society. The first demonstrates the weakness of an individualized approach to guilt, as well as the limitations of the International Criminal Court; and the second reveals the overlooked strength of individual and local processes seeking accountability for the use of force.

Brants discusses the inability to address collective guilt in international criminal law, examining dilemmas presented by the ICC. She asserts that '[C]riminal law shares the guilt of the landscape – it becomes a means of not having to face the truth, a sheet to cover one's face.' She notes that 'international criminal justice cannot fulfil its own proclaimed goals of retribution, deterrence, redress, restoration of stable social relations, and the establishment of a legitimate collective memory, all of which require a "truthful account" of what took place.' Brants concludes that: 'the result is that too much law leads to too little justice. Where cosmopolitanism appears to want to be all things to all people, it suffers inevitably from contradictions and even a tendency to self-destruct, and, as a self-proclaimed part of the cosmopolitan ideal, international criminal justice is similarly afflicted, even in the details of the legal principles that are institutionalized in substantive international criminal law.'

Bailliet seeks recognition of the shifting trends of local and national institutional processes by which to pursue the emancipatory vision of true cosmopolitan justice. She points to dilemmas related to deployment of US armed troops abroad in security engagements from the perspective of institutional cosmopolitanism. Bailliet seeks to describe how existing local and national legal and quasi-legal structures were utilized by an individual soldier to voice contestation and dissent against the engagement of US troops in Iraq (characterized as lacking both legality and legitimacy). She examines the processes of 'bottom-up' discourses of minorities and local communities challenging the executive branch for defying its juridical legitimacy within the national intra-system jurisdictional level. Rather than presenting the local, domestic, and international legal orders as being in competition, she seek to present them as both overlapping and presenting gaps which are filled by social actors in order to buttress the gradual evolution of the international rule of law.

Part III reviews dilemmas presented by regional institutions and their treatment of 'the other', as represented by minorities, migrants, and detainees.

Topidi examines the impact that Turkish membership mighty have on the future of the EU, and vice versa, with special consideration of the values of diversity, equality and non-discrimination. She discusses the empirical examples of the headscarf debate, minority languages, and religious beliefs, freedom of expression and political participation in order to consider whether EU norms contribute in the direction of a more humane governance model.

Hudson asserts that 'cosmopolitan justice needs more than courts and conventions'. She characterizes cosmopolitan justice as the counterpart of cosmopolitics, examining the situation of migrants and detainees accused of engaging in terror. Hudson suggests that 'cosmopolitan justice is a discursive form of justice: it gives those who come before it the opportunity to tell their stories, to give an account of who they are, what they have or have not done, and what their needs are. She calls for cosmopolitanism from both above and below to provide hospitality to 'the stranger'.

Franko Aas delineates a 'discursive and political development of cosmopolitanism against a seemingly contradicting trend: the growing border-consciousness and border-defensiveness of Western societies'. Using the example of European borders and border policing, she argues that borders are not only a source of demarcation but also of pan-European solidarity and integration. Aas suggests that 'at the same time, the coupling of universalistic ethics with the essence of Europeanness can, paradoxically, transform cosmopolitanism into a language of exclusion'. She states: 'Borders point to the continued importance of space and power relations inscribed in space. They serve as a potent reminder that in the abstract totality of the globe, the local and the national carries an enduring salience.' Aas concludes that 'it is precisely this entanglement – political, discursive and practical – between migration and illegality which sustains the humanitarian anarchy in Europe's borderlands.'

Part IV contains three chapters that address the notion of commercial cosmopolitanism and its challenges. The first chapter highlights the importance of recognizing transnational economic law as a relevant arena for cosmopolitan analysis, the second chapter offers critical consideration of dilemmas and contradictions within this arena, and the third chapter discusses commercial cosmopolitanism in practice. Wai asserts that transnational economic law permits simultaneous consideration of state and non-state normative orders, and their interrelationship. He highlights the spread of private ordering through the use of the *lex mercatoria* and international commercial arbitration. Wai also cites the growth of voluntary norms of corporate social responsibility and their increased relevance for social regulation in many areas of traditional concern for public law, such as human rights, corruption, environment and labour. He explains that 'private dispute resolution may be less inclined to consider matters of either domestic or transnational public policy. A business law dispute heard in a state court with state laws in the background might be more alert than an arbitration tribunal with *lex mercatoria* in the background to as to how the contractual relation was related human rights or consumer concerns.' He concludes that the institutional form to achieve cosmopolitan justice in the global economy will be a blend of traditional and novel, of individual, state, and international all in an evolving and interlinked relation.

Langford narrates the story of how cosmopolitanism from below ('the world's first global internet and street campaign') prevented the development of a multilateral investment treaty in the late 1990s but left in place a decentralized, fragmented system. He warns that international arbitration tribunals apply an 'expanisve' interpretation of property rights when interpreting bilateral (and trilateral) investment and trade treaties. He offers responsive options, such as the rejection of bilateral investment treaties (BITs), exhaustion of domestic remedies, use of international human rights courts, and integration of human rights within arbitration tribunals.

Føllesdahl explains that 'new forms of economic globalization have rendered developed states less able to protect their citizens – not to mention the governments of developing countries ... economically weaker states often face several new challenges under these forms of globalization. Sometimes conventions or regional cooperation help states maintain control, but many poor or weak states may be unable to uphold strict labour and human rights standards against corporations – especially multinationals who can credibly threaten to move to other, more friendly jurisdictions.' He addresses the responsibilities of corporations and investors in a case study examining the normative constraints on the Norwegian Government Pension Fund in light of cosmopolitan justice. Føllesdahl explores responses to corporate engagement in human rights violations, corruption, and environmental damage in the form of investment strategies which may pursue engagement or divestment.

The Epilogue is provided by Hylland Eriksen, who discusses the concept of quotidian cosmopolitan justice and its link to a fractured notion of hospitality, warning that 'cosmopolitanism may degenerate into missionary liberalism, but it may also degenerate into indifference'.

Rather than simply defending the merits of either cosmopolitan evangelism or its equally unnuanced, nihilist critique, the collected papers presented in this volume present a range of approaches. They underscore that cosmopolitan justice (in its empirical and theoretical guises) is very much a work in progress – perhaps offering a response to the fragmentation of international law and the challenge of the contemporary transnational legal order.

References

Calhoun, C. (2001) 'The Necessity and Limits of Cosmopolitanism: Local Democracy in a Global Context', Paper presented to UNESCO/ISSC conference, 'Identity and Difference in the Global Era', Candido Mendes University, Rio de Janeiro, 20–23 May 2001.

Douzinas, K. (2007) *Human Rights and Empire: The political philosophy of cosmopolitanism*. Abingdon: Routledge-Cavendish.

Mignolo, W. D. (2000) 'The Many Faces of Cosmopolis: Border Thinking and Critical Cosmopolitanism', *Public Culture* 12(3): 721–48.

Santos, B. d'Sousa (ed.) (2007) *Another Knowledge is Possible: Beyond Northern Epistemologies*. London: Verso.

Santos, B. d'Sousa and C. A. Rodriguez-Garavito (eds), (2005) *Law and Globalization from Below*. Cambridge: Cambridge University Press.

Tsing, A. L. (2005) *Friction: An Ethnography of Global Connection*. Princeton, NJ: Princeton University Press.

Part I

Chapter 1

Cosmopolitan sovereignty

Sam Adelman

> Cosmopolitan sovereignty, the only type of global sovereignty on offer, claims the garments of value (freedom, dignity, emancipation) but is realised in the ubiquitous violence of economic competition, war as police action and empty but ever-present legality. Law as validity without significance is the main form of the social bond.
>
> Costas Douzinas[1]

1.1 THE 'NEW' COSMOPOLITANISM

Cosmopolitanism is resurgent. In its new incarnation it 'is a way of thinking that declares its opposition to all forms of ethnic nationalism and religious fundamentalism as well as to the economic imperatives of global capitalism. It perceives the integrity of contemporary political life as threatened both by the globalization of markets and by regressive forms of revolt against globalization, and aims to reconstruct political life on the basis of an enlightened vision of peaceful relations between nation states, human rights shared by all world citizens, and a global legal order buttressed by a global civil society' (Fine, 2003: 452). The cosmopolitan vision (Beck, 2006) is of an unbounded, virtually deterritorialized common moral community in which the principle of sovereignty is subordinated to that of humanity.[2]

For cosmopolitan thinkers like Beck and Habermas, the European Union is a cosmopolitan laboratory in which the means of securing peace under the rule of

1 Douzinas (2007b: 290).

2 Hannah Arendt (1951: xi), who did not regard herself as a cosmopolitan thinker, argued that 'human dignity needs a new guarantee which can be found only in a new political principle, a new law on earth, whose validity this time must comprehend the whole of humanity, while its power must remain strictly limited, rooted in and controlled by newly defined territorial entities' with the crucial proviso that this power 'must remain strictly limited, rooted in and controlled by newly defined territorial entities'.

law are being developed in a continent historically riven by violence through the construction of a post-sovereign community that presents the world with a vision of its cosmopolitan future. Notwithstanding its myriad democratic deficits, for Giddens this model of cosmopolitan democracy is 'the most important and promising experiment in transnational governance'.[3] 'Europe' is an idea, ideal and ideology as much as a physical space, the harbinger of Kant's dream of perpetual peace. If so, it has been a long time coming for it was in 1795 that Kant asserted that 'The peoples of the earth have entered in varying degrees into a universal community, and it is developed to the point where a violation of laws in one part of the world is felt everywhere. The idea of a cosmopolitan law is therefore not fantastic and overstrained; it is a necessary complement to the unwritten code of political and international law, transforming it into a universal law of humanity' (Kant, 1991: 107–8).[4] Cosmopolitan law would be tantamount to a new social contract that would facilitate internationally what Hobbes' covenant had secured internally: the forging of law and order from anarchy and chaos. As Kant was aware, however, since the dawn of modernity, sovereignty has been the rock on which cosmopolitanism has always been in danger of foundering. Since the possibility of potentially despotic world state could not be countenanced, the predilection towards violence of nation-states could best be controlled, he argued, through the construction of a league of republican states (with paradoxically coercive powers) in which individual freedoms had already been achieved and which would respect the categorical imperative of hospitality as the basis for world citizenship. Unfortunately, the history of the League of Nations and the UN has revealed the unwillingness of sovereign states to cede sovereignty, and thus exposed the limitations in his prescription that the new cosmopolitanism seeks to overcome. This recalcitrance has not deterred cosmopolitan dreamers from the time of the Stoics, from whom the concept originated (Douzinas, 2007: ch. 7).

The concept received a shot in the arm at the end of the Cold War, when circumstances appeared so propitious that Fukuyama (1992) notoriously proclaimed the triumph of liberal democracy and capitalism at the end of history. Now, it was hoped, the provisions in the International Bill of Rights would decisively shift the organizing principle of the international from sovereignty to human rights. For Beck and Habermas, cosmopolitanism is less an ideal than an inevitability arising from inexorable pressures towards interdependence and interconnectedness in the global age. Beck argues that successful states will be those which abandon the national outlook and the sovereign

3 Cited in Ward (2003: 2107).

4 Emerging to complement constitutional and international law, Kant envisaged a cosmopolitan law under which individuals would have rights as 'citizens of the earth'. See Archibugi (1995).

prerogatives that characterized the Westphalian system during modernity,[5] while Habermas:

> presents cosmopolitanism as the *logical culmination* of the principles of right on which enlightenment was founded. The underlying argument is that the universal principles of right and law, though once swamped by the particularistic self assertion of one nation against another, are 'best suited to the identity of world citizens, not to that of citizens of a particular state that has to maintain itself against other states'. For Habermas, there is a sense in which the rational necessity of cosmopolitanism is not up for discussion, and a democratic community cannot opt out of the project of realising constitutional principles at the national, transnational and global levels.
>
> (Fine 2007: 58, citing Habermas 2006: 133; emphasis in original)[6]

In fact, the implosion of the Soviet Union and Yugoslavia unleashed a tide of nationalism and ethnic conflict.[7] In Kosovo, the delivery of liberal democracy and the rule of law came from on high, packaged in bombs, in a militarized humanitarian intervention of dubious legality that set the tone for what followed in Iraq, Chechnya, and elsewhere. Fundamentalisms flourished, with Islamism finding its *doppelgänger* in neo-conservatism, and neo-liberalism imposing the violence of the market. Since 2001, it is sovereignty – a principle more universally adhered to than human rights – that has been resurgent. Ostensibly the means of promoting democracy and human rights, the 'war on terror' privileged realism, unilateralism, pre-emptive regime change and celebrated might. Regime change may have brought about a change in the tone of US foreign policy in 2009, but the new president had no qualms in insisting that 'State sovereignty must be a cornerstone of international order.'[8] In his speech in Cairo in July 2009, Obama sounded like

5 Beck argues that the methodological nationalism that characterized the social sciences throughout the twentieth century is counterproductive and redundant, and that it is illogical to use the state as the point of departure in analysing law, politics, culture and society. See Beck (2005, 2006) and Beck and Grande (2007).

6 It is striking how Habermas and Beck conclude, albeit for different reasons, that cosmopolitanism is somehow inevitable, leading one to contemplate the role of German history in the inflection they give to the concept.

7 The fact that most cosmopolitan thinkers accept that people are products of specific histories and therefore do not dispute the significance or legitimacy of national boundaries exacerbates the difficulties involved in seeking to reconcile their universalist vision with the homogenised erosion of individual particularity (see Sypnowich, 2005). Jews long symbolized the particularity of the rootless cosmopolitan, the alien other and the 'legitimate' target of Nazi and Bolshevik oppression. In the contemporary period it is the capitalist global elite whose wealth enables them largely to transcend the limitations of nationality that regularly serves to highlight the immiseration of the majority of the world's population; see the discussion on citizenship below.

8 Speech in Cairo, 7 July 2009: http://www.america.gov/st/texttrans-english/2009/July/2009070706 2839abretnuh3.549922e-02.html.

a model cosmopolitan in calling for an international order in which sovereignty and human rights are both protected. The question this chapter addresses is whether this is possible.

The paradox of neo-conservatism is that the 'coalitions of the willing' sought to redraft international law in pursuit of its own cosmopolitan vision. 'At the technical juridico-political level, the foundations of the "new" international law are being laid through a complex mosaic of the individual and collective right to "pre-emptive" self-defence, justifications for the use of United Nations unsanctioned use of force for the violent achievement of "regime change," and the equally violent disregard for the hitherto relatively settled norms of international humanitarian law' (Baxi, 2005: 35). This involved a systematic attempt to make transnational institutions, the building blocks on which the new cosmopolitanism is supposedly being constructed, more supine in the teeth of sovereign rationality. It is difficult to imagine a less cosmopolitan body than the UN Security Council[9] but this is perhaps appropriate in the dystopia in which 'Global capitalism has denuded the world of meaning and humanitarian violence has drained the moral universe of value. Human rights and cosmopolitanism contribute to this loss' (Douzinas, 2007b: 293).

Habermas has sought to rehabilitate Kant's vision in terms appropriate to the twenty-first century by synchronizing the legitimacy of the constitutional nation-state with the authority of cosmopolitan law and institutions through constitutional patriotism (Habermas, 2001). 'Constitutional patriotism refers *both* to a shared attachment towards universalistic principles *and* to the actualisation of these principles in the form of particular national institutions. It is this "both–and" quality that allows constitutional patriotism to nurture a disposition of attachment to one's country and be compatible with the transformed self-consciousness of world citizens' (Fine, 2007: 42; emphases in original). He sees the EU as a novel form of political community that performs in the post-national era the role of the nation-state in modernity. In doing so, he has been confronted by a problem common to cosmopolitan arguments, namely the democratic and legitimacy deficits that arise from the lack of accountability of meta-national institutions (Kymlicka, 2001; Fine, 2007). The problem is compounded by the fact that rights are overwhelmingly contingent upon membership, i.e. citizenship of states whose sovereignty rests on what Weber acutely described as a monopoly of legitimate

9 The use of the veto by the permanent members of the UN Security Council means that it operates more often than not as an anti-cosmopolitan body. The International Criminal Court constitutes a step forward but it too is deeply flawed, with countries like the US and Israel making sovereign decisions to opt out, and its failure to indict Blair creating the perception that it is an instrument of West Western justice – leading the African Union to further the cosmopolitan cause by refusing to accept the legitimacy of its indictment of Sudanese president Bashir. As such, the ICC is an apt symbol of the contradictory and uneven nature of the cosmopolitan project. The international economic institutions have always been anti-cosmopolitan organizations.

violence. On the one horn of the dilemma confronting cosmopolitanism is whether the effective enforcement of global citizenship requires a global state with a similar monopoly. On the other is the possibility that retention of this monopoly by nation-states will hole the project below the waterline.

1.2 HUMAN RIGHTS

In a juridico-political order that remains overwhelmingly sovereign-centric, states are the guarantors of the rights that they have so persistently violated. The paradox of universal human rights is that in order to be protected at all they must be constitutionalized or legislated as civic or citizen rights under sovereign jurisdiction. Apart from the European human rights regime, the erosion of the sovereign monopoly of law caused by the growing lawmaking powers of non-state actors has hardly dented the capacity of sovereign states to determine the parameters and enforcement of human rights law. It might be argued that the ICC is still in its infancy and universal jurisdiction is emergent but inchoate but the cosmopolitan faith in the capacity of transnational institutions has thus far been misplaced, not least because of the extent to which they remain mediated by sovereign rationality. This is equally true of the EU even if member states have split, shared, pooled or otherwise diluted their sovereignty to a greater degree than elsewhere. Far from disappearing, sovereignty is adapting to meet the changed circumstances wrought by globalization.[10]

Despite the erosion of sovereign immunity and impunity through the gradual emergence of universal jurisdiction and the establishment of tribunals from Nuremberg to the ICC, human rights continue to defer to sovereignty and will do so as long as their promises and possibilities are overdetermined by the sovereign rationality they are designed to control. Unless and until this is achieved they will, to paraphrase Marx, be human rights in but not for themselves. This interpretation assumes that they are capable of constituting a genuine alternative organizing principle but only if they break the bonds of sovereign rationality. However, there is a second possibility more disconcerting to the cosmopolitan vision: that human rights are part of the problem of contemporary politics and that they may even be

10 Claims about the construction of a novel post-sovereign order tend to underplay the continued role of traditional, modern sovereignty in the Union. The power of the Council of Ministers (in effect a gathering of sovereigns) far outweighs that of the parliament, and this 'residual' sovereignty has regularly been used by member states to opt out of aspects of the Union deemed incompatible with that sovereignty, such as the social chapter and the common currency. The fact that no member state has thus far refused to enforce a decision of the European Court of Human Rights or the European Court of Justice provides support for the cosmopolitan argument about the possibility of constructing an effective supranational rights regime, with two major provisos: it is a regime in which civil and political rights take priority over socio-economic rights and in which the relative rightlessness of non-citizens is still a significant problem.

aporetic (Agamben, 1998; Ranciere, 2004). Is it possible to think human rights outside and not merely against sovereignty?

Within three years of the end of the Second World War a contradiction was locked into the reformulated international juridico-political order. In 1945, sovereignty was further entrenched as the foundational principle of international relations and international legal subjectivity in the UN Charter. In contrast, in 1948 the UDHR proffered an almost diametrically opposed paradigm in which the protection and promotion of human rights would constitute the basic norm of the international order. Contemporary cosmopolitanism may be viewed as an attempt to resolve this contradiction through a recalibration of the balance between the individual and the state and the emergence of global citizenship rights less and less contingent upon sovereign prerogative. The implicit assumption is that human rights and sovereignty are *equally* capable *in principle* of constituting the basic norm of global order, but this will only become possible when the terrain on which the debate occurs is no longer determined by sovereign rationality.[11] In one sense the problem is less a matter of relative weight than of genealogy. The problem of rights may be as longstanding as the existence of people in political communities, but in *modernity* it takes a particular form from the mythical moment in which Hobbes' covenant is concluded. Rights become an issue as soon as the Leviathan emerges in the original exception. *Modern* rights are coextensive with the form of sovereignty that provokes them and henceforth determines the conditions in which they will be fought for.[12] If it were not for Westphalia, the relationship between the individual and the political community would doubtless have remained a burning issue, but not in the form that it would now assume. Supposedly inherent and inalienable natural rights, the ceding of which is a paradoxical precondition for the social contract, take on a different character when they become the gift of the sovereign and a basis of struggle. Rights and sovereignty now share genealogy and genetics. At the birth of the modern Western political order it is as if the evil, selfish and violent dizygotic twin emerges first and proceeds to torment its sibling.

To some extent the point being made is banal – of course human rights are designed to limit sovereign excess, but they must be both more than this and different if the cosmopolitan vision is to be realized. They must respond to the

11 The closest analogy is the equality-difference debate in liberal feminism, which implicitly accepts men as the yardstick and patriarchy as the terrain of contestation. As radical feminists have argued, the terms of the debate and the terrain on which it is fought must be changed. I discuss this aspect of human rights at greater length in a forthcoming monograph entitled *Sovereignty, Human Rights and Global Order*, and do so irrespective of other problems associated with the dominant (liberal) conception of human rights such as their unstable philosophical foundations.

12 Kant regarded the Westphalian system, which celebrates the absence of external constraints, as depraved. He belaboured the fact that rulers could glory in their 'power to order thousands of people to immolate themselves for a cause which does not truly concern them, while he himself need not incur any danger whatsoever' (Kant, 1991: 103, cited in Fine, 2007: 23).

emergence of decentred, deterritorialized postmodern sovereignty (Hardt and Negri, 2000), not least by extending their reach to include non-state actors. They must expand the limited conception that inheres in too much cosmopolitan thinking that results in an overemphasis on civil and political rights over socio-economic and cultural rights, and on the individual at the expense of the collective.[13] On one level the history of human rights has unfolded as a series of appropriations and re-appropriations (Baxi, 2006). In the eighteenth century, the attack on sovereignty during the French Revolution also constituted the universalization of the particular demands of white, Christian, largely bourgeois men in the form of the Declaration of the Rights of Man and Citizen. In the twentieth century, global capitalism sought to re-appropriate them in the form of trade-related, market friendly human rights, and neo-conservatives have sought in this century to fashion them in their own image in the guise of liberal humanitarian interventionism. Baxi argues that the traditional UDHR human rights paradigm 'is steadily, but surely, being *supplanted* by that of trade-related, market-friendly human rights (TRMFHR) under the auspices of contemporary globalization' (Baxi, 2006: 235; emphasis in original).[14] To resonate beyond the West, cosmopolitanism must go beyond liberalism and address the suspicion that it is but one more neo-colonial incarnation of the Euro-American tendency to universalize its particular needs. Against Baxi's argument that human rights are the products of struggle and Santos' assertion that a meaningful cosmopolitanism can only be constructed from below (Santos, 2002), neo-Kantian cosmopolitanism has yet to demonstrate the superiority of its essentially metaphysical deontology in which the philosophically problematic notion of natural law remains central. The idea that all human beings have equal worth in a single moral community is noble, if not utopian, but it difficult to reconcile with the importance of local contexts, histories, interpretations and traditions, i.e. culture, without preserving the sovereign entities it is designed to constrain – a difficulty compounded by its ever-closer associations with capitalist globalization.

When Kant revived the cosmopolitan ideal, he did so not by sketching his prescription for a common normative and moral order on a *tabula rasa*, but in response to the depredations of the Westphalian system. Caught between the Scylla of human rights and the Charybdis of sovereignty, cosmopolitanism unsuccessfully seeks to square the circle. Thus Held, for example:

> While states are hugely important vehicles to aid the delivery of effective regulation, equal liberty, and social justice, *they should not be thought of as ontologically privileged.* They can be judged by how far they deliver these public goods and how far they fail; for the history of states is marked, of course, not just by phases of bad leadership and corruption but also by the

13 I think this is a valid point despite the notable work on global justice of writers like Thomas Pogge.
14 See also Adelman (2008).

> most brutal episodes. A cosmopolitanism relevant to our global age must take this as *a starting point*.
>
> (Held, 2005: 10; my emphases)

Similarly, Nussbaum suggests that cosmopolitan must reconcile itself to the desirability and inevitability of sovereignty in calling for a new social contract in the form of a 'global bargain' as the basis for global citizenship.[15] The cosmopolitan hope appears to be that global public reasoning will bring law and order to the anarchy and chaos of the displaced internal state of nature through governance in the same way sovereignty did through government, thereby obviating the need for the potentially despotic world state against which Kant warned; that a cosmopolitan league of republican states (whose human rights records are hardly glittering) can gainsay the history of modern sovereignty.[16] Far from arguing in favour of a global state, the point I am making is that the relationship between sovereignty and statehood (and they are not theoretically coextensive) remains undertheorized in cosmopolitan literature. Indeed, one of the main paradoxes of cosmopolitanism and capitalist globalization (the logic of which is complete deterritorialization) is the extent to which they suggest the continued importance of sovereignty as a bulwark against market fundamentalism and cultural homogenization.

Rejecting the possibility of transcendental justice achieved through a perfect set of institutions, Sen argues that:

> Perfect global justice through an impeccably just set of institutions, even if such a thing could be identified, would certainly demand a sovereign global state, and in the absence of such a state, questions of global justice appear to the transcendentalists to be impossible.
>
> (Sen, 2009: 25)[17]

The 'war on terror' provoked transnational surveillance states into passing an avalanche of security legislation, resulting in perhaps the greatest state of anomie

15 'National sovereignty … has moral importance, as a way people have of asserting their right to give themselves laws' (Nussbaum, 2005: 214).

16 Space precludes a fuller discussion of any periodization of sovereignty, which undoubtedly existed in the ancient, premodern world – Rome being a good example. Similarly, contemporary notions of sovereignty, ranging from Hardt and Negri to Beck, are discussed in the context of postmodernity or a second modernity under capitalist globalization. Unless otherwise indicated, all references to sovereignty in this paper should be understood as referring to modern sovereignty which, I argue, endured from the Peace of Westphalia in 1648 to the adoption of the Universal Declaration of Human Rights in 1948.

17 Sen makes a valid point, notwithstanding my reservations about his liberal reformist approach to justice in general and my deeper reservations about his approval of Nagel's reactionary stance on global justice in the same section (Nagel, 2005).

in human history, creating lawless spaces, symbolized for Agamben by the camp: 'the hidden matrix and *nomos* of the political space in which we are still living' (Agamben, 1998: 174). The ideal of global citizenship in a cosmopolitan order is thus increasingly contradicted by the production of rightlessness across the world, leading Agamben to argue that:

> [G]iven the by now unstoppable decline of the nation-state and the general corrosion of traditional political-juridical categories, the refugee is perhaps the only thinkable figure for the people of our time and the only one in which one may see today – at least until the process of dissolution of the nation-state and of its sovereignty has achieved full completion – the forms and limits of a coming political community.
>
> (Agamben, 2000: 16)

1.3 CITIZENSHIP

Citizenship is an inherently exclusive concept. Like a Blakean antinomy, it is comprehensible only in relation to what it is not. Based on the idea of membership of a political community, it determines who is included and excluded, and hence their entitlements. For cosmopolitans, membership of the human community takes precedence over that of territorially delineated polities.[18] As Hannah Arendt cogently argued, the problem with this understanding of citizenship is that it is always at the mercy of sovereignty. She lucidly alerts us to the distinction between civic rights and human rights (putatively universal rights based on human-ness).[19] Despite assertions of global citizenship, human entitlements remain overwhelmingly determined by the accident of birth or sovereign prerogative. The biggest unsolved political problem of modernity, sovereignty is also the largest impediment to the cosmopolitan vision.

The refugee is the aporetic symbol of human rights for Arendt as well, the stateless person who ostensibly has universal rights by virtue of his humanity but finds himself unable to exercise his civil and political rights when he is ejected from sovereignty's fateful biopolitical embrace:[20] 'The conception of human rights,

18 Held elucidates eight principles that he regards as underpinning contemporary cosmopolitanism, the first of which is 'that the ultimate units of moral concern are individual human beings, not states or other particular forms of human association. Humankind belongs to a single moral realm in which each person is regarded as equally worthy of respect and consideration' (Held, 2005: 12). Note the mismatch between this assertion and international legal subjectivity which, in a sovereign-centric order, overwhelmingly privileges states over individuals.

19 For a typically coruscating critique of essentialist conceptions of the human, see Douzinas (2007a).

20 The 1951 Convention covers only 'political' refugees with a well-founded fear of persecution. The role of sovereignty in the creation of 'economic' refugees attracts no international legal protection at all in a global economy in which borders are increasingly porous to goods, services and information, but not to those who produce them.

based upon the assumed existence of a human being as such, broke down at the very moment when those who professed to believe in it were for the first time confronted with people who had indeed lost all other qualities and specific relationships – except that they were still human' (Arendt, 1951: 295).

For Benhabib, the history of post-war Europe is that of the gradual reconciliation of human rights and sovereignty through the willing subordination of the latter and the conformity of domestic law to the ethically higher form of legality provided by the former. The resultant *nomos* will be consistent with Kant's idea of world citizenship in a federation of republican states and subject to his conception of universal hospitality[21] and will comprise a superior form of positive law.[22] Kant argued that hospitality arises not from altruism, kindness or generosity, but from the categorical imperative to treat others as ends rather than means. It includes the right to temporary residence, the refusal of which is tantamount to the destruction of the stranger at the border of the polity. It is a right that 'occupies that space between human rights and civil and political rights, between the rights of humanity in our person and the rights that accrue to us insofar as we are citizens of specific republics', a right that 'expresses the dilemmas of a republican cosmopolitan order in a nutshell: how to create *quasi-legally binding obligations* through voluntary commitments and in the absence of an overwhelming sovereign power with the ultimate right of enforcement?' (Benhabib, 2006: 22, 23; my emphasis). In Benhabib's view, hospitality is the basis on which meta-national human rights claims can be constructed.

> Throughout the international system, as long as territorially bounded states are recognized as the sole legitimate units of negotiation and representation, a tension, and at times even a fatal contradiction, is palpable: the modern state system is caught between *sovereignty* and *hospitality*, between the prerogative to choose to be a party to cosmopolitan norms and human rights treaties, and the obligation to extend recognition of these human rights to all.
>
> (Benhabib, 2006: 31; emphases in original)

21 The paradox if not the aporia of human rights is that, despite (to paraphrase Kantorowicz's analysis of sovereignty and the king's two bodies) the transcendent whiff of incense in which they are shrouded, they are ultimately entirely immanent and positive, the always provisional outcome of a process of continuous negotiation; and the better for it.

22 The paradoxical relationship in human rights between natural law and positivism is encapsulated in the fact that although they are supposedly inherent, inalienable and universal, these rights are enforceable only through positive law mediated by sovereign states, i.e. either made or accepted by them through the voluntary assumption of treaty obligations, itself a basic principle of sovereignty in international law. At this conjuncture there is little evidence to suggest the emergence of a 'freestanding' human rights regime by which sovereign states are bound irrespective of their wishes, including customary international law. The only court in which states can be condemned without acceptance of its jurisdiction is that of public opinion.

In her idiom, this problem is more acute for liberal democracies trapped between constitutional universalism and territorial sovereignty in which, unlike citizens, denizens are resident in the *polis* but are not part of the *demos*. As such, they are subject to laws which they have not contributed to giving to themselves. The myriad problems with popular sovereignty notwithstanding, Benhabib argues that every act of self-legislation by a sovereign people is also an act of self-constitution in which the 'people' define who they are and, crucially, who they are not. So long as citizenship is contingent upon membership of a particular polity there is no way out of this aporetic construction of otherness through what Derrida called an alien universalism in which 'the foreigner who, inept at speaking the language, always risks being without defense before the law of the country that welcomes or expels him; the foreigner who is first of all foreign to the legal language in which the duty of hospitality is formulated, the right to asylum, its limits, norms, policing, etc. He has to ask for hospitality in a language which by definition is not his own' (Derrida, 2000: 15). To the refugee, sovereign and foreign are two sides of the same coin. Since exclusion on this basis of will presumably be moot in the cosmopolis, exploitation and oppression will manifest themselves in the well-rehearsed resort to second class citizenship.

Benhabib is greatly influenced by Arendt, for whom the homogeneous sovereign power of the people reflects an originary violence at the heart of Western politics that reduces some of its 'citizens' to mere existence and then to extinction (Birmingham, 2007: 771). Sovereignty's inherent impulse towards universality makes it incapable of dealing with singularity or particularity, which it therefore seeks to obliterate. This observation is echoed in Agamben's assertion that 'the production of a biopolitical body is the originary activity of sovereign power' (Agamben, 1998: 6). Against the 'full' life anticipated in the cosmopolitan vision, sovereignty produces bare life, or what Arendt called naked life.

Whereas Arendt sought a way out of this impasse through the establishment of a new principle of humanity that might secure human rights – a 'right to rights' – for Agamben this is not possible under contemporary political conditions.[23] Human rights are not the antidote to sovereignty but a utopian illusion, because to the extent that they are juridicalized they are part of the means by which sovereignty generalizes the state of exception and makes it permanent through the ban. Simultaneously inside and outside the law – or, more accurately, forever on the

23 It is not clear how Arendt's demand for a new principle of humanity based on a right to rights provides a solution to the problem of sovereignty. Historically, the nub of the problem is that rights flow from citizenship in a fateful juxtaposition of nation, state and sovereignty. Since human rights *qua* human rights are predicated upon sovereignty, and which is in turn predicated upon territory and citizenship, the absence of citizenship renders human rights incoherent. Human rights are thus revealed to arise not by virtue of humanness but rather on the basis of citizenship in sovereign nation-states that have historically been the biggest violators of the human rights they are supposed to guarantee.

threshold – sovereignty includes individuals in the law in order to exclude them from it.[24] In short, so long as a decision on the exception is possible on Schmittian lines (Schmitt, 1985) neither law nor human rights are guaranteed and the very basis of liberal legal cosmology – the notion that sovereignty is subordinate to the rule of law – is revealed as chimerical.[25]

1.4 SOVEREIGNTY

For Agamben this is no accident. So long as sovereignty subsists in Westphalian terms cosmopolitanism will always be on shaky ground because, as Weber argued, the core feature of the modern state is its monopoly on legitimate violence and to a lesser extent its monopoly on law.[26] States continue to assert their monopoly on legitimate violence and no serious cosmopolitan thinker advocates the construction of a meta-national body that could legitimately exercise this power. In sovereign rationality legitimate violence extends as far as requiring or tolerating death, exemplified in states' ability to make war and impose the death penalty.[27] At the same time, sovereignty's *raison d'être* is self-reproduction, which is contingent upon the reproduction of its subject-objects, and it is for this reason that Agamben defines it in terms of the production of bare life. While it must retain its capacity to kill precisely in order to differentiate itself from other forms of power, when it slides into thanatopolitics it runs the risk of sovereign suicide.[28] In contrast, the state's monopoly on law has been seriously eroded under globalization by the increasing lawmaking capacities of non-state actors.[29] The difficulty confronting cosmopolitanism is that while the erosion of the monopoly of law carries the potential for the construction of a juridico-political order in which sovereign states are increasingly subordinated to a 'higher' external, meta-national legal

24 On the relationship between human rights as law and ethical claims, see the debate between Sen (2004) and Baxi (2007: ch. 2).

25 Schmitt strove mightily to demonstrate that sovereignty is a juridical concept, in support of his desire to 'prove' the legality of the Nazi regime. In contrast, Agamben (1998, 2005) views it as an always potentially extra-legal form of pure power.

26 By this I mean that what was accepted as law within its jurisdiction required the state's imprimatur no matter where and how the law originated, e.g. customary law or international law. The essence of this monopoly was the sovereign state's ability to mediate all law within its jurisdiction.

27 So long as the sovereign capacity to decide the exception exists, the use of the death penalty can be suspended but not abolished.

28 Space precludes a discussion of the literature on the relationship between sovereignty and biopolitics in which Foucault stands on one side of the spectrum (regarding biopower as positive and as having superseded an increasingly redundant sovereignty), Agamben on the other (arguing that sovereignty, at least in the West, has always been biopolitical – which he views entirely negatively), and Esposito (2008) somewhere in between.

29 Transnational corporations are a good example, but network organizations in various state/non-state combinations as well as the WTO provide clear signs of the erosion of this monopoly.

regime in which human rights will hopefully be front and centre (and, of course, the converse), the continued monopoly of legitimate violence threatens to undermine the cosmopolitan vision. The co-implication of cosmopolitanism with violent liberal humanitarian interventions and attempts to redraft international law is a double-edged sword. For example, the 2005 UN General Assembly passed a resolution on the international community's duty to intervene, although not legally binding, may appear laudable at face value but it also amplifies the possibilities that it will be used by 'coalitions of the willing' in pursuit of sovereign self-interest.[30] As Beck notes, the 'language of human rights opens up a highly legitimate, authoritative discourse of power which, on the one hand, allows oppressed and endangered groups to legitimize their rights and ... (possibly) to get them enforced in domestic struggles. On the other hand, it also gives governments and non-governmental organizations a permanent and fundamental right to intervene in both word and deed anywhere in the world' (Beck, 2005: 64).

The assertion that the Westphalian system is in decline is commonplace. As Anghie (2004) and Krasner (1999) – who argues that sovereignty is organized hyprocrisy – have shown, it was based on partial reality at best. Decolonization produced a plethora of formally equal states, most of which have never enjoyed substantive political or economic equality.[31] Similarly, the principle of non-interference in the internal affairs of other sovereigns has always been honoured more in the breach than the observance by colonial and imperial powers, and economic might of powerful states, the international economic institutions and the markets makes a mockery of the principle that states are bound only by obligations voluntarily assumed. Only relatively big economic and military powers have been able to choose whether to split, share, pool or otherwise limit their sovereignty and have always done so in pursuit of perceived self-interest. Hegemonic powers have seldom seen the need to do so.

Douzinas distinguishes three types of sovereignty. Bare sovereignty is a precondition for community, and there is no community without jurisdiction – literally, the speaking of the law. Bare sovereignty is thus the basis on which a people gives law to itself. It is 'the setting of the origin and the ends of a

30 The General Assembly stated that its member states 'are prepared to take collective action ... should peaceful means be inadequate and national authorities are manifestly failing to protect their populations from genocide, war crimes, ethnic cleansing and crimes against humanity. We stress the need for the General Assembly to continue consideration of the responsibility to protect populations from genocide, war crimes, ethnic cleansing and crimes against humanity and its implications, bearing in mind the principles of the Charter and international law' (General Assembly Resolution UNGA A/RES/60/1 on 2005 World Summit Outcome, 24 October 2005).

31 Political sovereignty is of a different order, an issue I address below. Suffice to mention for the moment that the main goal of cosmopolitanism is to circumscribe domestic sovereignty when it violates human rights. Whereas most liberal cosmopolitan thinkers rarely address the structural causes of socio-economic rights violations, there is an extensive global justice literature that does so. See for example Pogge (2005).

community, the act or acts by means of which a community gives itself to itself' (Douzinas, 2007: 273–74). Theological sovereignty is embodied in the sovereign, who henceforth becomes the unitary source and voice of the law. Schmitt argued that sovereignty, like all political concepts, is a secularized form of theology and it is therefore unsurprising the contemporary sovereigns commonly represent themselves as having been anointed rather than elected (see Kantorowicz, 1957). It is still a concept suffused by an admixture of God, King and people. Theological sovereignty is 'the precipitation of bare sovereignty into the definite figure of the sovereign … The finite source of the law assumes the transcendent, grandiose epiphany of the sovereign, a fake God incarnate, the king's second mystical body' (Douzinas, 2007: 279).

The third form of sovereignty is cosmopolitan sovereignty, which paradoxically seems to take us back to Hobbes' originary mythical exception, to the moment in which the sovereign emerges from community but is thereafter never of that community. As originator and guarantor of the law, his ultimate power lies in his ability to suspend the law, to declare the state of exception. As Douzinas observes, in 'modernity the setting of ends, including the ends of the law, was the prerogative of the sovereign. War is the ultimate expression of sovereign end' (Douzinas, 2007: 288). My construction is slightly different: the end of sovereignty is sovereignty itself – in other words, self-reproduction – and death the primary means to this end. Along with Derrida, I would argue that the death penalty is as emblematic of sovereignty as war (so long as the sovereign capacity to decide the exception exists, the death penalty cannot be abolished but merely suspended). In any event, Douzinas argues that the 'return of war indicates that sovereignty is not retreating but losing its ability to make sense' (Douzinas, 2007: 288). In an era dominated by the 'war on terror':

> no common law or ethics, no world constitution or supranational right has or can emerge. War is called police action and economic competition, violence has taken a lawful, humane, civilised form, nesting everywhere and nowhere, linked to any number of ends but not to a supreme end. Community without commonality, law without justice, terrifying sovereign action that has made the exception permanent; these are the normative contours of the new world order.
> (Douzinas, 2007: 289)

The fact that sovereignty and statehood have never been fully coextensive provides support for cosmopolitanism. At the same time however, even the weakest states have demonstrated the most anti-cosmopolitan proclivities in respect of their own populations. In the early part of this millennium sovereignty seems to disappear without going away. Ever malleable, it is seemingly capable of endless metamorphosis.[32] Perhaps the most difficult theoretical problem it

32 The debate about the contemporary nature of sovereignty was largely precipitated by Hardt and Negri (2000).

throws up is the cleavage between the conceptual and chronological histories of the concept.[33] In varying forms it has proved tenaciously persistent and compatible with every form of government in every epoch. If, as Douzinas argues, today it 'has degraded, it is passing away and is replaced by humanity', this retreat is relative, as it 'is absorbed and condensed into a super-sovereign centre' (Douzinas, 2007: 269, 271).[34] It is modern, Westphalian sovereignty – the notion of supreme authority in a territorially defined entity free from external interference – that is being degraded, not sovereignty *per se*.[35] This degraded but still sacred principle may well be the rock on which attempts to save humanity from global warming will prove to have foundered.[36]

Cosmopolitan sovereignty 'exists in the form of a subjectivity without foundation, a personality that enjoys complete self-determination' (Douzinas, 2007: 277). The sovereign is able to decide the law and its and its limits because he is the 'ungrounded ground of the law' (Norris, 2003: 9), of the law but always potentially outside it.

1.5 CONCLUSION

The cosmopolitan dilemma is that we are seemingly unable or unwilling to live without sovereignty but face immense difficulties in controlling it. Does this suggest that cosmopolitanism is flawed in principle, or that it is not radical enough? Short of a global revolution, is the cosmopolitan ideal of world citizenship without a world state possible, given the fact that citizenship is contingent on sovereignty?

Much depends on how sovereignty is defined. It is theoretically possible to distinguish sovereignty from statehood and government and doing so to render the concept redundant. If it is understood as a bundle of capacities such as the ability of states to tax, to negotiate treaties or to legislate, it is possible in principle to place the exercise of governmental power under the rule of law.[37] Problems

33 Thus while Fine (2003, 2007) for example argues that the state is an historically contingent form the theory of the exception suggests that sovereignty is not and that the forms that it has assumed over time are different manifestations of an essentially pure power.

34 In contrast, see Hardt and Negri (2000), who argue that postmodern sovereignty is decentred and deterritorialised.

35 In modernity sovereignty was understood exclusively as state power. The theoretical difficulty referred to above is highlighted by the work of Schmitt and Agamben and illustrated by the fact that the historical contingency of sovereignty is different to that of the state.

36 See my forthcoming paper, 'Rethinking Human Rights: The Impact of Climate Change on the Dominant Discourse', in Humphreys, S. (ed.) (2009), *Human Rights and Climate Change*, Cambridge: Cambridge University Press.

37 Like the notion that sovereignty is juridical, the rule of law is a cardinal myth of liberal legal cosmology. We are always ruled by people.

begin to emerge, however, as soon as the fundamental duty of government to provide for the security of its citizens arises, because this is the point at which governmentality begins to blur into sovereignty, when defence of the people and the nation result in crude Schmittian categorizations of friends and enemies, in 'collateral damage', in violations of international law and the selective delivery of democracy and human rights to the weak.

Although reform of the main international institutions is undoubtedly necessary, cosmopolitan conceptions of global justice tend to place too much faith in their efficacy. The UN Security Council will remain dysfunctional so long as the permanent members are able to exercise their sovereignty in the form of the veto. The international economic institutions are undemocratic and unaccountable so long as they are mediated by the sovereign prerogatives of the powerful. Circumscribing sovereign immunity and impunity through the establishment of institutions like the ICC and principles like universal jurisdiction is necessary but insufficient.

The trouble is that sovereignty is more than an aggregation of capacities, more than the sum of its parts. As the theory of the exception reveals, it is a metaphysical concept that enables this unique power to stand outside history and law, or at least forever on the threshold between law and anomie. Sovereignty is more than a series of institutions or the exercise of power by an individual or a group. It is more than the constitutional and institutional framework within which the people are able to give themselves law because the pact under which this is achieved is also the means by which they can be dispossessed. We should not be deluded into believing that 'Europe' is incapable of relapsing into barbarism. The EU is a collection of sovereigns in which there is no pan-European monopoly of violence, but member states continue to kill. It is not the harbinger of a post-sovereign order but of a different sovereign order in which it appears that the attributes of statehood are negotiable, but not sovereignty itself.[38]

Liberal cosmopolitanism struggles to resolve the tension between the universal and the particular, the global and the local through an inchoate form of global citizenship that resembles the seductive delusion of popular sovereignty.[39] If a global order beyond modern sovereignty is currently inconceivable, it is nonetheless imperative work towards rather than waiting for Derrida's Godot-like democracy to come or Benjamin's cataclysmic messianic divine violence. In the meantime, a meaningful cosmopolitan future can only be constructed through grinding, time-honoured forms of struggle for solidarity from below against cosmopolitan sovereignty.

38 Distinguishing between sovereignty and statehood also enables us to assess the legitimacy of non-state actors, whose power has exploded with privatization, and to determine when and to what extent sovereign power is being sub-contracted to companies like Halliburton and the now renamed Blackwater, by the US, for example.

39 Schmitt's attempt to rationalise the legality of Nazism revolved around the argument that the regime was the distillation of the will of the Volk. Arendt scathingly criticised the Rousseauean conception of popular sovereignty.

Bibliography

Adelman, S. (2008) 'Between the Scylla of Sovereignty and the Charybdis of Human Rights: The Pitfalls of Development in Pursuit of Justice', *Human Rights and International Legal Discourse (HR&ILD)*, 2: 1.

Agamben, G. (1998) *Homo Sacer: Sovereign Power and Bare Life* (Stanford: Stanford University Press).

—— (2005) *State of Exception* (Chicago and London: University of Chicago Press).

Anghie, A. (2004) *Imperialism, Sovereignty and the Making of International Law* (Cambridge: Cambridge University Press).

Archibugi, D. (1995) 'Immanuel Kant, Cosmopolitan Law and Peace', *European Journal of International Relations*, 1(4): 429–56.

—— (2005) *State of Exception* (Chicago and London: University of Chicago Press).

Arendt, H. (1951) *The Origins of Totalitarianism* (New York: Harcourt Brace).

Baxi, U. (2005) 'The "War on Terror" and the "War of Terror": Nomadic Multitudes, Aggressive Incumbents, and the "New" International Law', *Osgoode Law Journal*, 43: 7.

—— (2006) *The Future of Human Rights* (2nd edn) (Delhi: Oxford University Press).

—— (2007) *Human Rights in a Posthuman World: Critical Essays* (Delhi: Oxford University Press).

Beck, U. (2005) *Power in the Global Age: A new global political economy* (Cambridge: Polity Press).

—— (2006) *The Cosmopolitan Vision* (Cambridge: Polity Press).

Beck, U. and Grande, E. (2007) *Cosmopolitan Europe* (Cambridge: Polity Press).

Benhabib, S. (2006) *Another Cosmopolitanism* (Oxford: Oxford University Press).

Birmingham, P. (2007) 'The An-Archic Event of Natality and the "Right to Have Rights"', *Social Research*, 74: 3.

Brock, G. and Brighouse, H. (2005) (eds), *The Political Philosophy of Cosmopolitanism* (Cambridge: Cambridge University Press).

Derrida, J. (2000) *Of Hospitality. Anne Dufourmantelle invites Jacques Derrida to Respond* (Stanford: Stanford University Press).

—— (2005) *Rogues: Two Essays on Reason* (Stanford: Stanford University Press).

Douzinas, C. (2007a) 'The Many Faces of Humanitarianism', *Parrhesia*, 2: 1–28.

—— (2007b), *Human Rights and Empire: The political philosophy of cosmopolitanism* (Oxford: Routledge-Cavendish).

Esposito, R. (2008) *Bíos: Biopolitics and Philosophy* (Minneapolis: University of Minnesota Press).

Fine, R. (2003) 'Taking the "Ism" out of Cosmopolitanism: An Essay in Reconstruction', *European Journal of Social Theory*, 6(4).

—— (2006) 'Cosmopolitanism and Violence: Difficulties of Judgment', *British Journal of Sociology*, 57(1).

—— (2007) *Cosmopolitanism* (Oxford: Routledge).

Fukuyama, F. (1992) *The End of History and the Last Man* (New York: Free Press).

Habermas, J. (2001) *The Postnational Constellation: Political essays* (ed. Max Pensky) (Cambridge: Polity Press).

—— (2006) *The Divided West* (ed. Ciaran Cronin) (Cambridge: Polity Press).

Hardt, M. and Negri, A. (2000) *Empire* (Cambridge, MA: Harvard University Press).

Held, D. (2005) 'Principles of Cosmopolitan Order', in Brock, G. and Brighouse, H. (eds), *The Political Philosophy of Cosmopolitanism* (Cambridge: Cambridge University Press).
Kant, I. (1795) *Perpetual Peace: A Philosophical Essay* (London: George Allen & Unwin).
—— (1991) *Kant: Political Writings* (ed. Hans Reiss) (Cambridge, Cambridge University Press).
Kantorowicz, E. H. (1957) *The King's Two Bodies: A Study In Mediaeval Political Theology* (Princeton, NJ: Princeton University Press).
Krasner, S. D. (1999) *Sovereignty: Organized Hypocrisy* (Princeton, NJ: Princeton University Press).
Kymlicka, W. (2001) *Contemporary Political Philosophy: An Introduction* (Oxford: Oxford University Press).
Nagel, T. (2005) 'The Problem of Global Justice', *Philosophy and Public Affairs*, 33.
Norris, A. (2003) 'The Exemplary Exception', *Radical Philosophy*, 119.
Nussbaum, M. (2005) 'Beyond the Social Contract: Capabilities and Global Justice', in Brock, G. and Brighouse, H. (eds), *The Political Philosophy of Cosmopolitanism* (Cambridge: Cambridge University Press).
Pogge, T. (2005) 'A Cosmopolitan Perspective on the Global Economic Order', in Brock, G. and Brighouse, H. (eds), *The Political Philosophy of Cosmopolitanism* (Cambridge: Cambridge University Press).
Rancière, J. (2004) 'Who is the Subject of the Rights of Man?', *The South Atlantic Quarterly*, 103: 2/3.
Santos, Boaventura de Sousa (2002) *Toward a New Legal Common Sense* (London: Butterworths).
Schmitt, C. (1985) *Political Theology: Four chapters on the concept of sovereignty* (Cambridge, MA: MIT Press).
Sen, A. (2004) 'Elements of a Theory of Human Rights', *Philosophy and Public Affairs*, 32.
—— (2009) *The Idea of Justice* (London: Allen Lane).
Sypnowich, C. (2005) 'Cosmopolitans, Cosmopolitanism, and Human Flourishing', in Brock, G. and Brighouse, H. (eds), *The Political Philosophy of Cosmopolitanism* (Cambridge: Cambridge University Press).
Ward, I. (2003), 'The End of Sovereignty and the New Humanism', *Stanford Law Review*, 55: 2091.

Chapter 2

Does a world state really lead to a graveyard of freedom?[1]

Ronald Tinnevelt

2.1 INTRODUCTION

Several normative theories and policy models have recently been developed to deal with the transformation of state sovereignty and the problem of democratic legitimacy in a globalizing era: cosmopolitan democracy, global governance networks, directly deliberative polyarchy, world polity etc. The main question that drives these proposals is what kind of global institutional scheme best fits the requirements of moral cosmopolitanism – the idea that human beings are the ultimate units of moral concern.

Although the differences between these models are considerable, they all share the same questionable presumption. Despite recent more 'centralizing' developments within the international realm – such as the realization of the ICC, the judicial functions of the WTO or the quasi-legislative functions of the ILO[2] – and a growing transnational character of risks, the idea of a world state is not accepted as a possible global institutional scheme. Most legal and political theorists simply assume that a world state is a tyrannical institution and immediately argue for some form of global or network governance. And where the idea of a world state does surface it mainly plays a negative role – either as a means to discredit other theories or to argue for non-global or non-cosmopolitan forms of justice and democracy.

If legal and political theorists are truly concerned about the requirements of moral cosmopolitanism, however, should they not examine the viability of *all* possible supranational regimes and give good reasons why some form of world state is a non-starter for scientific research and institutional reform? An often-heard criticism is that a world state would be ungovernable and unable to accommodate the political expression of cultural differences. However this critique merely seems to be aimed at a specific form of the world state – Kant's notion of a universal monarchy or unified global state – but not necessarily at a federal world republic or minimal world state. Many arguments, moreover, are not always clearly stated and might not be all that difficult to refute.

1 The last part of the title comes from Kant's *Toward Perpetual Peace* (1999: 336).
2 Compare Brunkhorst (2006).

This paper will focus on the viability of a world state. Given limited space, however, the aim of this paper is also limited. Instead of arguing that we are moving in the direction of a state-like structure on the global level, or that some form of world state is best capable of securing the core values of moral cosmopolitanism, this paper will only: (1) present a taxonomy of arguments against the world state, (2) and explore whether they have any power of persuasion against two possible forms of the world state: (a) a unified global state and (b) a minimal world state. So this paper does not take all forms of world state into consideration,[3] nor does it present an in-depth comparison between the idea of the world state and other important arrangements of international relations (like that of 'world society' or 'world polity'[4]). Although a minimal world state is better equipped to deal with these arguments than a global state, we will argue that such a regime contains certain centralizing tendencies that are inherent to the assumptions and principles upon which it is built. Before addressing these points, however, we start with a general analysis of the idea of a world state.

2.2 THE IDEA OF A (WORLD) STATE

Within the current debate on cosmopolitanism and global justice there are, fortunately, exceptions to the general rule that the idea of world state is not seen as a topic of serious reflection.[5] Alexander Wendt and Otfried Höffe are probably best known. Yet one needs to be sensitive to the fact that ideas like world government or a world state are sometimes used with different meanings. Some authors, for example, apply the category of world government to both global governance and world state.[6] Not every proponent of world government, then, would welcome a world state. So what constitutes a world state?

Walzer's analysis of seven possible political arrangements of international society is helpful in this regard. He develops a continuum of political arrangements based on degree of centralization.[7]

What is striking about this outline, is that Walzer reserves the term 'world state' strictly for the idea of a global state. Neither a federation of nation states nor a multinational empire fall into this category. A global state is characterized by the fact that every person in the world is directly connected to a single centre. It is a state without any kind of 'political realization of difference'.[8] Walzer,

3 For a very interesting discussion of the ideas of 'Weltstaat' and 'Weltstaatlichkeit', see Albert and Stichweh (2007).
4 For John Meyer's work on world society and world polity, see Krücken and Drori (2009).
5 Wendt (2003), Höffe (2007), Cabrera (2004), Deudney (2007), Tännsjo (2008) and Marchetti (2008).
6 Craig (2008: 133).
7 Walzer (2003).
8 Ibid, 171–2.

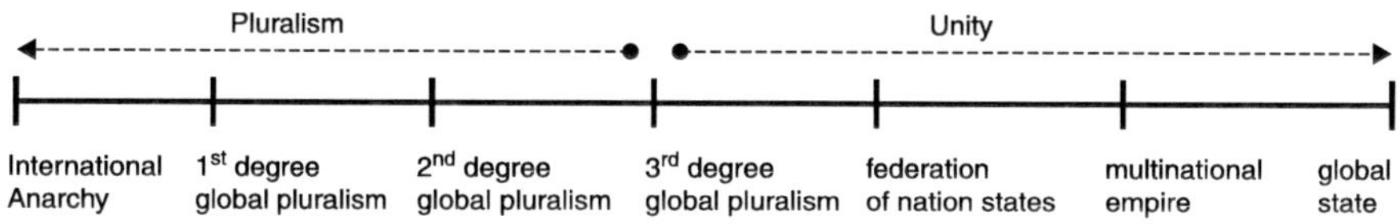

Figure 2.1 Political arrangements according to degree of centralization.

furthermore, neither discusses the political character nor the responsibilities of such a state.

Although Walzer is right to put the global state at the far right end of his continuum, he cannot argue that the notion of a 'world state' only applies to this specific arrangement. In essence, the idea of a world state primarily points to the fact that there is a state-like structure with world-wide jurisdiction and global responsibilities. But it does not imply that such a regime can not be a multi-level one. If a federation can be recognized as a state, so could a federation of nation states. So instead of merely applying the idea of a world state to the most centralized regime on this continuum, it can apply to the entire range between a federation of nation states and a global state.

A lot depends, however, on one's definition of a state. Just take Nozick's view on what it takes for an institution to be recognized as a state. By slightly weakening the classical Weberian conditions – by opting for a *de facto* monopoly on the use of force and dropping the fact that a state claims to be the 'sole authorizer of violence' – Nozick is capable of recognizing even his 'dominant protective agency' as a state.[9]

But what are the specific features of a state? Within contemporary political and legal discourse, unfortunately, no wide agreement can be found. The word 'state' is not only used in several different ways (referring for instance both to the body politic and the government), but many rival definitions can be found.[10] Given the complex character of the modern state and the length of this paper, we will stick to the classical definition of Weber: a territorial administrative and legal order that claims a monopoly on the legitimate use of force and 'binding authority, not only over the members of the state, the citizens … but also to a very large extent, over all actions taking place in the area of its jurisdiction'.[11] Most of these features, can be organized under the heading of four criteria: 'legality, supremacy, territoriality, and comprehensiveness'.[12]

9 Nozick (1974: 117).
10 Compare Dunleavy (2007) and Morris (2004).
11 Weber (1947: 156).
12 Caney (2005: 150).

To make sense of the many manifestations of the modern state (federal state, multinational state etc.), however, some of these criteria need to be relaxed. The idea of *comprehensiveness* is a case in point. According to this feature a political unit should be recognized as a sovereign state 'if it has ultimate authority over a territorially defined group of people and it has authority *over all issues* and not simply some'.[13] Another criterion is that of (supreme) authority. Federal systems of government cannot properly function without some level of shared sovereignty.

But we should be careful not to relax the criteria for modern statehood too much. If we do, the idea of a world state would cover far too many different arrangements of international relations to still be a meaningful concept. Giving up the requirement of the monopoly on the use of force, for example, could 'suggest that a world state is already here (the UN?) or just around the corner'.[14]

Although most proponents of a world state emphasize the importance of a monopoly on the use of force, some are wary of concentrating too much power at the top. Cabrera for instance opts for a 'dispersal and balancing of global coercive authority'.[15] Deudney, similarly, defends a 'fully non-hierarchical, fully republican, world federal government'.[16] Given their preference for a non-hierarchical system of mutual restraint, one should be careful of too quickly labelling their positions as forms of a world state.

2.3 A SUBSIDIARY AND FEDERAL WORLD REPUBLIC

Given that there are many manifestations of the world state to the left of the global state, which regime should we use to contrast the global state with? Comparing the models of Wendt, Höffe, Tännsjö, Yunker and others, one will quickly notice that whereas they all reject the idea of a full-blown world state, their proposals occupy different points on the continuum. To circumvent problems of demarcation, we will take the idea of a *minimal world state* as our point of comparison.

What, however, constitutes the minimal character of such a state? A minimal world state can be called 'minimal', according to Höffe and others, because it is only responsible for a residual state of nature. Following Kant's peace proposal Höffe argues that this state of nature is characterized by two dimensions: an inter-state state of nature and a global-civic state of nature. The first concerns the relations between states, the second the relations between citizens of different states and the relations between states and the citizens of foreign states.[17]

13 Caney (2005: 150).
14 Wendt (2003: 506).
15 Cabrera (2004: 114).
16 Deudney (2007: 20).
17 Höffe (2007: 215).

Given the nature of this two-dimensional residual state of nature, Höffe is able to claim that his minimal world state is merely a complementary world republic that is organized on the basis of the principle of subsidiarity and the model of dual federalism. According to the first principle 'powers or tasks should rest with the lower-level sub-units of that order unless allocating them to a higher-level central unit would ensure higher comparable efficiency or effectiveness in achieving them'.[18] Dual federalism, on the other hand, points to the fact that the central and lower-level governments 'take on their ... responsibilities independently of each other'.[19]

Whether Höffe is right to opt for dual instead of cooperative federalism, is not something that should concern us here. What is important, however, is that the minimal world state is merely a secondary state. As such it does not demand a fully centralized rule. It is a democratic multilayered political regime 'encompassing differing degrees of responsibility and relative power at all levels of political decision-making'.[20]

Such a secondary state would, in principle, only be responsible for global issues. But which issues are global? Here proponents of the minimal world state differ. Whereas some emphasize that a minimal world state would only need to maintain peace and secure universal rights, others argue that such a state also has a *de facto* responsibility for the 'juridical, social and ecological constraints of [the global] market'.[21]

2.4 ARGUMENTS AGAINST A WORLD STATE

Having given a very general sketch of the idea of a (minimal) world state, we need to go back to our two original questions: what arguments are traditionally raised against the world state, and to what extent do these arguments have any power of persuasion against the ideas of a minimal and global world state? In the remainder of this paper we will use the following classification of arguments: Kantian, liberal nationalist, exclusion, disanalogy arguments, and realist.[22] These five types of arguments fall roughly in two broad categories. Practical arguments that centre on the *feasibility* of a world state – such as its ungovernability or unaccountability – and normative ones that deal with its *desirability*.[23] In the sections below, these arguments will be briefly discussed and critically assessed.

18 Føllesdal (1998: 190).
19 Höffe (2007: 215–16).
20 Marchetti (2008: 167).
21 Höffe (2007: 249).
22 Here we build on Lu (2006), Höffe (2007), Horn (1996), Heater (1996), Cabrera (2004), Tännsjö (2008) and Marchetti (2008).
23 Compare Marchetti (2008: 155).

2.4.1 Kantian arguments

A world state, according to critics, is undesirable because it is an extremely weak and inefficient form of political organization (*ungovernability objection*) and because it inescapably poses the risk of global tyranny (*tyranny objection*). The main reason why these two types of arguments are called Kantian, is not because they are somehow intrinsically tied up to the fundamental presuppositions of Kant's philosophy, but because legal and political theorists always refer to Kant when they employ these arguments. Within his political and legal writings, however, Kant offers a far wider range of arguments than just the ungovernability and tyranny objections.

2.4.1.1 Ungovernability objection

Many philosophers have claimed that the advantages of centralization – such as a more effective delivery of public goods – are counterbalanced by even greater disadvantages when political structures become too large. Kant famously argued that 'as the range of government expands laws progressively lose their vigor'.[24] Typical of this *restricted-size argument*, is that the character of a political structure is a matter of only secondary importance. All types of political institutions have a natural limit in terms of territory and populace. Other versions of this argument, however, apply specifically to democratic forms of government. It is pointed out that participation, representation or classic forms of protest become hopelessly problematic beyond a certain scale. Cabrera calls this the *democratic distance argument*.[25]

Whether or not this argument is convincing depends, among other matters, on one's conception of democracy. The right scale for a council democracy will be different from that of a representative structure. What Dahl's calculations, for instance, have shown, is that direct participation in the collective decision-making process of large states is unfeasible.[26] But even if one embraces a less participatory form of democracy, one will have to accept that an increase in the population of a political unit will lead to an increase in the amount of power that is transferred to government officials and a decrease in the influence of every individual citizen.

One way of sidestepping the argument of restricted size, is to accept the solution that Rousseau 'seems' to be giving in his *Considération sur le gouvernement de Pologne* and Montesquieu in his *Esprit des Lois*: the idea of federalism or federal republic. The word 'seems' is bracketed because Rousseau – although he sometimes suggests that federalism can provide a solution to the impossible

24 Kant (1999: 336).
25 Cabrera (2004: 93ff).
26 Dahl (1998: 106–7).

choice between destruction by foreign force or internal vice – in the end prefers small and isolated republics.[27]

A second way of countering the restricted size and democratic distance objection, is by emphasizing the importance of intermediary institutions between the world state and nation-states. Continental and subcontinental unions like the EU can help ensure more robust forms of accountability and representation.[28] This argument for the intermediary role of continental regimes is both defended by critics (such as Held and Habermas) and proponents of the world state (like Höffe and Cabrera).

A third way of countering the democratic distance objection is by pointing at the dissimilarities between the national, international realm and supranational realm. One could admit that large, supranational political structures are unable to simply adopt the *modus operandi* of classical democratic states, but deny that this is a problem. The competences that are transferred to supranational organizations, after all, are typically such that they are less demanding in terms of democratic legitimacy and citizen involvement. Moravcsik, for instance, explicitly warns us not to use the ideal of the democratic nation-state as the evaluation standard for larger political entities. The baseline, according to him, 'should be the real-world practices of existing governments acting imperfectly under complex constraints'.[29] Applying this kind of real-world analysis to the European Union, he comes to the surprising conclusion that the EU is not undemocratic, but 'merely specializing in those aspects of modern democratic governance that typically involve less direct political participation'.[30]

However, as the fierce reactions against his views on European democracy already make clear,[31] many authors in the field of supranational democracy do not believe that there are 'natural' limits, in terms of size, to democratic modes of government. For them, the transfer of competences beyond democratic control can never be justified, and always carries within it the risk of despotism.

A final reply (though less convincing and mainly aimed at the problem of small republics) is given in the federalist papers. Addressing the anti-federalist's claim that good government and effective control are only possible in a decentralized (and more or less homogeneous) society, Publius argues in favour of the enlarged size of republics and claims that a large republic is the best remedy for corruption, lack of control etc. With this, however, we come very close to the *bounded citizenship objection* (see below).

27 Riley (1973: 11). More, of course, needs to be said then about the idea of federalism.

28 Cabrera (2004: 94).

29 Moravcsik (2004: 27).

30 Ibid.

31 cf. Føllesdal and Hix (2006).

2.4.1.2 Tyranny objection

The tyranny objection consists in fact of two interrelated arguments: (a) the claim that a world state – because of its need for hierarchical centralization – poses a great and maybe even inevitable risk of tyranny, and (b) the objection that, unlike a tyrannical nation-state, a tyrannical world state leaves no exit possibilities. One way of responding to the first objection is to argue that – provided a system of checks and balances and a critical public sphere is in place – the risk of tyranny needn't be greater at the world state level than at the level of the nation state.

It is, however, doubtful whether such a reply is fully convincing with regard to the global state. Depending on its competences, a global state would need such a rigidly hierarchical form of government that there will always remain a strong risk of tyranny. The proponents of a minimal world state, on the other hand, don't necessarily face this kind of risk. By pointing at the important differences between a global state and a subsidiary and federal world republic, proponents of a minimal world state could argue that 'an important set of pressures for hierarchical centralization'[32] is absent. The most important ones being that a minimal world state would not need a foreign policy and would only rule on global issues.[33]

The no-exit objection, however, does pose a serious challenge to proponents of both models of the world state. Leaving aside the absurd reply of space travel, there doesn't seem to be a way of *directly* countering this argument. The only way to address the no-exit objection is by indirectly questioning the relevance of this objection (for example by arguing that we can take away the reasons for exit or by arguing that a world state does not necessarily imply a logic of extreme hierarchical centralization). Considering that we already discussed the second aspect, we need to focus on the first point.

One could indirectly question the relevance of the no-exit objection by asking whether it is realistic to expect totalitarian regimes to guarantee exit possibilities, or whether other states actually have the financial and social resources to deal with migrants. But one could also address the members themselves and ask whether they can realistically make use of such an option.[34] The last argument has a long tradition that goes back – at least – to Hume's oft-quoted words in *Of the Original Contract*: 'Can we seriously say that a poor peasant or artisan has a free choice to leave his country, when he knows no foreign language or manners, and lives from day to day by the small wages which he acquires?'[35]

Even if world statists, however, are able to question the relevance of the general version of the no-exit argument, there are other versions that pose different challenges. Pettit, for example, formulates an interesting version of the no-exit

32 Deudney (2006: 276).
33 Marchetti (2008: 158), Tännsjö (2008: 117) and Horn (1996: 246–7).
34 Horn (1999: 251).
35 Hume (2006: 193).

objection in a recent paper. A state, according to Pettit, can only be a 'non-arbitrary source of interference'[36] if it allows its citizens the freedom to leave if they so wish. Such a relation between consensual entry and consensual exit, however, cannot be guaranteed on the level of a federal world republic. A federal world republic not only has no outside, but it can only function as a *world* state if member states are irrevocably incorporated within a larger political structure. Although proponents of a federal world republic can only counter the consequentialist objection by arguing in favour of voluntary entry, they cannot deny that a minimal world state is no voluntary association.

At this point, one could claim that secession need not be forbidden or argue that the disadvantages that are associated with the absence of a right to exit might outweigh the advantages gained by solving collective action problems and the security dilemma. But even then the no-exit objection will still be relevant.

2.4.2 Liberal nationalist arguments

Because democracy and redistribution are dependent on a high level of trust and common understanding, there are strong limits to the scale of political communities. Democracy and social justice require bounded communities (*bounded citizenship objection*). Although this argument closely resembles the restricted size and the democratic distance objection, the underlying rationale is different. Whereas the restricted size and democratic distance objection mainly address the *objective* conditions for democratic communities to sustain themselves, the bounded citizenship objection is primarily concerned with the *subjective* conditions for genuine forms of citizenship and democracy – with the glue that holds democratic political communities together. The restricted size and bounded citizenship objection, however, are often used simultaneously. The anti-federalists, for example, argue for the necessity of small communities because good government requires a certain amount of homogeneity. The importance of bounded communities, however, is not the only reason why liberal nationalists argue against a world state. Another often heard critique is that such a state poses a serious threat to the concrete ethical life of political communities (*pluralism objection*).

2.4.2.1 *Bounded citizenship objection*

Contrary to the pluralism objection, the bounded citizenship objection is not necessarily an argument against a unified global state. Such a state, after all, need not be a (fully) democratic one. The bounded citizenship objection is primarily aimed at proposals for some form of transnational democracy, in our case a form of democratic world state.

36 Pettit (2009: 6).

Liberal nationalists offer different reasons for their skepticism. The most important is the believe that there is substantially less room for optimism regarding supranational forms of democracy than proponents of world government claim. According to liberal nationalists they ignore the empirical conditions of *genuine* forms of citizenship and democracy.[37] The best version of democracy is one where people do not merely vote according to personal self-interest, but where they are committed and responsible citizens. And such a form of democracy requires an amount of solidarity, common understanding and trust that can only be generated in nationally bounded communities.

It is difficult, however, to see why this objection implies a rejection of supranational forms of democracy; even within the theory of liberal nationalism itself.[38] It is one thing to claim that democracy works best in nationally unified political units, but it is quite another to say that all non-national democratic decision-making process are therefore illegitimate or insupportable. While the bounded citizenship objection provides an important reason for realizing democracy in national units, there may be other arguments that go against the central preference for national decision-making.

Take the example of a multinational federal state. While in this case the bounded citizenship objection could be invoked to argue that the substate nations are the primary units of democracy, the idea of a multinational state in itself entails the existence of at least some competences and decision-making at the federal level itself. Since most liberal nationalists endorse the legitimacy of multinational federal states, they *ipso facto* endorse the legitimacy of having some form of 'transnational' decision-making. So the fact that they can and do endorse the legitimacy of federal decision-making, shows that the general preference of national political units can in some cases be overridden by other concerns. What these cases are, is clearly stated by global democrats and world statists: solving collective action problems, securing peace etc.[39]

But there is also another way to respond to the bounded citizenship objection. One could acknowledge that shared understandings are needed to motivate citizens, but deny that these 'must be nationally based'.[40] Or one could, as Dryzek does, claim that 'a shared problem, or problem set'[41] is sufficient to guarantee effective forms of deliberation and democratic decision-making.

Fortunately it isn't necessary to confront liberal nationalists head on to counter their argument. One could also use a more innocent version of Moravcsik's claim. Given that a minimal world state constitutes a multi-level political system that is based on federalism and subsidiarity, there is no need for a close unity between all

37 Miller (2000: 81 and 96).
38 Here I follow De Schutter and Tinnevelt (2009).
39 Compare Caney (2005: 159–60).
40 Cabrera (2004: 106).
41 Dryzek (2008: 483).

people on the global scale. Thinner forms of legitimation might suffice. Habermas makes such a claim when he discusses the democratization of the UN:

> A negative consensus would suffice in place of civic solidarity, namely, shared outrage at the aggressive warmongering and human rights violations of criminal gangs and regimes or shared horrors over acts of ethnic cleansing and genocide.[42]

Depending on what functions and political authority international organizations have, different levels of trust, solidarity and commonality are needed.

2.4.2.2 *Pluralism objection*

To what extent does a world state necessarily nullify cultural differences? At first sight it seems difficult not to agree with this kind of critique. If unity requires centralization and pluralism decentralization, then extreme centralization – as is the case in a global state – will leave no room for a political realization of social or cultural differences. But a global state, as we discussed above, is certainly not the only conceivable form of a world state. Especially with regard to a minimal world state it is difficult to imagine why the concrete ethical life of political communities would be seriously threatened. If the competences of such a subsidiary and federal world republic are limited there is no reason why states should not be able to have their own system of social justice or 'define the rights of their citizens in different ways'.[43] Within a multi-level political system, nation-states can still be the privileged sites of democracy.

Why, furthermore, should it be the case – as liberal nationalists claim – that a system of independent national communities is the only way to protect cultural differences and that any transfer of political authority to higher-level coercive bodies is harmful to pluralism and national self-determination?[44] Don't we need to acknowledge that in today's globalizing world, the cultural identities of small nations are often better promoted if they join supranational institutions than if they don't? The fate of the identity of small nations within Europe, for instance, is significantly strengthened by the official language policy of the EU. Danish, as a result, enjoys equal official status with the other EU languages.

If pluralism and national self-determination, moreover, are indeed such fundamental values it is difficult to see why liberal nationalists support the idea of multinational federal states. Even as a second best option, multinational federalism still shows that unity and pluralism can be united at levels beyond the nation-state.

42 Habermas (2006: 109–10).
43 Miller (2000a: 93)
44 See for example Miller (2007: 268).

2.4.3 Exclusion arguments

Beyond the liberal nationalist objection that democracy requires bounded communities that are united around a common feeling of national belonging, the idea of creating a world state is sometimes also objected to in more cruder terms. Political identification – according to this type of argument – requires boundaries. The core of this objection is not so much that feelings of political commitment are necessarily bound to specific cultural or linguistic elements, but rather that feelings of belonging to a certain group are essentially feelings of not belonging to certain other groups. The 'distinctiveness of cultures and groups', as Walzer argues in his *Spheres of Justice*, 'depends upon closure'[45] (*collective identity objection*).

A similar objection is given by Schmitt and Mouffe in their analysis of the domain of the political. The distinction between friend/enemy or we/they – between competing collective identities – is characteristic of this domain. It constitutes its 'condition of possibility'.[46] A 'completely pacified globe', according to Schmitt, 'would be a world without the distinction between friend and enemy and hence a world without politics'[47] (*antagonism–agonism objection*). The main reason why we use this term, and not simply antagonism or agonism objection, is because Schmitt and Mouffe differ in their interpretation of the we/they distinction. Although the we/they distinction could become the 'locus of an antagonism', Mouffe stresses the importance of a 'common symbolic space' within which the conflict between 'we' and 'they' takes place.[48] Within this space the conflicting parties recognize each other's legitimacy.

2.4.3.1 The importance of closure for political associations

Because the collective identity objection and antagonism/agonism objection overlap and are sometimes used interchangeably, we will not discuss them separately.[49] But what kind of general criticism do they share and to what extent is this argument against the world state really convincing?

In his criticism of the project of European political integration – which he decries as an attempt at a 'pure democracy' – Manent gives an interesting account of this type of claim. 'Pure democracy is democracy without a people – that is, democratic *governance*, which is very respectful of human rights but detached from any collective deliberation.'[50] Manent's critique, interestingly, does not constitute another version of the 'no demos' thesis. His main problem is not the absence of a common language or a shared history. What he criticizes, is the ideal

45 Walzer (1983: 39).
46 Mouffe (2005: 16).
47 Schmitt (1996: 35).
48 Mouffe (2005: 16, 20).
49 For a good discussion see Abizadeh (2005).
50 Manent (2007: 7).

of a completely unified humanity. Most proponents of the European version of democratic empire, according to Manent, have forgotten that collective differences or 'separations between and among human groups' are not only *inevitable* aspects of politics, but also *essential* ones.[51] Limitation and differentiation are essential aspects of any kind of political regime. A global political community, hence, should be dismissed.

Similar arguments can be found within a wide variety of political philosophical positions. At the heart of this type of criticism is the assumption that the self-referential nature of collective self-determination and identity formation implies a distinction between insiders and outsiders. Collective self-legislation necessarily presupposes a 'clearly defined self' to which one can ascribe collectively binding decisions.[52] Self-legislation is always also self-constitution.[53]

The consequences of this dynamic for our discussion of the (minimal) world state is rather straightforward. Since there is no 'external other' or 'constitutive outside', a world state is an impossible ideal. The same applies to proposals for a strong kind of global democracy. Without a politically organized global community, it is almost impossible to fully democratize the global forces of domination. Although one could reply that a minimal world state need not annul the importance of *membership* in bounded political communities, this misses the point of the exclusion argument. According to this type of argument, no bounded political community can ever develop at the global level.

At first sight this argument sounds convincing. If collective self-legislation implies self-constitution then sovereignty implies exclusion. On further consideration, however, things are more complicated. Even if one admits that the formation of political identities requires the drawing of a boundary, one can still question why this boundary should be thought of in *spatial* terms. Why should political identity formation and self-legislation presuppose a *geographically* external other? Isn't it possible to construct difference and otherness *imaginatively*[54] or 'through a temporal differentiation between its present and its past delimitation of the temporal dimension'? History, in the last case, becomes 'the Other in terms of which the global Self is defined'.[55] A global democratic community, in other words, develops by distinguishing itself from what it is not: a voluntary association of strategically oriented nation-states. If this is true, there is no reason why a global political community is conceptually impossible. Whether or not a global political community will develop, however, is a different question.

51 Manent (2007: 7).
52 Habermas (2006: 76).
53 Benhabib (2004: 45).
54 Abizadeh (2005: 58).
55 Wendt (2003: 527).

2.4.4 Realist arguments

Because of a perceived lack of understanding of empirical questions and real world politics, proposals for some form of world state and government are often dismissed as purely utopian.[56] They fail to live up to the dictum formulated by Rousseau, that of 'taking men as they are, and the laws as they can be'.[57] In this regard, contemporary defenders of a world state can be criticized for precisely the same reasons as the first advocates of a perpetual peace project. The proposals of Pierre Dubois, William Penn, Abbé de Saint-Pierre, or Jeremy Bentham were often seen as little more than the pompous daydreams of utopian theorists.

Twentieth-century political realists, likewise, tend to accuse their internationalist contemporaries of a similar naiveté. Given the constraints imposed on politics by the egoistic passions of human beings, the self-interested motivation of states and the anarchical nature of the international order, it is very unlikely that a stable form of world state will ever come into being (*infeasibility objection*). And even if a world state would one day be feasible the process of creating such a state would 'do more harm in a moment than it would guard against for ages'[58] (*consequentialist objection*).

2.4.4.1 *The infeasibility objection*

Should all attempts to outline the contours of some form of world state be rejected as utopian and therefore irrelevant? A first thing to note is that, in the course of the past centuries, utopian ideas have influenced world politics – often for the worse – but sometimes for the better. Looking at the early proposals for an international political order, Archibugi rights emphasizes that:

> [T]he writings of Hugo Grotius and Émeric Crucé informed some of the ideas approved at Westphalia; that Saint-Pierre was physically at the gates of Utrecht ... and that Hans Kelsen prepared and circulated drafts for a new League of Nations statute long before governments agreed on the founding of the United Nations.[59]

One should, in other words, not be too quick to dismiss 'utopian thinking' as completely at odds with the real world of politics. Ideas, moreover, are patient. Often, the passing of time suffices to make realistic those proposals that were deemed utopian not so long before. At the time of Penn's *Essay towards the*

56 Here and below I build on Tinnevelt and Geenens (2008).
57 Rousseau (1997: 41).
58 Ibid (1917: 112).
59 Archibugi (1998: 199).

Present and Future Peace of Europe (1693), nobody would have thought that his proposal for a European League would one day turn into reality.

A lot depends, however, on the type of world state that one tries to defend and the way in which it is established (see above). Whereas a unified global state will indeed strain our power of imagination, a minimal world state will not. The leap from Walzer's third degree global pluralism or Habermas's proposal for a world domestic politics without a world state, to a subsidiary and federal world republic isn't that far. All these regimes consist of democratic states at the national level, networks of continental regimes at the transnational level, and a world organization with limited competence at the global level.

To this we might add that the 'interconnected threats and challenges'[60] we face in our globalizing age and the global public goods that need to be provided, might be able to unify the different strategic agendas and provide the right incentive for making a move to the right of Walzer's continuum more realistic.[61]

These counterarguments, however, all have a provisional character. As long as some form of world state hasn't been established, the infeasibility objection cannot be dismissed.

2.4.4.2 *The consequentialist objection*

Can we execute the idea of a world state without changing the condition of peace into its opposite? According to Rousseau – and to a certain extent Kant – we probably can't. Both point at the tension between the idea of a world state and its execution.[62] Let us admire such a fair project, Rousseau writes in his criticism of Saint Pierre, but 'console ourselves for its failure by the thought that it could only have been carried out by violent means from which humanity must needs shrink'.[63]

One way of by-passing the consequentialist objection is to stress the importance of collective self-governance and argue for 'transitional phases' or even a 'gradual reform according to principles'[64] instead of trying to coercively establish a state-like political structure at the global level. Kleingeld's reinterpretation of Kant's view on international relations is illuminating in this regard. Kant, according to Kleingeld, neither regards the world state as conceptually contradictory, nor does he really reject this idea as undesirable or infeasible. In fact, he 'combines the defence of a voluntary league with an argument for the ideal of a world federation with coercive powers'.[65] The only way to approximate the world

60 Annan (2005: 6).
61 Marchetti (2008: 155–6).
62 Compare Maus (2006: 474–80).
63 Rousseau (1917: 111–12).
64 Compare Höffe (2007: 206) and Langer (1986).
65 Kleingeld (2004: 304).

state is through the intermediate stage of the voluntary establishment of a league of nations.

Although defending a gradual reform according to principles could imply that the transition from a voluntary league of states to a world state will never be completed – consequently reaffirming the importance of the infeasibility objection – it does refute the consequentialist objection.

2.4.5 Disanalogy arguments

The establishment of a world state, according to critics, is not only unrealistic but also superfluous. This is not only the case because global problems and security threats can also – and probably even more effectively – be dealt with on lower levels of governance (*superfluous objection*), but also because there are significant differences between the state of nature between individuals and the state of nature between states (*no social contract objection*).

2.4.5.1 The superfluous objection

Whether or not this objection strikes a chord seems – at first sight – to be a matter of empirical research and not of philosophical analysis. Without a thorough comparison of the functioning of a world state and for example that of a system of global governance, it seems almost impossible to determine which model can more effectively secure peace and solve collective action problems.[66] But on further consideration, different reasons can be given why one can doubt that the latter – or a similar regime, for that matter – is more effective than the former.

One of these reasons is based on the important difference between what Höffe calls a 'willingness to establish peace' and a 'reliable protection of the peace'.[67] Although our current constellation consists of different dispute settlement procedures and many international organizations have the authority to impose sanctions, the entire system can still be seen as a more or less voluntary association of states that lacks the capacity to ensure full compliance. Full compliance can only be secured within the context of a world organization with *effective* sanctioning power. We need not deny, therefore, that some form of peace is possible within a system of global governance, but we can argue that such a peace is a provisional and maybe even unstable one.

But even if we suppose that global governance is a more effective regime than the world state, the previous counterargument resurfaces in a different guise. Considering the 'huge number of international organizations' that are required to deal with global problems and protect peace, it is unclear who should settle

66 Meyer's analysis of the 'statelessness of world society' is interesting in this regard, see Krücken and Drori (2009: 194ff).
67 Höffe (2007: 204).

disputes between them, and 'do so in accordance with the law rather than a given power constellation'.[68] In the long run, then, the superfluous objection might not be all that convincing.

2.4.5.2 *No-social contract objection*

The no-social contract objection, finally, has a long tradition within legal and political theory. Although theorists like Locke and Rousseau more or less explicitly claim that a social contract between states is needed, they – for different reasons – are not prepared to argue for some form of world state. One of these reasons is that no structural analogy exists between the state of nature between individuals and that between states.

Similar accounts can be found in the work of many contemporary legal and political theorists. Postnational arrangement of international society, according to them, should not literally mirror the construction of the nation-state. Habermas, for instance, argues that the constitutionalization of international law should not be seen 'as a logical continuation of the evolution of the constitutional state leading from the national to a global state'. Both processes have different starting points. There already exists a constitution – such as the Charter of the United Nations – at the global level and the actors (states) are members of an international body. What is absent from the state of nature between states is not 'a constitution that founds an association of free and equal consociates under law', but a supranational organization with 'executive and sanctioning powers'.[69]

The no-social contract objection, however, is untenable. From the fact that the national, international, and supranational order differ in many ways, one cannot directly infer that no form of world state is desirable. A disanalogy between constitutionalism at these three political levels, for instance, does not dispel the claim that a stronger hierarchy and unity between the different constitutional sites and courts of justice is needed to end the present fragmentation of our international constitutional order. So one can acknowledge the fact that, within our globalizing world, the model of the nation-state is not the only (and maybe not even the best) source of political imagination and still embrace some form of the world state. The no-social contract objection merely cautions us not to see 'democracy beyond borders' or 'justice beyond borders' only through the lens of the full-blown ideal of the democratic nation-state.

2.5 RESTRAINED COMPETENCES?

Given the important differences between the model of a unified global state and that of a subsidiary and federal world republic, the latter seems far better equipped

68 Höffe (2007: 204).
69 Habermas (2006: 132).

to deal with the traditional arguments against the world state than the former – especially with regard to the realist and Kantian arguments, and the pluralism objection. By recognizing the importance of the dual principles of federalism and subsidiarity, the proponents of a minimal world state create room for a multi-level political system in which nation-states are still the privileged sites of democracy.

The only arguments that cannot be fully countered are the no-exit and the feasibility objection. Especially the latter one will continue to expose the idea of a minimal world state to strong realist critique. As long as a minimal world state hasn't been established, Morgenthau's well-known warning will retain its original appeal: 'There is no shirking the conclusion that international peace cannot be permanent without a world state, and that a world state cannot be established under the present moral, social, and political conditions of the world.'[70]

These two objections, nevertheless, don't have enough power of persuasion to reject the model of a minimal world state. Instead, they show the relevance of further research. There is one important worry, however, that still hasn't been fully addressed – one that is closely related to the ungovernability objection and the safeguards that proponents of a minimal world state install to prevent unrestrained interpretations of its responsibilities and a 'bloating of government and bureaucracy'.[71] Are these safeguards able to prevent a gradual expansion of the responsibilities of the minimal world state? Can such a state, in other words, remain a complementary or secondary state in the long run? If not, the model of a minimal world state will move to the right of Walzer's continuum and will again be exposed to some of the arguments that were rejected above.

What I would like to argue – but am not fully capable of doing, given the size of this paper – is that the principles of subsidiarity and all-affectedness contain a tendency to hierarchical centralization. Let's start with the first.

Claiming that powers should, as far as possible, rest with the lower-level subunits, only makes sense in the context of fair background conditions – among else an 'initial fair, global distribution of resources'.[72] We cannot, as Gosepath rightly claims, 'demand self-help from those who unfairly have less than others, but are still able to help themselves'.[73] This implies that a minimal world state is not only responsible for maintaining peace and securing international and global civic laws, but also for guaranteeing global justice. Although this broader range of functions *de facto* only remains in play as long as such a fair, global distribution of resources hasn't been guaranteed, it still points to the fact that a minimal world state will have a tough job staying minimal.

A second problem is related to the 'all-affected principle' that proponents of a minimal world state use to deal with the boundary problem within their multilevel

70 Morgenthau (1985: 536).

71 Höffe (2007: 223).

72 Gosepath (2001: 153).

73 Ibid (2001: 154).

political system. This problem basically revolves around the following question: who can take part in decision-making regarding cross-border issues? The solution that the all-affected principle offers seems rather straightforward and convincing at first sight. Depending on the scale and nature of political problems, the required solution and the proper scope of the relevant democratic communities will differ. Local problems demand local responses and constituencies, whereas global political problems require supranational solutions and will affect a global constituency.

The main problem with the all-affected principle, however, is not only that it will lead to a 'multiplication of sites of representation and discursive involvement'[74] or that it lacks a determinate content, but primarily that there is no principled line between global, international, and national problems. The traditional distinction between national and international affairs is vague, 'politically contested and insufficient when it comes to problems to do not only with war and peace, but also with the environment, international justice and so forth'.[75] How can disputes regarding the right delineation of national and international issues be solved? And who is responsible for deciding where those boundaries lie?

One way of revolving possible disputes is to follow the judgment of the German Federal Constitutional Court on the Treaty of Lisbon and declare one-sidedly and maybe once and for all which decisions should be taken on the national level and which on the European level.[76] Such a solution, however, runs counter to the basic intuitions of the model of a minimal world state and gives individual states the opportunity to withdraw from international institutions at any moment they see fit and for any kind of self-centred reason. These decisions will therefore need to be taken by higher-level political institutions.

If we add to this the fact that the process of globalization will lead to an increase in transboundary issues and the scale of 'all affected', a certain centralizing tendency is inevitable. Höffe's distinction between the *de jure* and *de facto* responsibilities of the minimal world state nicely illustrates this point. *De jure* limited to a small set of responsibilities, it will *de facto* be responsible for much more.

So although a minimal world state is better capable of countering the traditional arguments against the world state than a global state, it still keeps a very fragile balance between a simultaneous need for centralization and decentralization.

Bibliography

Abizadeh, A. (2005) 'Does Collective Identity Presuppose An Other? On the Alleged Incoherence of Global Solidarity', *American Political Science Review*, 99: 45–60.

Albert, M. and Stichweh, R. (eds) (2007) *Weltstaat und Weltstaatlichkeit: Beobachtungen globaler politischer Strukturbildung*, Wiesbaden: Vs Verlag.

Annan, K. (2005) *In Larger Freedom: Towards development, security and human rights for all*, New York: United Nations.

74 Benhabib (2006: 218).
75 Tännsjö (2008: 125).
76 Compare articles 249 and 252 of the judgment.

Archibugi, D. (1998) 'Principles of Cosmopolitan Democracy', in D. Archibugi, D. Held and M. Kohler (eds), *Re-imagining Political Community*, Stanford: Stanford University Press.
Benhabib, S. (2004) *The Rights of Others: Aliens, Residents and Citizens*, Cambridge: Cambridge University Press.
—— (2006) *Another Cosmopolitanism*, New York: Oxford University Press.
Brunkhorst, H. (2006) 'How Much Democracy does Global Constitutionalism Need?', in R. Tinnevelt and G. Verschraegen (eds), *Between Cosmopolitan Ideals and State Sovereignty: Studies in Global Justice*, Houndmills: Palgrave.
Cabrera, L. (2004) *Political Theory of Global Justice: A Cosmopolitan Case for the World State*, London and New York: Routledge.
Caney, S. (2005) *Justice beyond Borders: A Global Political Theory*, Oxford: Oxford University Press.
Craig, C. (2008) 'The Resurgent Idea of World Government', *Ethics and International Affairs*, 22(2): 133–42.
Dahl, R. A. (1998) *On Democracy*, New Haven and London: Yale University Press.
De Schutter, H. and Tinnevelt, R. (2009) 'Is Liberal Nationalism Incompatible with Global Democracy', *Metaphilosophy*, 40(1): 109–30.
Deudney, D. H. (2007) *Bounding Power: Republican Security Theory from the Polis to the Global Village*, Princeton and Oxford: Princeton University Press.
Dryzek, J. (2008) 'Two Paths to Global Democracy', *Ethical Perspectives*, 15(4): 469–86.
Dunleavy, P. (2007) 'The State', in R. E. Goodin, P. Pettit and T. Pogge (eds), *A Companion to Contemporary Political Philosophy*, vol. 2 (2nd edn), Malden, MA: Blackwell, 793–803.
Føllesdal, A. (1998) 'Survey Article: Subsidiarity', *The Journal of Political Philosophy*, 6(2): 190–218.
Føllesdal, A. and Hix, S. (2006) 'Why There Is a Democratic Deficit in the EU: A Response to Majone and Moravcsik', *Journal of Common Market Studies*, 44: 533–62.
Gosepath, S. (2001) 'The Global Scope of Justice', *Metaphilosophy*, 32(1/2): 135–59.
Habermas, J. (2006) *The Divided West*, Cambridge: Polity Press.
Heater, D. (1996) *World Citizenship and Government: Cosmopolitan ideas in the history of Western political thought*, Houndmills: Macmillan Press.
Höffe, O. (2007) *Democracy in an Age of Globalisation*, Dordrecht: Springer.
Horn, C. (1996) 'Philosophische Argumente für einen Weltstaat', *Allgemeine Zeitschrift für Philosophie*, 21(3): 229–51.
Hume, D. (2006) *Political Essays* (5th edn), Cambridge: Cambridge University Press.
Kant, I. (1999) *Practical Philosophy*, ed. M. J. Gregor, Cambridge: Cambridge University Press.
Kleingeld, P. (2004) 'Approaching Perpetual Peace: Kant's Defence of a League of States and his Ideal of a World Federation', *European Journal of Philosophy*, 12(3): 304–25.
Krücken, G. and Drori, G. S. (eds), (2009) *World Society: The Writings of John W. Meyer*, Oxford: Oxford University Press.
Langer, C. (1986) *Reform nach Prinzipien. Untersuchungen zur politischen Theorie Immanuel Kants*, Stuttgart: Klett-Cotta.
Lu, C. (2006), 'World government', in E. N. Zalta (ed.), *The Stanford Encyclopedia of Philosophy*, http://plato.stanford.edu/archives/win2006/entries/world-government.

Manent, P. (2007) *Democracy Without Nations: The fate of self-government in Europe*, Wilmington: Intercollegiate Studies Institute.
Maus, I. (2006) 'From Nation-State to Global State, or the Decline of Democracy', *Constellations*, 13(4): 465–85.
Marchetti, R. (2008) *Global Democracy: For and Against. Ethical Theory, Institutional Design and Social Struggles*, London and New York: Routledge.
Miller, D. (2000) *Citizenship and National Identity*, Cambridge: Polity Press.
—— (2007) *National Responsibility and Global Justice*, Oxford: Oxford University Press.
Moravcsik, A. (2004) 'Is there a "Democratic Deficit" in World Politics? A Framework for Analysis', *Government and Opposition*, 29(2): 336–63.
Morgenthau, H. J. (1985) *Politics among Nations: The Struggle for Power and Peace* (6th edn), New York: McGraw Hill.
Morris, C. W. (2004) 'The Modern State', in Ge. F. Gaus and C. Kukathas (eds), *The Handbook of Political Theory*, London: Sage.
Mouffe, C. (2005) *On the Political*, London: Routledge.
Nozick, R. (1974) *Anarchy, State, and Utopia*, New York: Basic Books.
Pettit, P. (2009) 'Legitimate International Institutions: A Neorepublican Perspective', in J. Tasioulas and S. Besson (eds), *The Philosophy of International Law*, Oxford: Oxford University Press (forthcoming), http://papers.ssrn.com/sol3/papers.cfm?abstract_id=1313211.
Riley, P. (1973) 'Rousseau as a Theorist of National and International Federalism', *Publius*, 3(1), 5–17.
Rousseau, J. J. (1917) *A Lasting Peace through the Federation of Europe and The State of War*, London: Constable.
—— ([1762] 1997) *'The Social Contract' and Other Later Political Writings*, Cambridge: Cambridge University Press.
Schmitt, C. (1996), *The Concept of the Political*, Chicago: University of Chicago Press.
Tännsjo, T. (2008) *Global Democracy: The Case for World Government*, Edinburgh: Edinburgh University Press.
Tinnevelt, R. and Geenens, R. (2008) 'The Coming of Age of Global Democracy? An Introduction', *Ethical Perspectives*, 15(4): 427–51.
Tinnevelt, R. and De Schutter, H. (2008) 'Global Justice as Justice for a World of Largely Independent Nations? From Dualism to a Multi-level Ethical Position', *CRISPP*, 11(4): 519–38.
Walzer, M. (1983) *Spheres of Justice: A Defense of Pluralism and Equality*, New York: Basic Books.
—— (2003) *Arguing about War*, New Haven, CT: Yale University Press.
Weber, M. (1947) *The Theory of Social and Economic Organization*, trans. A. M. Henderson and T. Parsons, New York: Oxford University Press.
Wendt, A. (2003) 'Why a World State is Inevitable', *European Journal of International Relations*, 9(4): 491–542.

Part II

Chapter 3

Guilty landscapes

Collective guilt and international criminal law

Chrisje Brants

3.1 INTRODUCTION

In the grand scheme of the cosmopolitan project, the development of a global legal order is both a necessity and a given, leading to peace under the rule of law and driven by a shared morality and commitment to human rights (Fine, 2003; Habermas, 2001; Beck, 2006). Or is it that the shared morality and human rights commitment lead to the global legal order? Given that morality, human rights and legal order are all normative socio-political constructions, the question of causation is impossible to answer. And yet increasingly the development of a body of substantive and procedural rules of international humanitarian criminal law,[1] culminating in the establishment of the International Criminal Court (ICC), is assumed to be the means by which conflict, tyranny and lawlessness will be transformed into peace, the rule of law and democracy. In that sense, international criminal law seems to be more than just one of the forms of transitional justice, whereby war-torn societies seek a reckoning with the past. Not only does the unprecedented proliferation of international courts and tribunals reflect a deep-seated faith in the ability of international criminal law to heal the wounds of mass murder (Heller, 2008: 975), it has come to be regarded as an integral part of the great transition to a cosmopolitan world, one of the microcosms of the proposed cosmos whereby Enlightenment ideals and legal principles will bring about the required state of humanitarian morality.

Much is expected of it and it has great aspirations. Its most important aims, found in the prevailing discourse of international legal culture – at least, the discourse of international politicians and many, if not most lawyers – and in the preambles to the statutes of the different ad hoc tribunals and the International

1 I use this term in order to distinguish between criminal law under which the international core crimes of genocide, crimes against humanity and war crimes are judged, and what is traditionally understood by the term international criminal law, that is concerned with cooperation between states in order to facilitate or allow national law to be applied. To make for easier reading, I will simply refer to international criminal law in the rest of this contribution.

Criminal Court include not only ending impunity with regard to genocide, crimes against humanity and war crimes, but also establishing and/or reinforcing the rule of law and democracy by reconciliation, conflict solution, deterrence and retribution; providing a platform for the recognition of and redress for victims; and, through all this, contributing to collective memory and history for the sake of future generations.[2] Intriguingly, while in most jurisdictions of the developed world the legitimacy of domestic criminal law and justice (which has, *mutatis mutandis*, the same interrelated aims) is increasingly challenged in the wake of and parallel to diminishing faith in the rational discourse of democracy and law, and the rise of populism, international criminal law's claim to cosmopolitan legitimacy that derives from its stated aims is more or less taken for granted.

It should be noted that international criminal law (like human rights) makes a claim to universality, while at the same time in its institutionalized form it is both substantively and procedurally dependent on consensus between sovereign nation states, and the jurisdiction of the ICC takes second place to that of domestic legal orders. That, however, is only one of its inherent contradictions, although in the political realities of the world it is one that raises immediate questions about the cosmopolitan potential of international criminal law. Yet to doubt that potential, to question its universal aims and claims, is something of a heresy. As if, given the gravity of the crimes and the memory of the holocaust, inquiring into what exactly international justice can realistically achieve somehow means a negation of those crimes and their victims. However, if we want to take the legitimacy of international criminal justice seriously – upon which its contribution to the cosmopolitan ideal depends – we cannot simply take its claims at face value, but must scrutinize them carefully, one by one and in their interdependence and contradictions.

Given the contradictory nature of its aspirations – indeed of the cosmopolitan ideal in general – international criminal justice could be said to bear the seeds of its own destruction, with not only a tendency to shoot itself in the foot but also a propensity to 'mission creep'. Baxi (2006) and Adelman (2008) have noted how globalization tends not to favour, indeed undermines, the traditional human rights paradigm by the promotion of trade-related, market-friendly human rights. Teitel (2005) has argued persuasively that the goal of history telling that colours the truth-finding process of an international criminal trial will inevitably also foster and be meant to foster normative regime change and nation building. It is but a small step from retroactive history-making legitimizing the trial of prior leaders, to legitimizing proactive intervention with the humanitarian aim of stopping atrocities and making the trial possible in the first place. The legitimacy of transitional justice then creeps forward to mesh with the legitimacy of humanitarian intervention. It could also be said that history telling can stand in the way of

2 See extensively on the relationship between these politically directed aims: Alvarez (2004: 321–2); Brants (2007: 26–38).

another accepted axiom of international criminal justice, namely that a fair trial, conducted according to the principles of due process, is essential to the establishment of the rule of law in societies in transition, because it is a demonstration of how civilization and humanity can prevail over barbarity (Brants, 2010). This contribution will take a closer look at this claim made for fair trial, and more specifically at one of its most important principles, that of individual guilt in relation to the other aims of international criminal justice. Can it be that even in such details its contradictory and self-defeating potential makes itself felt?

3.2 NOTIONS OF GUILT

The principle of individual guilt in criminal law permeates Western legal culture and is commonly regarded as one of its great achievements. The precise legal language in which the principle finds its way into jurisprudence and law serves to contain any notion of guilt that threatens to escape and overflow into collective guilt, whereby a whole people or their descendants are held guilty for crimes committed by individuals (the German people for the Holocaust, for example, or those with white skins for slavery). Or into metaphysical guilt, the existential state in which man is simply guilty because of the very fact of his being. In 1998 the Dutch artist Armando, plagued by troubled memories of World War II, created a work called 'Guilty landscape'.[3] It has been interpreted by some to symbolize metaphysical guilt: Armando's landscape and trees are the blind witnesses to the atrocities of war that took place in and around them, so that they are infested with guilt and therefore guilty themselves. Man is absent from this guilty landscape, which is precisely why it serves as a metaphor for the *condition humaine* that is permanently at risk of being overwhelmed by guilt (Mooij, 1997: 8).

Interpreted thus, collective and metaphysical guilt are the exclusive terrain of philosophy and art, banned from criminal law lest we descend into legal cultural atavism. Yet, art also teaches us that 'guilty landscapes' are not only blind, if guilty, witnesses, but also accusers, who confront collective humanity with what was done in its name. 'We are building a new world' is the title of a painting of the desolate wilderness that was Flanders during and after World War I (by the English war artist Paul Nash; it hangs in the Imperial War Museum in London): here it is not the landscape that bears the guilt, but man who, having failed abysmally, has now abandoned the ruin he created. And the Wallonian painter and poet Henri Michaux sees both guilty landscapes and guilty humanity:

3 Armando, *Schuldig landschap*, is part of the collection at the Het Valkhof museum in Nijmegen, in the Netherlands.

Landscapes to cover the wounds, the steel, the shell splinter, the
Evil, the era, the rope around the neck, the mobilisation.
Landscapes to smother the screams.
Landscapes like a sheet to cover one's face.[4]

Something of the ambiguity of the original verse is lost in translation, because the poet compares the gradually healing landscape of France after World War I to a *drape*, which can mean sheet, curtain or shroud in French, although some of the metaphorical meaning is still retained in English. These are landscapes behind which we can hide, but they themselves also hide the scars of war: a sort of natural cover up, not only of the broken countryside and the dead but also of the crimes that were committed, while at the same time this panders to our need not to face the unbearable guilt we have incurred because of them.

The principle of individual guilt, part of our legal cultural heritage, governs the criminal law of nation states and functions in relatively stable societies in peace-time and within the parameters of (neo-) enlightenment principles. In such criminal law, overblown notions of guilt are easily refuted with an appeal to those same principles.[5] But the individual guilt of national criminal law concerns the individual evil of crime, not the greater collective evil of war. It is no coincidence that artists relate the guilt of landscapes and humanity to armed conflict and to the chaos and mass destruction that are the result. In the great evil of war, as Armando and Michaux would have us understand, collective or metaphysical guilt – the two are distinguishable, but nevertheless overlap – eventually removes from view all traces of any individual share. 'Where all are guilty, no one is', wrote Hannah Arendt (2003: 23).

This is a dilemma that increasingly plagues international humanitarian criminal law that is concerned with situations of mass atrocity, precisely because it is based on enlightened (Western) national legal systems, and therefore also on the principle of individual guilt. International criminal law is part of, and claims a role in, transitional justice: the process of transition through which societies, torn apart by armed conflict, pass on the road to a future in which law and justice are the leading and binding principles of stability. But international criminal law only appears on the stage if, during that conflict, crimes against humanity have occurred that are systematic, on a massive scale and almost invariably perpetrated in a collective

4 Michaux (1961). Original in French; my translation.

5 This is not to say that some form of collective guilt does not figure in domestic criminal law in most European countries. Indeed, its prevalence is increasing. It would go beyond the scope of this paper to delve into the deeper causes of the collectivization of legal guilt in late modernity. Suffice it perhaps to say (as an oversimplification) that increasing manifestations of collective interest in, and claims to protection against, risk and danger to the detriment of the individual interest in, and right to, the protection of fundamental principles in criminal law, bring the prospect of collective guilt ever closer.

context. In coming to a verdict about the guilt of individuals – i.e. searching for the 'truth' about events – we cannot simply pull the sheet over our head, but must face the unbearable. The principle of individual guilt would seem to preclude this, so that, increasingly, for that reason international criminal law stands accused of being not fit for purpose. There is, so it is said, selective fact-finding, but no truth, law, but no justice. In the light of such criticism, the problem of collective guilt and the question whether it should remain banned from the realm of criminal law, cannot be ignored. In this context, the principles of enlightenment do not convince – indeed, if they embody rationality, truth and morality, they mean that we must take collective guilt seriously in international criminal law.

3.3 OBJECTIONS TO THE PRINCIPLE OF INDIVIDUAL GUILT IN THE CONTEXT OF INTERNATIONAL CRIMES[6]

According to a number of critics, whose arguments have been most extensively articulated by the American Mark Drumbl (2005a: 539–610; 2007), the transplantation of principles of national law, and particularly the principle of individual guilt, to an international context makes no sense, because we are dealing with a quite different type of criminality in quite different circumstances in the international context than those for which national criminal law was designed. Strictly according to the letter of substantive international criminal law as it is to be found in the statutes and case law of the international courts and tribunals, it is conceivable that international crimes, even genocide, could be committed by a single individual. But this is primarily a matter of theory. In practice, international crimes are committed almost exclusively on a mass scale by large numbers of perpetrators and in the context of systemic violence, and in any event, there are, by definition, large groups of victims (Van Sliedregt, 2003: 5; Ohlin, 2006: 73).[7] Partly for that reason, international crimes share a certain collectiveness. Most authors seem to derive a concept of collective action in this context from Dworkin: it is impossible to analyse such criminal acts according to the individual share of each participant or to reduce them to the statistical function of an individual deed. On the contrary, they are committed by 'individuals acting together in a way that merges their separate actions into a further, unified act that is together theirs' (Dworkin, 1996: 19–20).

6 I use this term to refer to the three categories of core crimes with which international criminal law is concerned.

7 Genocide only exists if there is intent to destroy a national, ethnic, racial or religious group as such in whole or in part; ordinary crimes such as murder or rape do not become crimes against humanity unless they are part of a large or systematic attack on a civilian population, while war crimes must be part of a plan or policy. See Articles 6, 7 and 8 of the ICC Rome Statute.

Drumbl maintains that this collective element forms the essence of international crimes (Drumbl, 2005a: 571; cf. Fletcher, 2005: 1077). The perpetrators commit violence as part of and on behalf of a group, in the name of ideological values and ideas that are experienced and accepted as imperative within the culture of that group. Some group members play a leading, intellectual role; others are the foot soldiers who translate ideas and ideology into collective mass atrocity. Others again – the bystanders, usually the majority – simply watch, but tacitly approve, or at least do not distance themselves from the violence, let alone protest against it. The victims also form a collective, targeted because they too are members of a group, one that is defined as threatening and hostile. These circumstances warrant two conclusions. Firstly, such crimes cannot be committed without the collective cooperation of the whole group, although the degree of collective perpetration and each individual's part, and blameworthiness, may differ. Secondly, what we have here is an inversion of values, norms and definitions that means that the criminality with which international criminal law is concerned, is not self-evidently deviant in the societies 'where or at the time at which it is committed (even though it may deviate from international norms of *ius cogens* and elementary human decency)' (Drumbl, 2005a: 567).

Now, normal people do not suddenly fly in the face of such compelling basic norms and become mass murderers. International crimes are committed within a group culture of fear and violence that is not only rationalized and justified by techniques of neutralization, but that becomes a culture of normality in which situations are redefined, thereby allowing individuals to regard behaviour as perfectly legitimate that they would, under other circumstances, certainly view as deviant.[8] In this opaque reality, violence is shorn of its criminal nature and victims of their true status (Galtung, 1990: 292). The development of a rationalizing vocabulary (in which the mass media play an important part) is indispensable to such justification of international crimes. On the one hand, the perpetrators' need and search for a legitimate identity, for example as the saviours of their people in the face of a group of dangerous others, may lead to the systematic portrayal of victims as a life-threatening plague of vermin that must be exterminated.[9] On the other hand, more subtle but no less effective, there is the (official) vocabulary of moral neutrality. Civilian dead after bombing attacks become *collateral damage*, the destruction of villages or crops is 'punishment' or 'deterrence'. Removing prisoners to countries where they face certain torture and possibly death is called *extraordinary rendition*. The deportation of groups of the population – often the

8 The concept of the *culture of normality* was first used in a criminological context by Box (1983) and Coleman (1987), to explain crime committed by and on behalf of corporations. Brants (2007: 314 ff.) has transported the notion to the context in which international crimes occur.

9 The Nazis protrayed the Jews as rats. More recently, *Radio Télévision Libre des Milles Collines* in Rwanda consistently referred to Tutsis as cockroaches (see *Prosecutor v Akayesu* ITCR-96–4-T, T.Ch.1, 2 September 1998, §§148–9).

precursor to or even part of genocide – goes not by a neutral name but by one with a positive linguistic connotation: ethnic *cleansing*.[10]

Contrary to what is the case in the 'normal' circumstances in which national criminal law functions, international criminal law must deal with an abnormal context that is redefined as normal, in which the accused are those who conformed to prevailing norms, while those who resisted were the deviants.

> This broad participation [in atrocity], despite is catalytic role, is overlooked by the criminal law, thereby perpetuating a myth and a deception ... In situations of mass violence, the assumptions of the domestic model are reversed: most people are implicated in the atrocity, and non-participation – at least, open opposition – is the deviant act.
>
> (Drumbl, 2007: 172)

According to Drumbl, in these circumstances it is an anomaly to design international trials as an analog of national criminal process and therefore to require proof of individual guilt as the basis for punishment. He adds that, while guilt and blameworthiness in the national context are based on the degree to which an accused can be said to have acted (or neglected to act) freely and independently, this is precisely what is in doubt with regard to the majority of people who are implicated in a collective atrocity. However, because the principle of individual guilt is incorporated into international criminal law, this has important consequences for the (historical and) narrative value of the investigation by the court and its verdict: such trials are unable to encompass the scope and complexity of the relationship between collectivity and violence, and one of the results is that bystanders remain outside of the reach of the criminal law, which essentially affords them a form of amnesty – a variation on Hannah Arendt (Drumbl, 2005a: 570). Some scholars go a step further: only the very small minority for whom it can be proved that they were leaders, gave orders or personally and frequently committed murder, will stand trial; the great majority who were part of a rampaging mob, who encouraged, stood watching, supported a criminal regime or looked the other way, will face no such consequences. Because criminal law is obsessed with individual guilt of a few, it allows the many to perpetuate the myth that they are not implicated and therefore bear no guilt (Fletcher, 2005: 1077). And so criminal law shares the guilt of the landscape – it becomes a means of not having to face the truth, a sheet to cover one's face.

Moreover, because it cannot take into account the specific characteristics of mass atrocity and judge members of society according to the way in which they participated in international crimes, international criminal justice cannot fulfil its own proclaimed goals of retribution, deterrence, redress, restoration of stable

10 See more extensively: Brants (2007: 315–16).

social relations, and the establishment of a legitimate collective memory, all of which require a 'truthful account' of what took place. This is the more damaging, because, in a burgeoning international legal culture, international criminal law is regarded as *the* legitimate response to mass atrocity, so that other context-specific or traditional ways of responding (such as reintegration and reconciliation rituals) are excluded as being insufficiently 'fair' and are accepted only as subordinate to international criminal law.[11] The result is that too much law leads to too little justice. It is hardly surprising that those who see the problem as the result of the principle of individual guilt draw two conclusions: first, that the important and formal predicate of international law that collective guilt is to be avoided at all costs, must be reconsidered; and second, that the collective context of international crime requires that we look for sanctions that can take it into account (Drumbl: 2007; Fletcher: 2002).

3.4 OBJECTIONS AGAINST COLLECTIVE GUILT IN THE CONTEXT OF INTERNATIONAL CRIMES

It is not entirely true that international criminal law does not take the collective nature of international crimes into account, for it plays a role both in sanctioning and in how individual guilt is dealt with. In the preamble of the ICC Statute, the Court's (complementary) jurisdiction is limited to *the most serious crimes of concern to the international community*, which, in combination with the principle of individual guilt, puts the focus on those who bear the greatest responsibility: people who give orders, who plan and direct policy and strategy, who create or manipulate the social circumstances in which international crimes occur, or who, despite their position of leadership, make no attempt to stop such crimes. There are of course, practical considerations at work here – it is hardly feasible to drag a whole nation one by one before the court – but the principle of individual guilt is also a choice of principle, with historical roots.

Although the International Military Tribunal at Nuremberg must be regarded as the cradle of international criminal law as we now know it, the debate on collective guilt is of earlier date.[12] In the twentieth century (before then, collective punishment for atrocities in wartime usually took the form of military revenge), it was the First World War that started the discussion: what was to happen to the Germans and Turks in whose name international crimes *avant la lettre* (the name

11 This is partly the result of the principle of subsidiarity or complementarity, according to which the ICC's jurisdiction is determined: the international court has no part to play unless national states are unwilling or unable to prosecute the crimes concerned *in a fair and impartial manner* (Article 17, ICC Statute; my emphasis).

12 See for an extensive historical overview, Bass (2000). There is a wealth of literature on the Nuremberg trials. I have based this section on Sands (2003) in particular.

came later) had been committed – conducting a war of aggression, terrorizing the civilian population and plundering Belgium and Northern France, torpedoing passenger ships in unrestricted submarine warfare, and the mass murder of Armenians (and Greeks) in the Ottoman Empire? And to the military and political leaders who were responsible for such strategies and policies? The Allied victors had already started to formulate an answer during the war, and it was one that depended primarily on power politics.

The British and, to a much lesser extent, the Americans favoured criminal trials for those with the greatest responsibility (the German Kaiser, in particular). But little came of it, although the Treaty of Versailles did provide for the trial of war criminals before their own national courts.[13] Neither was any legal infrastructure developed that would have made international trials possible. The Ottoman Empire collapsed and was partially divided among the European Allies, while the German people were collectively punished on the basis of many other provisions contained in the Versailles Treaty. The punitive and revengeful sanctions imposed on Germany plunged that country into economic misery, hunger and political chaos, while the highest responsible figures went free,[14] resulting, if perhaps only indirectly, in the rise of Hitler and his Nazi Party.

During World War II, the question again arose of what to do with the Germans and Germany. This time, the Americans were the *auctores intellectuales* of the answer. The first proposals, however, came from Stalin (perhaps not surprisingly) but also from Churchill, advocate of criminal trials after World War I, to simply shoot the most important German Nazis (albeit that Stalin was thinking of a minimum number of 50,000, and Churchill of a maximum of 50). The Americans would not hear of this, but a high-level debate did develop between the United States and its Allies about what should be done. The American minister of finance, Henry Morgenthau, favoured the 'pastoralisation' of Germany, which involved annexation of the most important industrial regions, destruction of the rest of German heavy industry and the forced resettlement of a large part of the population (and, the British objected, most likely a substantial number of deaths). A milder version of this plan was actually agreed between Churchill and Roosevelt, but after the latter's death in the spring of 1945 it disappeared from the table. All attention (including that of Churchill, now convinced) was turned to designing a fair and just criminal procedure for trying the top Nazis. Only this, it was argued, would lay the foundations for a new and legitimate regime in Germany and for a lasting peace. Such a procedure would be based on the Anglo-American

13 A few submarine captains and army officers stood trial in the German Weimar Republic, and a few Turkish officers and provincial governors in Turkey. The trials, however, were little more than symbolic gestures towards the victors, and served little purpose, beyond flaming resentment and political unrest in the defeated countries.

14 Queen Wilhelmina of the Netherlands gave the Kaiser sanctuary, General Ludendorff escaped to Sweden, and General Hindenburg became (second) president of the new republic.

concept of fair trial and due process, and therefore also on the principle of individual guilt.

The essence of the mantra of international criminal law – repeated again and again by international lawyers in theory and in practice – that collective guilt and collective sanctions have no place in an international criminal trial, has therefore two basic points of departure that are rooted in history. On the one hand, the lesson learnt from Versailles is that collective guilt and collective sanctions do not result in peace, reconciliation, deterrence; rather the opposite. On the other hand, only a fair trial will serve to demonstrate what can be achieved under the rule of law, namely that civilized values and justice in the sense of retribution after procedural fairness can and must prevail over barbarity and arbitrariness. Otherwise, international criminal law loses it legitimacy, degenerates into victors' justice and becomes counterproductive.

Some authors, troubled by the criticism of the principle of individual guilt, believe that the idea of collective guilt simply has no basis in reality. Richard Goldstone, the first prosecutor at the International Tribunal for the Former Yugoslavia, said of the suspects at Nuremberg: 'one sees a group of criminals. One does not see a group of representatives of the German people – the people who produced Goethe, or Heine or Beethoven'.[15] Aside from whether Goldstone's view of reality corresponds to that of other people, as Drumbl succinctly remarks, this is a spurious argument: the same German people also brought forth Mengele, Goebbels and Himmler, and there is no reason why, if they may claim collective responsibility for the production of genius, they should not also be collectively responsible for producing mass murderers (Drumbl, 2005b: 1316). Other authors have appealed to the justice of proportional sanctions in combination with individual guilt: 'Collective sanctions may be effective, but they cannot be just if they sever the relationship between an individual's responsibility and the magnitude of his crime' (Heller, 2008: 999).

Others (e.g. Sloane, 2008: 199/200) are of the opinion that Drumbl is convincing on the failures of international criminal law to achieve its own goals because the principle of individual guilt does not connect with the social reality in which those goals must be realized. This then creates a dilemma that is not so easy to avoid. For it is one of the schizophrenias of international criminal law[16] that, by its own standards, allowing collective guilt and punishment in would lead to unjust trials and unjust, disproportionate sanctions, and frustrate the demonstration of fair and civilized justice under the rule of law. If international criminal law wishes to be the principled voice of civilization and reason, it cannot afford to water down its own principles. This Catch-22 situation has led Drumbl himself but also others to tread what appears to be a different path.

15 Quoted approvingly by Booth (2003: 184).
16 The term is Ratner's (1998).

3.5 FROM COLLECTIVE GUILT TO COLLECTIVE RESPONSIBILITY

Although there are those who assert that collective guilt is a plausible and sometimes healthy response to collective crime (Fletcher, 2004: 163), they remain a minority. It is more usual to find advocates of a 'third way' solution based not on collective guilt, but on collective responsibility. In this, they seem to base their arguments predominantly on the work of the German philosopher Karl Jaspers, although they do not always refer to it. Jaspers, partly in correspondence with Hannah Arendt, wrestled with the nature of German guilt with regard to what had happened to the Jews and others under Nazi rule, but also with the fact that such a criminal regime had been able to achieve – and retain – power. In *Die Schuldfrage* (1946), he distinguishes different forms of guilt, relevant from different perspectives and with different consequences.[17]

Criminal guilt attaches to each individual who commits an offence; this is the field of criminal law over which the courts have jurisdiction. Political guilt touches all citizens who have tolerated what has been done in the name of the state, for all bear co-responsibility for the way in which society is governed, although not all individuals are liable for the offences committed by some in the name of the state; only the victor can judge. Those who knew of serious crimes but did not resist, or those who made unethical choices so that specific crimes were committed or made possible, are morally guilty (it is moral guilt that creates the conditions in which criminal and political guilt can arise); this can only be judged according to one's individual conscience. And finally, there is the metaphysical guilt that arises out of sins against the moral ties that hold humanity together: everyone bears co-responsibility for all crime and injustice and is metaphysically guilty if no one acts to stop it; in the final event, this is the exclusive jurisdiction of God.

These distinctions are in themselves not unproblematic, but the point I wish to make here is that they are recognizable in many contributions to the debate on collective guilt in international criminal law, sometimes more or less literally:

> Even if it is really true that the German people as a whole desired the destruction of the Jews ... this question of this collective guilt must be judged by the world stage, by the conscience of the German people and ultimately by their maker, if there is one.
>
> (Ohlin, 2006: 73)

For others, they form a means of reasoning from collective responsibility in the direction of collective sanctions. If I understand Jaspers correctly, direct collective responsibility only arises in the case of political guilt. Metaphysical guilt is

17 I have used the (most recent version of the) English translation: *The Question of German Guilt*, 2000.

also collective, but it touches humanity as a whole, not only the group in whose name crimes have been committed – this makes metaphysical guilt the most relevant form in terms of human moral survival, and the least relevant for the problem that Drumbl and others are addressing. Moral guilt – however much its consequences may be collective – is an individual matter. Some authors make this distinction. Franck, for example, proceeds from the premise that the state no longer owns the individual; rather the individuals collectively own the state, so that collective responsibility must not be confused with personal guilt, although it most certainly arises when crimes against humanity are committed by or on behalf of the collective (2007: 537). And the philosopher Michael Waltzer has this to say on the political guilt from which collective responsibility derives:

> [C]itizenship is common destiny, and no one, not even [the regime's] opponents ... can escape the effect of a bad regime, an ambitious or fanatic leadership, or an overreaching nationalism. But if men and women must accept this destiny, they can sometimes do so with a good conscience, for the acceptance says nothing about their individual responsibility. The distribution of costs is not the distribution of guilt.
>
> (Waltzer, 1997: 297)

It is the distribution of costs that opens the way to collective sanctions, although it is a moot question whether the underlying concept of guilt has not escaped from the purely political into the realms of morality. Levinson, for example, starting from the functional perspective of law and economics, justifies group responsibility and group sanctions as serving to control misbehaving members of the group – 'delegated deterrence'. It is the group that risks bearing the consequences of crimes committed by some of its members and therefore has an interest as a whole that all behave in conformity with the norm, while the group is also best placed to exert (moral) pressure on its members. But the justification for collective sanctions is not purely instrumental: its basis is collective responsibility for the failure to observe the (moral and social) duty to prevent crimes occurring (Levinson, 2003: 349). Leaving aside that 'delegated deterrence' presumes rational choice and moreover clear (and civilized) norms that bind the group together (the lack of which is characteristic of precisely those circumstances in which international crimes occur), assuming the dereliction of a moral and social duty comes very close to assuming guilt.

Drumbl, who does not wish to use the term collective guilt, because guilt is a concept of criminal law and he doubts whether every member of a collective 'deserves punishment', would nevertheless call all members of perpetrator groups to account on behalf of victim groups, and subject them to collective sanctions. These include, as well as the more traditional sanctions such as embargos and other forms of trade limitations, for example removing the benefits of group violence, lustration, the redistribution of wealth and compulsory participation in community service and/or truth and reconciliation commissions (Drumbl, 2005b:

576–77). Although he does not want to bring all of this under the jurisdiction of (international) criminal courts, rather turning to the realm of political sanctions and national and traditional forms of transitional justice, it seems to me that he has done little more than switch labels, and what we are really talking about is collective punishment. It is also unclear why variations of collective sanctions and (punishment) rituals should be acceptable, but not collective punishment on the basis of collective guilt, and especially how collective sanctions avoid the injustice of collective punishment. Neither am I convinced by his answer, that there is some sort of universal norm rooted in democracy and participation of the community itself that can be a touchstone for the justice of such sanctions (Drumbl, 2007: 181–7). In many ways, Drumbl's search for the cosmopolitan ideal shows through his work and is certainly evident in this falling back on universal norms. But is there such a norm, other than in the enlightened Western principles that Drumbl finds wanting as the most important basis for the reaction to international crime? One cannot have one's cosmopolitan cake and eat it.

3.6 CONCLUSION

I began this contribution by noting that we cannot take the claims to universality that are made for and by international criminal law, and therefore its presumed legitimacy, at face value. Where cosmopolitanism appears to want to be all things to all people, it suffers inevitably from contradictions and even a tendency to self-destruct, and, as a self-proclaimed part of the cosmopolitan ideal, international criminal justice is similarly afflicted, even in the details of the legal principles that are institutionalized in substantive international criminal law. The metaphor of guilty landscapes bring us not only the message that we are all doomed to bear the guilt of our existence that is the fate of imperfect mankind, for otherwise we will lose our humanity. Such landscapes also hide the crimes they have witnessed, and accuse us of gladly accepting the cover up at the same time. That is the struggle of international criminal law with the problem of collective guilt.

Of course it is a struggle partly born of the nature of the crimes over which international criminal courts have jurisdiction. But more than anything it arises precisely out of the aspiration to be all things to all people, and therefore out of a failure to recognize the limits inherent in the option to use the criminal law to promote a global rule of law. I have no doubt that international criminal law does not make good on its own pretensions in terms of its proclaimed aspirations (Brants, 2007: 40). But I do doubt very much that this is the result of the principle of individual guilt. This is perhaps the place for a declaration of principle. While I am sceptical of the far-reaching claims of (some) cosmopolitanism and, in its wake, international criminal justice, I believe in enlightenment principles, in the idea of human rights and the notion of a fair trial. At the same time, international criminal law is but a small – though in its expressive value perhaps invaluable – part of a utopian project that strives to uphold a minimum of universal human dignity (a much less ambitious ideal than cosmopolitanism), for that is what is negated and denied by crimes against humanity. With international criminal law we can openly turn our backs on them and declare our solidarity with the victims (cf. Sloane, 2007, and Brants, 2007: 39–40). Perhaps this will help to write history, maybe some will be deterred in future, or victims find some consolation and that is a bonus, but not the *raison d'être* of international criminal law. In the final event, it is a matter of fundamental humanity, and that is not easily expressed in terms of substantive or procedural principles.

But having opted for the criminal law, we are bound by its principles. However relevant it may be for understanding how and why international crimes occur, the collective element is not something to which international criminal law should be asked to do justice. Of course, morally speaking, each individual always has a choice, and those who make the wrong choice are, together with a great many others, morally guilty. But, aside from the fact that moral guilt is not legal guilt, the question is whether the wrong choice should always be punished, or whether everyone who chooses wrongly deserves punishment, even whether those who make the right choice should suffer because of the moral failings of their 'group members'. The latter negates the very essence of human dignity, individuality. At the same time, criminal law – also international criminal law – does not ask anyone to be a hero, but in the exceptional circumstances in which international crimes are committed, only exceptionally heroic people conform to basic human standards, or rather deviate from what has become criminal conformity. It is for that very reason that it would be asking too much of international criminal law, destroying its justification, if we were to relinquish the principle of individual guilt. To be sure, if collective (political, moral and above all metaphysical) guilt are relevant to our thinking on the reality of crime, then nowhere more so than in cases of crimes against humanity. But we must recognize the limitations of our endeavour to deal with realities by means of the criminal law. For 'this guilt', wrote Hannah Arendt in a letter to Karl Jaspers dated 17 August 1946, 'in contrast to all criminal guilt, oversteps and shatters any and all legal systems' (quoted in Bass, 2000: 13).

Bibliography

Adelman, S. (2008) 'Between the Scylla of Sovereignty and the Charybdis of Human Rights: The Pitfalls of Development in Pursuit of Justice', *Human Rights and International Legal Discourse* 2: 1.

Alvarez, J. E. (2004) 'Trying Hussein: Between Hubris and Hegemony', *J. Int'l Crim. Just.* 2: 319.

Arendt, H. (2003) *Responsibility and Judgment*, New York: Random House Inc.

Bass, G. J. (2000) *Stay the Hand of Vengeance. The Politics of War Crimes Tribunals*, Princeton, NJ: Princeton University Press.

Beck, U. (2006) *The Cosmopolitan Vision*, Cambridge: Polity Press.

Booth, C. (2003) 'Prospects and Issues for the International Criminal Court: Lessons from Yugoslavia and Rwanda', in P. Sands (ed.), *From Nuremberg to the Hague: The Future of International Criminal Justice*, Cambridge: Cambridge University Press, 157.

Box, S. (1983) *Power, Crime and Mystification*, London: Tavistock.

Brants, C. (2007) 'Gold Collar Crime: The Peculiar Complexities and Ambiguities of War Crimes, Crimes against Humanity, and Genocide', in H. N. Pontell and G. Geis (eds), *International Handbook of White-Collar and Corporate Crime*, New York: Springer, 309.

—— (2007) 'No Man is an Island: The Legitimacy of International Criminal Process as a Form of Transitional Justice', in R. de Lange (ed.), *Aspects of Transitional Justice and Human Rights*, Nijmegen: WLP, 23.

—— (2010) 'Universal Crimes, Universal Justice? The Legitimacy of the International Response to Genocide, Crimes Against Humanity and War Crimes', in A. Crawford (ed.), *International and Comparative Criminal Justice and Urban Governance. Convergence and Divergence in Global, National and Local Settings*, Cambridge: CUP (forthcoming).

Coleman, J. W. (1987) 'Toward an Integrated Theory of White Collar Crime', *American Journal of Sociology* 93: 406.

Drumbl, M. A. (2005a) 'Collective Violence and Individual Punishment: The Criminality of Mass Atrocity', *Nw. U. L. Rev.* 99: 539.

—— (2005b) 'Pluralizing International Criminal Justice', *Mich. L. Rev.* 1003: 1295.

—— (2007) *Atrocity, Punishment and International Law*, Cambridge: Cambridge University Press.

Dworkin, R. (1996) *Freedom's Law. The Moral Reading of the American Constitution*, Cambridge, MA: Harvard University Press.

Fine, R. (2003) 'Taking the "ism" out of Cosmopolitanism: An Essay in Reconstruction', *European Journal of Social Theory* 6: 4.

Fletcher, G. P. (2004) 'Collective Guilt and Collective Punishment', *Theoretical Inquiries in Law* 5: 163.

—— (2002) 'Liberals and Romantics at War: The Problem of Collective Guilt', *Yale L. J.* 111: 1499.

Fletcher, L. E. (2005) 'From Indifference to Engagement: Bystanders and International Criminal Justice', *Mich. J. Int'l L.* 26: 1076.

Franck, T. (2007) 'Individual Criminal Liability and Collective Civil Responsibility: Do They Reinforce or Contradict One Another?', *Wash. U. Global Stud. L. Rev.* 6: 567.

Galtung, J. (1990) 'Cultural Violence', *Journal of Peace Research* 3: 291.

Habermas, J. (2001) *The Postnational Constellation: Political Essays*, Cambridge, MA: MIT.

Hart, H. L. A. (1968) *Punishment and Responsibility*, Oxford: Oxford University Press.

Heller, K. J. (2008) 'Deconstructing International Criminal Law', *Mich. L. Rev.* 106: 975.

Jaspers, K. (2000) *The Question of German Guilt*, trans. E. B. Ashton, New York: Fordham University Press.

Jens, D. O. (2007) 'Group Think: The Law of Conspiracy and Collective Reason', *J. Crim. L. and Criminology* 98: 147.

Levinson, D. J. (2003) 'Collective Sanctions', *Stan. L. Rev.* 56: 345.

Michaux, H. (1961) 'Landschappen (vertaling Gerrit Kouwenaar)', in *1900–1950, Bloemlezing uit de moderne buitenlandse poëzie in Nederlandse vertaling*. Samengesteld door Sybren Polet, Amsterdam: De Bezige Bij, 53.

Mooij, A. W. M. (1997) *Schuld in strafrecht en psychiatrie*, Deventer: Gouda Quint.

—— (1998) *Psychiatrie, recht en de menselijke maat. Over verantwoordelijkheid*, Amsterdam/Meppel: Boom.

—— (1999) 'Postmodernisme en gemeenschapsdenken in het strafrecht', in M. Moerings, C. M. Pelser and C. H. Brants (eds), *Morele kwesties in het strafrecht*, Deventer: Gouda Quint, 3.

Ohlin, J. D. (2006) 'Three Conceptual Problems with the Doctrine of Joint Criminal Enterprise', *J. Int'l Crim. Just.* 5: 69

Ratner, S. (1998) 'The Schizophrenias of International Criminal Law', *Texas Int'l Rev.* 33.

Röling, B. V. A. (1980) *Over het Kleine en het Grote Kwaad. Overpeinzingen over misdaad en oorlog*, Boerderijcahier 8001: uitg. Universiteit Twente.

Sands, P. (ed.) (2003) *From Nuremberg to the Hague: The Future of International Criminal Justice*, Cambridge: Cambridge University Press.

Sliedregt, E. van (2003) *The Criminal Responsibility of Individuals for Violations of International Humanitarian Law*, Den Haag: T.M.C. Asser Press.

Sloane, R. D. (2008) Book review of Mark. A. Drumbl, 'Atrocity, Punishment and International Law', *Am. J. Int'l L.* 192: 197.

—— (2007) 'The Expressive Capacity of International Punishment: The Limits of the National Law Analogy and the Potential of International Criminal Law', *Stan. J. Int'l L.* 43: 39.

Tallgren, I. (2002) 'The Sensibility and Sense of International Criminal Law', *Eur. J. Int'l L.* 13: 61.

Teitel, R. (2005) 'The Law and Politics of Contemporary Transitional Justice', *Cornell Int'l L.J.* 38: 837.

Waltzer, M. (1997) *Just and Unjust Wars*, New York: Basic Books.

Waters, T. W. (2008) 'Killing Globally, Punishing Locally? The Still-Unmapped Ecology of Atrocity', 55 *Buff. L. Rev.* 1331.

Chapter 4

Exposing checks and balances in war powers

A soldier's tale of cosmopolitan federalism

Cecilia M. Bailliet

4.1 INTRODUCTION

In 2009, as one of the most oxymoronic events of our time, President Obama received the Nobel Peace Prize and concurrently ordered the deployment of 30,000 additional troops to Afghanistan. He characterized the war as one of self-defence, thereby highlighting the military engagement's legality and legitimacy in relation to international law. President Obama further alluded to the notion of a just war, and invoked transnational cosmopolitan values by referring to the importance of supporting the emergence of democratic institutions in other countries:

> Whatever mistakes we have made, the plain fact is this: the United States of America has helped underwrite global security for more than six decades with the blood of our citizens and the strength of our arms. The service and sacrifice of our men and women in uniform has promoted peace and prosperity from Germany to Korea, and enabled democracy to take hold in places like the Balkans. We have borne this burden not because we seek to impose our will. We have done so out of enlightened self-interest – because we seek a better future for our children and grandchildren, and we believe that their lives will be better if other peoples' children and grandchildren can live in freedom and prosperity ... The one rule that lies at the heart of every major religion is that 'we do unto others as we would have them do unto us' and called upon all to reach for the world that ought to be- that spark of the divine that still stirs within each of our souls.[1]

We recall Adelman's warning in Chapter 1, that the 'the continued monopoly of legitimate violence threatens to undermine the cosmopolitan vision'. Rather than concede defeat to realist views, this chapter invites recognition of the shifting

1 Full text of the speech is available at: http://www.whitehouse.gov/the-press-office/remarks-president-acceptance-nobel-peace-prize.

trends of local and national institutional processes by which to pursue the emancipatory vision of true cosmopolitan justice.

I discuss dilemmas related to deployment of US armed troops abroad in security engagements from the perspective of institutional cosmopolitanism.[2] According to Beitz, institutional cosmopolitanism is traditionally linked to the aspiration of creating a supranational system to reduce the role of national governments. Rather than support the call for the creation of a world government; I review how existing local and national legal and quasi-legal structures were utilized to voice contestation and dissent against the engagement of US troops in Iraq (characterized as lacking both legality and legitimacy). Hence, I favour Pogge's definition of institutional cosmopolitanism as the assertion of global duties owed by individuals in an interdependent world.[3]

Habermas highlighted the 15 February 2003 demonstrations against the invasion of Iraq in the European capitals as constituting the birth of a European public which would serve as a counterbalance to the hegemonic unilateralism of the United States and defend international law.[4] In addition, Brennan and Ganguly described how millions more demonstrated in Latin America and Asia.[5] Yet, it is important to also acknowledge the examples of domestic political participation which placed significant pressure on the US federal government. Benhabib identifies the phenomenon of 'democratic iterations', which she defines as 'complex processes of public argument, deliberation, and exchange through which universalist rights claims and principles are contested and contextualized, invoked and revoked, posited and positioned throughout legal and political institutions, as well as in the associations of civil society.'[6] Indeed, she highlights the importance of republican federalism, as iterations may emerge within the legislature, judiciary, and executive branches. I examine the processes of 'bottom-up' discourses of minorities and local communities challenging the executive branch for defying its juridical legitimacy within the national intra-system jurisdictional level. Rather than presenting the local, domestic, and international legal orders as being in competition, I seek to present them as both overlapping and presenting gaps which are filled by social actors in order to buttress the gradual evolution of the international rule of law.

The chapter commences with presentation of the case of Lieutenant Watada, who refused to deploy to Iraq based on his belief that the military engagement was illegal according to both domestic and international law. This is followed by description of solidarity movements from below and constitutional

2 On institutional cosmopolitanism see Beitz (1994: 124).

3 Pogge (1994: 90).

4 Habermas (2006).

5 Brennan and Ganguly (2009: 41).

6 Benhabib (2009: 94).

dilemmas relating to separation of powers in the context of war and the legitimacy of deployment of National Guard troops abroad, in light of national disasters requiring a response. The conclusion calls for reflection upon the ongoing tension between state sovereignty and popular sovereignty when considering the legitimacy of the use of force and the struggle for cosmopolitan justice.

4.2 INVOCATION OF THE INTERNATIONAL RULE OF LAW BY AN INDIVIDUAL: THE EHREN WATADA CASE

Constitutions are traditionally considered the ultimate expression of sovereignty; nevertheless, when they incorporate international legal standards the framework for sovereign acts is altered.[7] A most compelling dilemma arises from the interest of the international system to limit the primary sovereign act of the use of force. One of the great quandaries of our time was that although all nations ratified the UN Charter and thereby accepted the conditions of use of force only in situations of self-defence or via mandate by the UN Security Council, the crime of aggression lacked a mechanism for prosecution at the ICC.[8] Given the lack of a universal institutional forum for the enforcement of the prohibition against aggression, social actors sought to express condemnation of violations in a variety of local, national and quasi-legal fora.

As noted by Berman, international legal norms may empower constituencies within a domestic polity and provide them with a language for influencing state policy.[9] Dahbour highlights the importance of an oppositional civil society to respond to arbitrary abuse of power by the State.[10] In June 2006, Lieutenant Ehren Watada refused orders to deploy to Iraq on grounds that he believed it to be an illegal war of aggression in contradiction of Article 2(4) of the UN Charter. He had submitted a letter of resignation, but was offered a position in the Battalion Headquarters, which he declined. Watada offered to deploy to Afghanistan instead, but was denied. He presented a constitutional argument based on consideration of the UN Charter as a treaty rendered supreme law of the land according to Article VI of US Constitution, for which the President has a duty to ensure

7 See Goldsmith and Levinson (2009: 1791).

8 May (2008: 3). See the ICC's Special Working Group on the Crime of Aggression's work on the definition, elements, and jurisdictional conditions of the Crime of Aggression: http://www.iccnow.org/?mod=aggression. The ICC's jurisdiction in this arena will enter into force in 2017.

9 Berman (2006: 1265).

10 Dahbour (2009: 21).

that that it be faithfully executed under Article II §3.[11] Lowe sets forth that the invasion of Iraq by the US was essentially an example of 'conflation of the unilateral right of self-defence with the right of the Security Council to take action to preserve international peace and security'.[12] Hence, Watada's action may be perceived as acting in the interest of the international community to uphold the international rule of law. Watada argued that because the US had a treaty obligation to uphold the UN Charter, the order to deploy to Iraq was illegal under both the US Constitution and international law, and he was therefore required not to obey. In essence, what is interesting is that Watada's strategy demonstrates how individuals who engage in advocacy linked to global citizenship can utilize state institutions within high-functioning democratic systems in their existing form, without needing to bypass or transform their structure, rather than seeking reform of practice.[13] Rather than seeking dissolution of national states in pursuit of transnational democracy, it may be argued that national institutions in democratic nations may actually be best situated to confronting dilemmas affecting the rule of law.

Watada asserted that his duty extended to upholding both the US Constitution and international law, and gave a speech at the Veterans for Peace National Convention in August 2006:

> It is my conclusion as an officer of the armed forces that the war in Iraq is not only morally wrong but a horrible breach of American law. Although I have tried to resign out of protest, I am forced to participate in a war that is manifestly illegal. As the order to take part in an illegal act is ultimately unlawful as well, I must as an officer of honor and integrity refuse that order … My moral and legal obligation is to the Constitution and not to those who would issue unlawful orders.

11 Court martial case *United States v 1 Lt Ehren K. Watada*, Army Trial Judiciary, Fourth Judicial Circuit, Fort Lewis, Washington (Feb. 5, 2007). Article VI: 'This Constitution, and the laws of the United States which shall be made in pursuance thereof; and all treaties made, or which shall be made, under the authority of the United States, shall be the supreme law of the land; and the judges in every state shall be bound thereby, anything in the Constitution or laws of any State to the contrary notwithstanding.' Watada attempted to resign but this was refused. Although he received an offer of safe placement in a non-combat position in Iraq, Watada turned this down. Aside from reassignment, retirement or removal from command is the usual solution in these cases. Watada also claimed that his participation would make him party to war crimes as he asserted that the US has failed to uphold Army Field Manual 27-10 on the laws of land warfare as pertaining duties of the Occupying power. He also cited the Geneva Conventions and the Nuremberg principles (Brecher and Smith, 2006).

12 See Lowe (2005: 672–5). He discusses how the invasion of Iraq was justified by reference to Iraq's defiance of UN Security Council resolutions from 1990 which required disarmament, along with Resolution 1441 of 2003. Nevertheless, he concludes that even if the resolutions were to be viewed as legitimizing the use of force, the UN Charter, Article 42, sets forth that such action is conditioned on a determination by the UN Security Council that it would be necessary.

13 On the question of 'globalizing democracy' see Smith (2009: 6).

> Aside from the reality of indentured servitude, the American soldier in theory is much nobler. Soldier or officer, when we swear our oath it is first and foremost to the Constitution and its protectorate, the people. If soldiers realized this war is contrary to what the Constitution extols – if they stood up and threw their weapons down – no President could ever initiate a war of choice again. When we say, '... Against all enemies foreign and domestic,' what if elected leaders became the enemy? Whose orders do we follow? The answer is the conscience that lies in each soldier, each American, and each human being. Our duty to the Constitution is an obligation, not a choice ... They [soldiers] must remember duty to the Constitution and the people supersedes the ideologies of their leadership ... The oath we take swears allegiance not to one man but to a document of principles and laws designed to protect the people.[14]

A principal dilemma which arises is that the assessment of an individual's invocation of state responsibility under international law is invariably complicated by assertions that the actual motivation is political, and the issue is then addressed as one involving the scope of freedom of expression: thereby culminating in tension between state sovereignty versus popular sovereignty. Essentially, there is a clash between the duty of the soldier to prove loyal to the state, show discipline, and preserve the reputation of the armed forces, versus the right of individuals, including soldiers, to communicate their beliefs regarding the legality of the military engagement. The problem is when a soldier defines the act of disobedience as defending the constitutional commitment to adherence to international public law; he/she presents an alternative interpretation of the loyalty to the state. A strategy by which governments may seek to avoid having courts delve into competing notions of loyalty to the state is by focusing on the method of communication of the objection. By characterizing the conflict as being essentially based on the scope of freedom of speech, it is possible to narrow the analysis to the form of communication rather than the substantive basis behind the speech.

The US Army tried to prosecute Lieutenant Watada for one charge of missing movement by design and four counts of 'conduct unbecoming an officer and a gentlemen', i.e. engaging in a political speech which criticized the legality and morality of the war was characterized as 'dishonourable' and 'disgraceful'

14 Lieutenant Ehren Watada, 'Soldiers Can Choose to Stop Fighting', address before the Veterans for Peace Convention (12 August 2006). President Bush received authorization 'to use the Armed Forces of the United States as he determines to be necessary and appropriate in order to- 1) defend the national security of the United States against the continuing threat posed by Iraq; and 2) enforce all relevant United Nations Security Council resolutions regarding Iraq'. 'Authorization for Use of Military Force Against Iraq Resolution of 2002', Public Law 107–243, 323 F. 3rd 133, 107th Congress (Oct. 16, 2002).

action.[15] The defence countered that Watada's speech was constitutionally protected:

> Amendment I
>
> Congress shall make no law respecting an establishment of religion, or prohibiting the free exercise thereof; or abridging the freedom of speech, or of the press; or the right of the people peaceably to assemble, and to petition the government for a redress of grievances.

The fact that Watada had the rank of a lieutenant and gave a speech in public and interviews in which he claimed to be speaking in defence and on behalf of soldiers who could not speak themselves demonstrates that he asserted his status as an officer of the Army as particularly grounding his dissent. His statements could be interpreted as impliedly encouraging others to disregard orders is a situation which may well not be constitutionally protected.[16] From the perspective of the military, such speech disrupts command, control and military authority, thereby imperiling the mission by spreading dissent, undermining morale and impairing discipline.[17] The reasoning behind the traditional limitation of soldiers' speech is the interest in preventing a military coup of the civilian leadership and ensuring military subordination to the civilian authority.[18] From this perspective, his institutional duty vis-à-vis the Army outweighed allegiance to the cosmopolitan ideal of respect for the international rule of law or perception of justice. Indeed, Watada's speech seeks to undermine the leadership of the armed forces during a time of military engagement. The defence countered that he was not in uniform,

15 Uniform Code of Military Justice, United States Code, Title 10, Chapter 47, Article 133 Conduct unbecoming an officer and gentleman: 'Any commissioned officer, cadet or midshipman who is convicted of conduct unbecoming an officer and a gentleman shall be punished as a court martial may direct.' The explanation defines such conduct as 'action or behaviour in an official capacity which, in dishonouring or disgracing the person as an officer, seriously compromises the officer's character as a gentleman, or action or behaviour in an unofficial or private capacity which, in dishonouring or disgracing the officer personally, seriously compromises the person's standing as an officer'. An example given is using insulting or defamatory language to another officer in that officer's presence or about that officer to other military persons.

16 See *United States v Voorhees* 16 Court Martial Reports 83, 95 (1954). On prosecution of speech by soldiers, see Moran (1980); see also Kester (1968: 1739).

17 *Parker v Levy* 417 U.S. 733 (1974) at 736. This case involved a doctor who urged African-Americans to avoid the war: 'I don't see why any coloured soldier would go to Viet Nam: they should refuse to go to Viet Nam and if sent should refuse to fight because they are discriminated against and denied their freedom in the United States.'

18 Wiener (1958: 269–70), noting that the violation of the principle of military subordination to the civilian power was a grievance charged against King George III in the US Declaration of Independence.

nor on duty, and he did not directly encourage others to engage in disobedience or take violent action against the government. It claimed that there was no danger to the morale or discipline among the troops, therefore Watada's speech was protected.[19]

The Army presented Professor Richard Swain, who teaches 'Officership' at the US Military Academy at West Point. Professor Swain outlined the principles that officers have no obligation to follow unlawful orders and that they are responsible for determining the legality of their orders. As pertaining the officer's oath, it applies to the Constitution and not a particular person or policy. He explains this in an article:

> The 'Constitutional Oath' clearly requires subordination to civil authorities, especially the commander in chief whose authority they carry ... Consequent to Article VI of the Constitution, officers must respect and protect the rights recognized by the Constitution and federal law to belong to their fellow citizens, and must be obedient to the laws of the United States and international treaties ratified in accordance with constitutional procedure. Even the order of the President does not relieve the officer of those obligations to obey the law as interpreted by the courts... For the obedience and loyalty owed the occupant of the office of President of the United States is inherent in both the latter's authority as Commander in Chief under Article 11 and in the wording of the commission issued under that authority. It is not personal, it is institutional and complete, so long as the President acts within the law, just as the loyalty owed the commanding general reflects an obligation to his or her office and not to his or her person.[20]

Officers who develop moral conflicts are expected to resolve them via the chain of command, and only tender their resignation should attempts at resolution prove unsuccessful. According to Swain, the oath remains valid even if the resignation is not accepted.[21] Hence, the counter-perspective is that individuals have an

19 See American Civil Liberties Union of Washington (2006).

20 Swain (2007: 8, 10).

21 Myers and Kohn (2007) offer an explanation for the lack of reference to moral resignation within the US: 'There may be some extraordinary or dire situation in which an officer must for personal reasons ask to be relieved or retired: for example, when people would be slaughtered for no explicable or conceivable reason or the existence of the country jeopardized with no conceivable justification. But one individual's definition of what is moral, ethical, and even professional can differ from someone else's. There is no tradition of military resignation in the United States, no precedent – and for good reason. Even the hint of resignation would encourage civilians to choose officers more for compliance and loyalty than for competence, experience, intelligence, candor, moral courage, professionalism, integrity, and character.'

interactional duty to address institutional injustice via disobedience or other calls for reform.[22]

The military judge rejected the stipulation of facts as constituting a confessional stipulation, characterizing it as being in breach of the pretrial agreement, and declared a mistrial. Watada was subject to a new court martial in February 2007, and thus filed a petition for extraordinary relief due to the fact that a second prosecution of the same charges would violate his Fifth Amendment right to be free from double jeopardy.

4.3 THE EMERGENCE OF SUB-NATIONAL COSMOPOLITAN SOLIDARITY AND LEGAL PLURALISM

As was the case during the war in Vietnam, there emerged a network of organized protests, marches and rallies against the Iraqi war and letter writing campaigns supporting conscientious objectors.[23]

The marches commenced in 2002 and continued through 2009, with participation totalling from the hundreds to the thousands. Several marches in Washington DC were organized by ANSWER (Act Now to Stop War and End Racism, dedicated to protesting against imperialist policies), the United for Peace and Justice coalition (opposing the government's policy of 'permanent warfare and empire building'), as well as Students for a Democratic Society. The Iraq Veterans Against the War linked the protection interests of military veterans with those of the Iraqi civilians, calling for:

- Immediate withdrawal of all occupying forces in Iraq.
- Reparations for the human and structural damages Iraq has suffered.

22 See Miklos (2006: 239–50). For further discussion of opposition to illegal war as expression of conscience see Bailliet (2006). For review of comparable cases from France and Germany, see Bailliet (2010).

23 The most famous epoch of civic engagement against the use of force by the United States occurred during the Vietnam War. Protests by individuals and groups such as Student Non-Violent Coordinating Committee and Vietnam Veterans Against the War, symbolic burning of draft cards, and conscientious objection/desertion by soldiers opposed to war sought to validate the primacy of the right of self-determination and the principle of non-aggression. Bertrand Russell and Jean Paul Sartre's 'International War Crimes Tribunal' (composed of 25 notable persons engaged in humanitarian and social arenas) in 1967 issued conclusions asserting that the United States had committed an act of aggression against Vietnam and Laos. In 1973, in part due to the lack of support for the war, the US withdrew its troops from Vietnam, signalling the restoration of the international rule of law. See Cover (1984–85: 200). See also Duffett (1968). The Tribunal also determined that the US violated the sovereignty of Cambodia, attacked civilians, used weapons prohibited by IHL, abused prisoners of war in violation of IHL, and engaged in genocide. Further, it concluded that Australia, New Zealand and South Korea has been accomplices of the US in the acts of aggression, and that Thailand, the Philippines and Japan had been complicit.

- Ending corporate pillaging of Iraq so that their people can control their own lives.
- Full benefits, adequate healthcare (including mental health), and other support for returning servicemen and women.[24]

Iraqi Veterans Against the War joined other organizations, including Amnesty International and the ACLU, to support Lieutenant Watada.[25] At the time of the court martial, over 600 persons attended a Citizens' Hearing held in Tacoma, Washington. The panel issued a report invoking violations of the Constitution and international public law, specifically highlighting the norms derived from Nuremberg:

> Our Citizens' Panel found the Iraq War to be illegal in both national and international law. In our document, we issued a Call to Conscience for Congress to hold hearings on the legality of both the war itself and the ways that the war is being conducted ... That the war in Iraq is a war of aggression that constitutes a crime against peace, under the terms of the Nuremberg Principles.... The oath to support and defend the Constitution implies that if in conscience a person believes an order to be illegal, he or she has an obligation to refuse the order.

The panel may be viewed as symbolizing the growing frustration within society for inadequate institutional responses at both the international and national levels to violations of the UN Charter and international humanitarian law.[26] The formation of the panel and the publication of a report strengthen the discourse of the civil society, as its quasi-judicial form seeks to utilize the 'code' of law and institutions to legitimize political engagement.[27] In this manner, local actors may offer an alternative vision of sovereignty, in which the society claims authority to demand respect from the state for international public law. In some respects, these actions may be considered examples of legal pluralism. As stated by Berman: 'The State does not hold a monopoly on the articulation and exercise of legal norms, then we can see law as a locus of various communities to debate different visions of alternative futures.'[28]

24 See: http://www.ivaw.org/about.

25 Watada demonstrated the power of the media as he attained celebrity status through coverage by MTV, see: http://www.mtv.com/videos/news/131887/army-officer-refuses-iraq-call-of-duty.jhtml≡=1551752.

26 It is significant that polling results confirming opposition to the war in Iraq be held by 64 per cent of the US population. See CNN Poll August 2007 at: http://www.pollingreport.com/iraq.htm.

27 See Cover (1983–84: 4).

28 Berman (2005: 1105).

Lieutenant Watada filed a petition for a writ of habeas corpus and an emergency request to stay the October 9 court martial to the US District Court. In November 2007, a Federal Judge of the US District Court for the Western District of Washington granted a preliminary injunction in favour of Watada due to abuse of discretion by the military judge resulting in double jeopardy.[29] In October 2008, the judge granted in part Watada's Second Amendment petition for a writ of habeas corpus, recognizing that the military court lacked jurisdiction to convene a court martial on the charges of missing movement and conduct unbecoming an officer and a gentleman.[30] The military court was ordered not to convene a court martial against Watada on those charges. In 2009, the US Army discharged Watada 'under other than honorable conditions'.

4.4 AMBIGUITY REGARDING THE SEPARATION OF POWERS IN RELATION TO WAR

Pogge highlights the importance of contemplating disputes arising with respect to the proper allocation of decision making powers between institutions in order to measure reliability of the system.[31] Lieutenant Watada had additionally claimed that the deployment of troops to Iraq violated Article I §8 of the Constitution, which recognizes Congress's general power to provide for the common defence, declare war, raise and support armies, provide and maintain a navy, call forth the militia to execute the laws of the union, suppress insurrections, and repel invasions. In contrast, according to Article II §2, the President is 'the Commander in Chief of the Army and Navy of the United States and of the Militia of the several States, when called into the actual service of the United States'.[32] The War Powers Act authorized Congress to declare War, or issue other authorization for military action, and limits the President to deploying troops in response to an emergency on condition that he or she receives Congressional authorization should the deployment prove longer than 60 days.[33] The War Powers Resolution requires that the President consult Congress before deploying troops and throughout the

29 *1 Lt. Ehren K. Watada v Lt. Col. John Head, Military Judge*, Army Trial Judiciary, Fourth Judicial Circuit, Lieutenant Gen. Charles Jacoby, Respondents Ft. Lewis Washington, Convening Authority, US District Court, Case. No. CO7–5549B45 Western District of Washington at Tacoma (Nov. 8, 2007).

30 *1 Lt. Ehren K. Watada v Lt. Col. John Head, Military Judge*, Army Trial Judiciary, Fourth Judicial Circuit; Lt. Gen. Charles Jacoby, Convening Authority, Ft. Lewis, Washington, Respondents, Case No. C07–5549BHS, Western District of Washington at Tacoma (Oct. 28, 2008).

31 Pogge (2008: 377).

32 See Flaherty (2006: 153); Ramsey (2006: 141); Bradley and Goldsmith (2005: 2047); Yoo (2005).

33 At the close of the Vietnam War, Congress enacted the War Powers Act of 1973, Public Law 93–148, 93rd Congress, H.J. Res. 542, Nov. 7, 1973.

hostilities.[34] There had been prior attempts to raise before the Federal Courts the issue of the boundaries of the President's constitutional powers as pertaining to deployment of troops, but the judiciary refused to engage, based on concerns for ripeness, the political question doctrine, or standing.[35] Herein lies a key weakness within the American system; there appears to be a *de facto* lack of forum for dispute resolution of conflicts between the legislative and executive bodies as pertaining issues related to security operations. The judiciary is passive with respect to resolving ambiguities related to the obligations of government officials in foreign policy.[36]

4.5 UNCERTAINTY REGARDING DEPLOYMENT OF THE NATIONAL GUARD AND LOCAL DISSENT AS EXAMPLES OF COSMOPOLITAN FEDERALISM AND CRISIS OF SOVEREIGNTY

Lieutenant Watada indicated that he was open to deploying to Afghanistan (which he characterized as a legal war), or performing alternative service: 'If they wanted to send me down to help the victims of Hurricane Katrina, I'll do that in a

34 The War Powers Resolution, 50 U.S.C.A. §§1541 et seq., was enacted in order to ensure that the President could not gradually build up American involvement in a foreign war without congressional knowledge or approval. It sets forth that the President can introduce the Armed Forces into hostilities pursuant to 1) a declaration of war, 2) specific statutory authorization, or 3) a national emergency created by attack upon the United States, its territories or possessions, or its armed forces. The President is required to withdraw forces within 60 days absent Congressional approval of the military action. See *Crockett v Reagan* 558 F. Supp. 893 (D.D.C. 1982), aff'd, 720 F. 2nd 1355 (D.C. Cir. 1983). See also *Campbell v Clinton* 52 F. Supp. 2d 34 (D.D.C. 1999), aff'd 203 F. 3rd 19 (D.C. Cir. 2000), cert. denied, 531 US 815, 121 S.Ct. 50, 148 L. Ed. 2nd 19 (2000), in which members of the House of Representatives unsuccessfully sought a declaration from the court that the President violated the War Powers Clause of the Constitution and the War Powers Resolution by conducting air strikes in the Federal Republic of Yugoslavia without Congressional authorization. The vote on Congressional approval ended in an exact tie and the President did not cease the operation within 60 days. The court declared that they lacked standing, as there was no concrete confrontation between the legislature and the executive. Indeed, the US has deployed troops over 100 times without a congressional declaration of war, e.g. Korea, Vietnam, Haiti, Lebanon, Nicaragua, and the Persian Gulf. In contrast, there have been five officially declared wars: the War of 1812, the Mexican War of 1846, the Spanish-American War of 1898, World War I, and World War II.

35 There were two cases which challenged the constitutionality of the Iraq invasion, both were dismissed by Federal Circuit Courts : see *Doe v Bush*, 323 F. 3rd 133 (1st Cir. 2003), dismissed on account of lack of ripeness and the lack of a fully developed dispute between the legislature and the executive; and *O'Conner v United States*, 72 Fed. Appx. 768, 2003 WL 21694593 (10th Cir. 2003), in which the issue addressing whether the President had unconstitutional intentions in pursuing the war was dismissed as a political question. These cases find precedent in previous cases addressing the first intervention in the Persian Gulf: See *Ange v Bush* 752 F. Supp. 509 (D.D.C. 1990) in which the issue of the constitutional validity of the deployment of troops to the Persian Gulf was characterized as a political question incapable of review by the judiciary. See also *Dellums v Bush* 752 F. Supp. 1141 (D.D.C. 1990), addressing the same deployment, where the Congressmen who filed the claim were found not to have standing.

36 See Goldsmith and Levinson (2009: 1791).

heartbeat. I'm willing to do anything it takes to help the people of America within the laws of America.'[37] Response to national disasters is usually provided by the National Guard, which is the only branch that serves both the federal and state governments. Traditionally, the National Guard has been described as citizen-soldiers who defend their communities during emergencies. Hence, it is important to address the legitimacy of the deployment of the National Guard abroad. The National Guard and reserve soldiers formed ca. 40 per cent of the troops in Iraq, many due to blockage of the latter's resignations and a 'stop-loss' extension of their contract effectuating a 'back door draft'.[38] The tension between local communities and the federal government enforcing this extension of duty was high, especially as the casualty rates escalated.

As an example of 'grassroots federalism' there was increased resistance within local town and city council meetings.[39] Running against the one-voice doctrine and foreign affairs pre-emption, the oppositional power took the form of *nomos* by passing resolutions citing concern for violation of the US Constitutional provision Article I section 8 cll. 15–16 concerning the power of Congress to 'provide for calling for the militia to execute the Laws of the Union, to suppress insurrections and repel invasions' and state constitutions identifying state assemblies as in charge of the state national guard in defence of the state.[40] The resolutions indicated disapproval of the impact of deployment of the National Guard to Iraq in terms of deaths, injuries (physical and psychiatric), disruption of family life, financial losses, interruption of careers, removal of police, firefighters, emergency medical technicians from local communities, at a time where there was no credible threat to the nation. There was a significant rise in desertion and suicide among soldiers as a consequence of combat trauma and family, interpersonal, financial, and legal and work crises at home.[41] Hence local processes addressing national norms actually buttressed international reclamations against military engagement abroad and highlighted the transnational aspects of the illegitimacy of the military engagement. Not only were Iraqi civilians suffering and communities disrupted, so were Americans. At the local level, rather than protecting the public good, the state's foreign engagements were viewed as having a directly negative impact.[42]

37 Statement recorded by Goodman (2006).

38 Scott Tyson (2006).

39 On grassroots federalism in Europe see Beck and Grande (2008: 157).

40 Finer (2005). On the foreign affairs pre-emption, 'translocal internationalism', and plural governance, see Resnik (2007: 31).

41 See Associated Press (2007). See also Von Zielbauer (2007), noting a case in which a soldier chopped off his trigger finger with an axe to prevent deployment. See also Lehmann (2004); Beannerman (2007).

42 Indeed, this is reminiscent of France in the 1800s, where concern for family and farm often overrode attempts to define military service as having legitimacy either with the people, local government institutions, or other communal actors. Rural local communities regarded conscription as a severe infringement of their way of life, and often counteracted it via bribery, selection of the most marginalized members of the community to fill quotas, arranging marriages of young men to widows, sending their youths into hiding, and self-mutilation among young men liable to conscription. See Forrest (1989: 65).

Opposition was further intensified by reactions of outrage to the delayed federal and state rescue response to Hurricane Katrina which hit Louisiana and Texas in 2005, impacting the majority African-American community of New Orleans the hardest. The world was struck by television images of thousands of poor men, women and children in devastating conditions, lacking food, water, medicine and basic security in the Super Dome, as well as in the deluged streets and homes. For many, this left a sensation that the African-American population was considered expendable. One college student noted: 'I believe African Americans do not want to fight in a war when they are treated like second rate citizens in their own country.'[43] Hence, there were echoes of Martin Luther King's Jr.'s speech 'Beyond Vietnam', in which he offered condemnation of what he deemed to be 'a cruel manipulation of the poor' in 'taking the black young men who had been crippled by our society and sending them eight thousand miles away to guarantee liberties in Southeast Asia which they had not found in southwest Georgia and East Harlem.'[44]

The flood in New Orleans in August 2005 underscored the precariousness of deploying the National Guard abroad; as Mississippi had 4,000 troops in Central Iraq while Louisiana had 3,000 troops in Baghdad (this constituted approximately one-third of their Guard units).[45] New Orleans' Mayor Ray Nagin was clear in his desperate plea for immediate assistance from the state and federal government. This prompted Governor Blanco to request provision of active duty federal troops,

43 See: http://www.blackcollegeview.com/vnews/display.v/ART/2004/11/01/41866fa805d09. A study assessing the significant drop in recruitment of African-Americans to military service found that 'More African-Americans identify having to fight for a cause they don't support as a barrier to military service' (Philpott 2005). See also Abruzzese (2007).

44 See: http://www.africanamericans.com/MLKjrBeyondVietnam.htm. He cited the image of black and white boys killing and dying together, while divisions and inequities remained unchallenged at home. He also objected to the violation of the principle of self-determination of the Vietnamese people. He was assassinated on the first anniversary of this speech.

45 Statistics taken from the *Washington Post*, cited by Solomon (2005). The flood in New Orleans was not the only natural disaster; during the summer of 2005, Gov. Brian Schweitzer of Montana requested the Pentagon to return National Guard troops and helicopters from overseas to help fight wildfires in his state. He noted that nine out of twelve of his state's Black Hawk helicopters were in Iraq and that they lacked the crews to operate the Chinooks. His request was refused. See 'MT's Governor Schweitzer on Lou Dobbs', available at: http://democraticgovernors.org/news/278/mt-gov-schweitzer-on-cnns-lou-dobbs. Similarly, in May 2007, Governor Kathleen Sebelius of Kansas was unable to provide National Guard troops immediately to respond to a tornado which destroyed the town of Greensboro. See Saulny and Rutenburg (2007). The crisis regarding the shortage of equipment and lack of readiness of the National Guard at home prompted a letter signed by all 50 state governors to President Bush in 2006, demanding re-equipment of deployed National Guard troops. On the Congressional attention see: http://www.signonsandiego.com/uniontrib/20070304/news_mz1c4caldwel.html. In California, Governor Schwarzenegger complained about the loss and non-return of National Guard equipment sent to Iraq, leaving the Guard lacking half of its equipment (Martin, 2007). Indeed, in October, fires erupted in California, forcing an evacuation of 350,000 homes and prompting immediate response by the federal government to supplement the Guard's personnel and equipment (Smith-Spark, 2007).

and a conflict ensued aboard Air Force One between the Governor and President Bush's advisors as to the chain of command over the state Guard troops and the federal troops. The failure to attain an immediate solution left an exasperated Mayor Nagin noting that the lack of coordination resulted in 'more people dying in my city'.[46]

4.6 REMOVAL OF STATE CONTROL OVER NATIONAL GUARD FORCES AND THE POTENTIAL FOR CONSTITUTIONAL CONFLICT

The background for the constitutional conundrums can be traced to the period of US intervention in Central America in the 1980s to combat left-wing movements. The Governors of California, Maine, Vermont, Massachusetts, Arizona, New York, and Washington opposed use of their National Guard units for training in Central America when President Reagan identified the Sandinista regime as a threat to national security.[47] From an international perspective, the military engagement was in violation of the UN Charter, Article 2(4), and this buttressed domestic reclamations addressing the legitimacy of the deployment.[48] In 1986, Representative Montgomery of Mississippi submitted the National Defense Authorization Act of 1987 that removed the gubernatorial consent requirement for use of National Guard for active duty outside the US (unless the units are needed for local emergency or unless the order is so intrusive that it deprives the state of effectively training the Guard for local service).[49] At present, governors may not object to location, purpose, type or schedule of active duty of National Guard units. Prior to this change, gubernatorial consent was required for use of National Guard over 15 days.[50]

However, in *Perpich v Department of Defense*, the US Supreme Court ruled that Congress can authorize the President to order members of the National Guard to active duty for purposes of training outside the United States during peacetime without either the consent of a state governor or the declaration of a national emergency.[51] Consequently, thousands of reserve guards were sent to the Persian Gulf without any declaration of a national emergency.[52] Thousands of reservists are stationed abroad in Iraq, Afghanistan and other locations for the war on terror, founded on a declared state of emergency which is continually extended and thus

46 CNN Interview with Mayor Nagin: http://transcripts.cnn.com/TRANSCRIPTS/0509/05/ltm.01.html.
47 Cooper (1991: 637).
48 Fidler (1994: 45).
49 10 U.S.C. section 672f (1988).
50 10 U.S.C. section 672b (1991). See also: http://www.unitedforpeace.org.
51 110 S. Ct. 24718 (1990).
52 Bovarnick (1991: 453).

results in further stop-loss renewal of contracts.[53] There were increased calls for congressional limitation on the power of the President to send reservists abroad, indicating concern for the consequences of the legislative reforms in practice.[54] Indeed, in 2007, the House of Representatives passed Resolution 63 (non-binding) which expressed Congressional disapproval of the President's decision to deploy more than 20,000 additional combat troops to Iraq.[55] Congress further called for a withdrawal of troops from Iraq, linking approval of a spending bill to a set timetable for such action. Senators Hillary Rodham Clinton and Robert C. Byrd called for a vote to end the Congressional authorization of the President to invade Iraq given five years earlier, given that the intelligence indicating that Iraq harboured weapons of mass destruction had proved wrong.[56] This development indicated further possibility of objection by soldiers: if the President were to order the armed forces to continue the operation contrary to the will of Congress; the military would be pressed to consider the legitimacy of the order and whether they

53 Wooten (2005: 1061): 'On September 14, 2001, in response to the terrorist attacks on the World Trade Center and the Pentagon just three days earlier, President George W. Bush declared a state of "national emergency" by virtue of the continued threat of terrorist attacks against the United States. That same day, the President invoked his power "to suspend certain laws relating to promotion, involuntary retirement, and separation of commissioned officers" and delegated that power to the Secretary of Defense. Under this authority, the various military institutions have enacted numerous "stop-loss" policies, by which military personnel are retained in service beyond the terms of their enlistment contracts. In other words, these policies aim to put a stop to the loss of military manpower during times of crisis by extending the service terms of members of the Armed Forces. Proclamation No. 7463, 66 Fed. Reg. 48,199 (Sept. 14, 2001) "A national emergency exists by reason of the terrorist attacks at the World Trade Center, New York, New York, and the Pentagon, and the continuing and immediate threat of further attacks on the United States.". The state of national emergency as announced in Proclamation 7463 has been extended annually, see 67 Fed. Reg. 58,317 (Sept. 12, 2002) (continuing the state of emergency through September 14, 2003); 68 Fed. Reg. 53,665 (Sept. 10, 2003) (continuing through September 14, 2004); 69 Fed. Reg. 55,313 (Sept. 10, 2004) (continuing through September 14, 2005), and is currently in effect, 70 Fed. Reg. 54,229 (Sept. 8, 2005) (continuing through September 14, 2006). Exec. Order No. 13,223, 3 C.F.R. 785 (2002). See 10 U.S.C. section 12305 (2000) "[D]uring any period members of a reserve component are serving on active duty ... the President may suspend any provision of law relating to promotion, retirement, or separation applicable to any member of the armed forces who the President determines is essential to the national security of the United States."'

54 See Mullins (1988: 328); see also Note (2006: 1815).

55 H. Con. Res. 63, 110th Congress, 1st Session (Feb. 12, 2007). Resolved by the House of Representatives (the Senate concurring).

56 Hulse and Healy (2007). As a compromise was temporarily reached between the Congress and the Executive, the Judiciary was spared intervening in the dispute. Nevertheless, the House presented a supplemental war spending bill that called for immediate troop withdrawals, resulting in defeat in the Senate and leaving the Pentagon frustrated that the delays in attaining funding were negatively affecting the army in Iraq. The Democratic Party sought to present its position as representing the will of the people; consider Representative John Murtha of Pennsylvania: 'Congressional Democrats will not stop championing the will of the American people until our troops come home' (Herszenhorn, 2007a, 2007b).

would be subject to adverse consequences if they obeyed it.[57] Hence, there remains a state of uncertainty which renders reliability of the system weak.

4.7 CONCLUSION

Watada's case is significant because it underscores the possibility of counter-hegemonic expressions of popular sovereignty within the local and national levels of government when measuring the legitimacy of deployment of troops to armed conflicts abroad. The interrelationship between international public law standards and the Constitution as complementary normative elements upholding the principle of the international rule of law is substantiated by the statements of the individual soldier and engaged civilians. These reclamations may be interpreted as affirming the gradual emergence of global citizenship. Oppositional civil society is active in reclaiming principles of federalism, separation of powers, authority, and accountability within state institutions even within the heart of what has been considered to be the 'Empire'.[58] Rather than dismantling sovereignty to achieve cosmopolitan values, it is reinterpreted. The process of normative contestation and development highlights the materialization of transnational democracy as implemented via state entities, identified by Benhabib as indicative of a 'cosmopolitanism to come'.

Bibliography

Abruzzese, S. (2007) 'Iraq War Brings Drop in Black Enlistees', 22 August, *The New York Times*.

American Civil Liberties Union of Washington (15 August 2006) Amicus Brief of American Civil Liberties Union of Washington in Connection with Article 32 Hearing, *United States v Ehren K. Watada*.

57 Corn (1998: 184). Further, the Army is currently struggling with the residual issue of whether officers erred by not standing up to the Secretary of Defense during the initial planning of the war, thereby highlighting tensions relating to interpretation of the constitutional oath and the principle of subordination of the military to the civilian authority. See Bumiller (2007).

58 This chapter calls for improved interaction between the Congress and the Executive in this arena, given the absence of involvement by the judiciary. In 2008, the Non-Partisan War Powers Commission, led by James Baker III and Warren Christopher, presented a proposal for a War Powers Consultation Act 2009 which would replace the 1973 War Powers resolution. It would have required the President to consult with Congress, in particular with a Joint Congressional Committee, in cases involving a 'significant armed conflict' – defined as combat operations that last or are expected to last more than a week. This was intended to clarify the role of both branches of government in situations involving deployment of American troops when interpreting the shared responsibilities delegated to them by the Constitution. This sought to mend the fissures presented by the Watada case and restore legitimacy to US deployments abroad. Nevertheless, by 2010 this initiative had not been passed. The report is available at: http://millercenter.org/dev/ci/system/application/views/_newwebsite/policy/commissions/warpowers/report.pdf.

Associated Press (2007) '2006 Suicide Rate for Soldiers Sets a Record for the Army', 17 August, *The New York Times*.
Bailliet, C. (2006) 'Assessing Jus as Bellum and Jus in Bello Within the Refugee Status Determination Process: Contemplations on Conscientious Objectors Seeking Asylum', *Georgetown Immigration Law Journal* 20(3): 337–84.
—— (2010) 'Constitutional Underpinnings for Conscientious Objection in Allegiance to International Public Law Norms pertaining to War', in C. Eriksen and M. Emberland (eds), *New International Law*, Leiden: Martinus Nijhoff.
Beitz, C. (1994) 'Cosmopolitan Liberalism and the States System', in *Political Restructuring in Europe: Ethical Perspectives*, London: Routledge.
Benhabib, S. (2009) 'Twilight of Sovereignty of the Emergence of Cosmopolitan Norms? Rethinking Citizenship in Volatile Times', in H. Gautney, O. Dahbour, A. Dawson and N. Smith (eds), *Democracy, States, and the Struggle for Global Justice*, New York: Routledge.
Beck, U. and Grande, E. (2008) *Cosmopolitan Europe*, Cambridge: Polity Press.
Beannerman, S. (2007) 'Iraq Reservists Face a "Perfect Storm" of Post-Traumatic Stress', 15 March, *Alternet*.
Berman, P. S. (2005) 'Conflict of Laws, Globalization, and Cosmopolitan Pluralism', *Wayne L. Rev* 51: 1105.
—— (2006) Book Review: 'Seeing Beyond the Limits of International Law', *Tex. L. Rev.* 84: 1265.
Bovarnick, J. (1991) 'Comment: *Perpich v. United States Department of Defense*: Who's in Charge of the National Guard?', *New England Law Review* 26: 453.
Bradley, C. A. and Goldsmith, J. L. (2005) 'Congressional Authorization and the War on Terrorism', *Harvard Law Review* 118: 2047.
Brecher, J. and Smith, B. (2006) 'Lt. Watada's War Against the War', 13 June, *The Nation*, available at: http://www.chsnews.com/stories/2006/06/13/opinion/printable1706260.shtml.
Brennan, T. and Ganguly, K. (2009) 'Crude Wars', in H. Gautney, O. Dahbour, A. Dawson and N. Smith (eds), *Democracy, States, and the Struggle for Global Justice*, New York: Routledge.
Bumiller, E. (2007) 'At Army School for Officers, Blunt Talk About Iraq', 14 October, *The New York Times*.
Cooper, M. F. (1991) Note: '*Perpich v. Department of Defense*: Federalism Values and the Militia Clause', *University of Colorado Law Review*, 62: 637.
Corn, Major G. S. (1998) 'Presidential War Power: Do the Courts Offer Any Answers?', *Military Law Review* 157: 184.
Cover, R. M. (1983–84) 'Nomos and Narrative', *Harvard L. Rev.* 97: 4.
—— (1984–85) *The Folktales of Justice: Tales of Jurisdiction, Cap. U. L. Rev.* 14: 179.
Dahbour, O. (2009) 'Introduction', in H. Gautney, O. Dahbour, A. Dawson and N. Smith (eds), *Democracy, States, and the Struggle for Global Justice*, New York: Routledge.
Duffett, J. (ed.) (1968), *Against the Crime of Silence: Proceedings of the Russell International War Crimes Tribunal*, O'Hare Books.
Fidler, D. P. (1994) 'War, Law and Liberal Thought: The Use of Force in the Reagan Years', *Ariz. J. Int'l and Comp. L.* 11: 45.
Finer, J. (2005) 'On Vermont's Ballots: Iraq War', 2 March, *The Washington Post*, p. A2.
Flaherty, M. (2006) 'The Most Dangerous Branch Abroad', *Harvard Journal of Law and Public Policy* 30: 153.

Forrest, A. (1989) *Conscripts and Deserters: The Army and French Society during the French Revolution and Empire*, Oxford: Oxford University Press.

Gautney, H., Dahbour, O., Dawson, A. and Smith, N. (eds) (2009) *Democracy, States, and the Struggle for Global Justice*, New York: Routledge.

Goldsmith, J. and Levinson, D. (2009) 'Law for States: International Law, Constitutional Law, Public Law', *Harvard L. Rev.* 122: 1791.

Goodman, A. (2006) 'Army Lieutenant Becomes First Commissioned Officer to Refuse Deployment to Iraq', 8 June, *Democracy Now!*

Habermas, J. (2006) 'February 15, or: What Binds Europeans', *The Divided West* 39 (trans. Ciaran Cronin).

Herszenhorn, D. (2007a) 'Democrats Say They Won't Back Down on War', 19 November, *The New York Times*.

—— (2007b) 'House Approves Funds for Military, with Strings', 15 November, *The New York Times*.

Hulse, C. and Healy, P. (2007) 'Clinton Proposes Vote to Reverse Authorizing War', 4 May, *The New York Times*.

Kester (1968) 'Soldiers who Insult the President: An Uneasy Look at Article 88 of the Uniform Code of Military Justice', *Harvard Law Review* 81: 1736–40.

Lehmann, C. (2004) 'Soldiers say Combat Stress Second to Personal Stress', 16 April, *Psychiatric News*.

Lowe, V. (2005) 'Security Concerns and National Sovereignty in the Age of World-Wide Terrorism', in R. St J. MacDonald and D. M. Johnston (eds), *Towards World Constitutionalism*, Leiden: Martinus Nijhoff, 655–79.

Martin, M. (2007), 'State National Guard Warns It's Stretched to the Limit', 11 May, *Chronicle Sacramento Bureau*.

May, L. (2008) *Aggression and Crimes Against Peace*, Cambridge: Cambridge University Press.

Miklos, A. (2006) 'Institutions in Cosmopolitan Justice', *Global Society*, 20(3): 239–50.

Moran, Major F. F. (1980) 'Free Speech, the Military and the National Interest', *AIR*.

Mullins, P. T. (1988) Note: 'The Militia Clause, The National Guard and Federalism: A Constitutional Tug of War', *George Washington Law Review*, 57: 328.

Myers, R. B. and Kohn, R. H. (2007) 'Salute and Disobey?', *Foreign Affairs*.

Note: (2006) 'Recapturing the War Power', *Harvard Law Review* 119: 1815.

Philpott, T. (2005), 'Analysis: Study shows 41% drop in number of black Army recruits since 2000', 4 March, *Stars and Stripes*, available at: http://www.stripes.com/article.asp?section=104andarticle=26657andarchive=true.

Pogge, T. W. (1994) 'Cosmopolitanism and Sovereignty', in C. Brown (ed.), *Political Restructuring in Europe: Ethical Perspectives*, London: Routledge, p. 90.

Ramsey, M. D. (2006) 'The Textual Basis of the President's Foreign Affairs Power', *Harvard Journal of Law and Public Policy* 30: 141.

Resnik, J. (2007) 'Foreign as Domestic Affairs: Rethinking Horizontal Federalism and Foreign Affairs Preemption in light of Translocal Internationalism', *Emory L.J.* 57: 31.

Saulny, S. and Rutenburg, J. (2007) 'Kansas Tornado Renews Debate on Guard at War', 9 May, *The New York Times*.

Scott Tyson, A. (2006) 'Army Using Policy to Deny Reserve Officer Resignations', 11 May, *The Washington Post*, p. A3.

Smith, N. (2009) 'Introduction: Altered States', in H. Gautney, O. Dahbour, A. Dawson and N. Smith (eds), *Democracy, States, and the Struggle for Global Justice*, Abingdon: Routledge, p. 6.

Smith-Spark, L. (2007) 'Have Lessons of Katrina Been Learnt?', 24 October, *BBC News*.

Solomon, N. (2005), 'The National Guard Belongs in New Orleans and Biloxi. Not Baghdad', 31 August, *Common Dreams News Center*, available at: http://www.commondreams.org/cgi-bin/print.cgi?file=/views05/0831–27.htm.

Swain, R. (2007) 'Reflection on an Ethic of Officership', *Parameters* 4–22.

Von Zielbauer, P. (2007), 'Army is Cracking Down on Deserters', 9 April, *The New York Times*.

Wiener, F. B. (1958) 'Courts-Martial and the Bill of Rights: The Original Practice', *Harvard Law Review* 72: 266.

Wooten, E. M. (2005) 'Note: Banging on the Backdoor Draft: The Constitutional Validity of Stop-Loss in the Military', *William and Mary Law Review* 47: 1061.

Yoo, J. (2005) *The Powers of War and Peace: The Constitution and Foreign Affairs After 9/11*, Chicago: University of Chicago Press.

Part III

Chapter 5

EU constitutionalization in Turkey

Exchanging visions and values on tolerance and diversity

Kyriaki Topidi

> [W]hat stain[s] a country's 'honor' [is] not the discussion of the black spots in its history, but the impossibility of any discussion at all.[1]

5.1 INTRODUCTION: A COSMOPOLITAN FRAME FOR A EUROPEANIZING PICTURE

The idea of a cosmopolitan Europe appears at first glance obscure, yet at the same time quite attractive. But what exactly do we understand by *cosmopolitan*, and why is it relevant for a country such as Turkey? Cosmopolitanism may be understood as a 'pervasive and ongoing cross-fertilization of identities and discourses',[2] which relies heavily on values connected to certain rights of the individual realized through a particular mode of governance. Within the debate on the most appropriate direction to be taken by a post-national Europe, various options have appeared in the last few years. From Habermas, an option that relies on a European Constitution as a means to create a more viable democracy,[3] to Weiler, an option that looks at the acknowledgement of religion as a means and a basis to increase tolerance,[4] or Delanty, one that supports a transnational citizenship based on the prevailing international concepts of human rights,[5] it has become relatively clear that cosmopolitanism begs for a renewed understanding of integration, a two-way process that operates both internally and externally. For thinkers such as Beck and Habermas, the EU's cosmopolitan future lies in the construction of a post-sovereign community that is governed by the rule of law.[6] Both authors seem to suggest the growing irrelevance of the state and the national outlook for world

1 Pamuk (2005).
2 Delanty (2005: 406).
3 Habermas (2001a, 2003).
4 Weiler (2003).
5 Delanty (2005: 414–15).
6 Beck (2006) and Habermas (2001b).

citizens. Constitutional principles thus acquire almost a life of their own nationally, transnationally and globally.

The recent and future enlargements of the Union have precisely challenged and tested empirically all the above visions of how cosmopolitan the EU has become.[7] Particularly for Turkey, the prospect of full membership has ignited the conflict 'between the old national and a new Cosmopolitan Europe',[8] that requires both the EU and Turkey to rethink their identities and the ideas that lie at their respective foundations.

Originating from a different disciplinary perspective, another line of thought suggests that due to its 'special form of soft world power', the EU is 'developing a special radiance and attraction'.[9] It is doing so in its attempts to put forward the idea that diversity as a part of a cosmopolitan integration is not a problem, but rather the solution.[10] The recognition of difference together with the integration of divergencies leads to the constitutional goal of tolerant interaction. As a common European identity seems an impossibility, shared values and principles operate as suitable substitutes towards a 'coherent' EU.[11] What Beck calls the 'language of human rights' embodies well the legitimate and legitimizing discourse that cosmopolitanism is based on, with the risk however that it carries by creating at the same time a right to intervention in the affairs of states anywhere in the world.[12]

What follows precisely tests these suitable substitutes to assess whether the power of norms that the EU claims to be adhering to is indeed contributing in the direction of a more human governance model. The point of departure is the recent developments in Turkey, a country that has undergone an avalanche of reforms since 2002, corroborating the potential of the process. Without entering a debate on the extent to which norms and values are sufficient to create a post-national European space, or whether a cultural niche for a European identity is nevertheless required, this chapter looks at the nature of the impact that Turkish membership might have on the future of the EU, and vice versa on the transformative impact of the Union on Turkey, through the prism of the values of diversity, equality and non-discrimination. After all, democracy defined in terms of human rights constitutes the core content of the Copenhagen criteria, the primary tool of accession negotiations. Put simply, this chapter, will attempt to link the process of

7 See also in this volume Adelman (2010) at 1–4, in particular his point about Europe being 'an idea, ideal and ideology as much as a physical space'.

8 Beck (2006: 164), as quoted in Baban and Keyman (2008: 108).

9 Beck (2009: 115).

10 Ibid, at 116.

11 In the same direction, Adelman (2010), in particular his footnote 11, hints at the possibility of a European supranational rights regime, with reference to the European Court of Human Rights state rights implementation record, that for a long time has informed the EU with regards to fundamental rights.

12 Beck (2005: 64).

Turkey's quest for EU membership with the process of instilling more rights in an Islamic political landscape within Turkey from a predominantly legal perspective.

To fulfil that task, the chapter will evolve following two axes: the internal and the external one. For the internal axis, it will focus on the constitutional battle that is currently taking place in Turkey, as well as on its legal outcomes. It will ask questions that pertain to the (im)possibility of creating yardsticks of tolerance and democracy, and will also address, within the current legal framework, the margins of protection of multiculturalism. The external axis will link Turkey's Westernization path with EU membership, tackling the obstacles and facilitating factors towards the achievement of this goal. It will also include an evaluation of Turkey's candidacy as a testing ground for EU enlargement and its compatibility with post-Islamic legal systems.

5.2 PROBLEMATIZING EUROPEANIZATION AND WESTERNIZATION IN TURKEY

Westernization constitutes a post-colonial concept that is subject to multiple and 'variable' definitions. Broadly, it is understood as a 'process whereby non-Western societies come under the influence of Western culture'.[13] While it is clearly perceived as a two-sided process, it is largely based on the willingness of the affected society to change towards a more Westernized prototype of society. In Turkey's case, this process has acquired more complicated features tainted by historical and socio-political elements, in particular the perspective of full EU membership.

While Islamic movements are often characterized by their resistance to modernity, they are also the result and product of specific socio-economic and political conditions.[14] Within the last few decades, Turkey has set an indicative frame for the observation of such movements. Parties such as the Welfare Party and its successor, the Virtue Party, have adopted in the past a rhetoric of social democracy, similar to other Islamic movements in the Middle East.[15] In fact, their rhetoric focused on the growing economic inequalities affecting the urban poor. Yet political Islam in Turkey has at the same time been evolving against the constant struggle between secularism and modernization.[16] Bearing in mind however that secularization is different in an Islamic state from that within a Western state,[17] this

13 'Westernization': Wikipedia, http://en.wikipedia.org/wiki/Westernization.

14 For a more nuanced approach on Islam as a progressive ideology, see for example Akyol (2007: 80–2).

15 For more on this point, see Delibas (2000: 90–91).

16 Akyol (2007: 82). Akyol speaks of the *neo-orthodoxy* of modern Muslims, who are less traditional yet more observant, reconstructing Islam not only as religion but more broadly as a system.

17 For more on this point see Krawietz (2008: 10–11).

bi-polarity has rendered Islamic political parties a 'counter-cultural model of modernity'.[18] Symbolically, the constant reference to the concept and notion of *justice*, both in the name and political agendas of political parties, is also indicative of this differentiation.[19]

Depicting therefore the current Turkish debate over Westernization as a pure Westernizers-versus-retrograde-Muslims contest provides an oversimplified version of the concept. Its historical roots may be traced back to the transition from the theocratic-oriented Ottoman Empire to a secular and modern Turkish Republic. The vehicle for transition was projected to be Westernization as a process leading to becoming a part of Europe.[20] Kemal Atatürk clearly instilled this understanding of modernity to the Turkish nation, when he argued that 'we Turks have always consistently moved towards the West.... In order to be a civilized nation, there is no alternative'.[21] The alternative to which Kemal was firmly opposed has been realized in the form of the post-1970 Turkish Islamist political movement.

Dogmatically, making a conceptual differentiation between Westernization and modernization is not unusual in Turkey's case. Islamist ideological circles insist on modernization because it is tightly linked to emancipation whereas, to them, Westernization represents 'enslavement to the West and estrangement from the Islamic civilization'.[22] Yet in Kemal's vision of progress, Islam was not considered a source of strength, let alone an element of Turkish identity that fostered the modern Westernized profile of the country. He therefore unambiguously promoted the renovation of the Turkish state at the cost of denial of Islamic identity, at least in the public sphere. As a reaction to the abandonment of the Islamic component of the Turkish identity, Islamists developed a view of Westernization as the 'ultimate betrayal of the nation',[23] blaming it for the backwardness and poverty of the country.

Although the republican history of Turkey has suffered a number of shocks, the surprise was considerable when for the first time in the 1995 general elections the so-called Welfare Party, a pro-Islamic political formation, came first in the vote. From that point onwards, one could begin questioning the so far unquestioned – yet imposed – orientation of the Turkish state towards the West. The debate over *Westernization* is therefore not new, but still very relevant, as today's Turkey is

18 Delibas (2000: 92).

19 The Egyptian National Charter of 1961 gives, for instance, policy directions on the establishment of social justice. Similarly Islamist parties in Morocco and Turkey have the word Justice in their names. See also Ende (2008: 32).

20 For a historical account of Turkish-European relations from the nineteenth century, see Erdogdu (2002).

21 Hale (2000: 38).

22 For more on this conceptual dichotomy, see Dagi (2002: 2–5).

23 Ibid, at p. 11.

governed by an Islamist political party, the Islamist Justice and Development Party (AKP), which promotes a rethinking of the West and Westernization.

AKP leaders, in particular Gül (the current President of the Republic) and Erdoğan (the current Prime Minister), have declared an understanding of *res publica* completely independent from religion, despite their ideological orientation, and have demonstrated firm attachment to certain democratic rights and freedoms.[24] At the same time, following the 2002 elections, Erdoğan regarded EU membership as an absolute priority for Turkey as well as an important step for the modernization of the country.[25]

This idiosyncratic and quite unique *rapprochement* between Western values and Islamist ideology and post-Islamic governance[26] takes place against the background of Turkey's bid to join the European Union.

5.3 THE INTERNAL CONSTITUTIONAL BATTLE: ETHNIC AND RELIGIOUS IDENTITY vs. REPUBLICAN VALUES

With a military that has taken upon itself the heavy task of serving as guarantor of the secular republican order[27] and an Islamist political party in power, it is not unexpected that the internal legal and political landscape might be far from settled. To enhance the Turkish paradox, reforms in line with the Copenhagen criteria and the *acquis communautaire* are led by AKP despite its Islamist ideological tag and in defiance of the past political attitudes of its predecessor parties. In a sense, this evolution subscribes to a parallel model of transformation that has seen non-violent Islamist political parties in the South Mediterranean Arab countries reach power with political agendas shifted to 'ordinary' (i.e. non-religious) priorities and declining religiosity.[28]

The current constitution, a product of Turkey's 1980 military coup, is restrictive in the regulation of basic political, social and human rights.[29] At the time of its enactment, despite the suspension of aid to Turkey, the then European Community (along with some European countries individually) undertook no

24 Abdullah Gül, interview, *Milliyet*, July 15, 2001.

25 Dagi (2002: 27).

26 *Post-Islamic* is here understood and defined in accordance with Asef Bayat's definition of post-Islamism as '[denoting] a departure, albeit in diverse degrees, from an Islamist ideologic package ... towards acknowledging ambiguity, multiplicity, inclusion and compromise in principles and practice.'

27 The army has staged in total four direct or indirect military interventions to protect and preserve the secular features of the republic. The most recent, also qualified as a post-modern coup, took place on 28 February 1997, when the Turkish military succeeded in sufficiently mobilizing public opinion to force the resignation of a coalition government led by the Islamist Welfare Party.

28 Emerson (2006).

29 For a detailed analysis of the 1980 coup see Aydin-Düzgit and Gürsoy (2008).

major intervention in favour of democracy and had thus no considerable impact in that direction.[30] Today, ahead of Turkey's Western path lie a number of domestically contested legal reforms. The following sections highlight a number of them.

5.3.1 Freedom of belief and the headscarf issue: identity or political symbolism?

The first example of rights pertains to religion. On March 7, 1989 the Turkish Constitutional Court annulled a law passed by Parliament allowing female students to cover their heads for reasons of religious belief. The Court's rationale was that the law at stake was contrary to the principle of secularism enshrined in Article 2 of the Constitution.[31] The historical experiences of the country afforded, according to the Court, constitutional status to the principle in dispute. The Court went on to define secularism as the 'principle which offers the individual the possibility to affirm his or her own personality through freedom of thought and which, by the distinction it makes between politics and religious beliefs, renders freedom of conscience and religion effective'.[32]

Such an argument, however, runs counter to the absolute interdiction of the wearing of the headscarf for example in higher education establishments,[33] especially as the mere manifestation of one's convictions from the standpoint of a student and not so much that of a teacher or a public servant.[34] As the ECtHR stated in *Şahin*, 'a balance must be achieved which ensures the fair and proper treatment of people from minorities and avoids any abuse of a dominant position',[35] in sum a balance between universality and diversity.

Both legally and politically, the headscarf has become an issue of contention between secular and Islamist circles or between those in favour of an assertive form of secularism opposed to those more comfortable with passive secularism. For the former, the headscarf represents a political symbol that departs from the secular character of the state. As the Turkish Constitutional Court stated in 1997, secularism implies the 'separation of religion and worldly affairs', the 'separation of social life, education, family and economy, law manners, dress codes etc. from

30 Ibid. The European Parliament constitutes a clear exception as it passed resolution calling for a return to normalcy. See for example Resolution on the Military Junta in Turkey, Brussels, April 10, 1981, *O.J.* C101/110, 4 May 1981.

31 Article 2 stipulates: 'The Republic of Turkey is a democratic, *secular* and social state governed by the rule of law, bearing in mind the concepts of public peace, national solidarity and justice; respecting human rights; loyal to the nationalism of Atatürk, and based on the fundamental tenets set forth in the Preamble.' (Emphasis added.)

32 Passage as quoted by the ECtHR in *Leyla Şahin v Turkey*, Application no. 44774/98, Grand Chamber Judgment, 10 November 2005, at para. 39.

33 In *Şahin*, the ECtHR found no violation of Article 9 ECHR arising out of the prohibition of the headscarf for students at university due to 'pressing social needs'.

34 On this point see *Leyla Şahin v Turkey*, Dissenting Opinion of Judge Tulkens, at para. 7.

35 *Leyla Şahin v Turkey*, at para. 108 of the judgment.

religion'.[36] For the latter, it is simply related to one's religious beliefs and by extension, identity. Furthermore, the banning of the covered students from higher education constitutes a human rights violation, according to Islamists, despite national and international fora ruling otherwise. Public opinion in Turkey surprisingly yet clearly, does not consider the issue as an important one, when compared to economic issues.[37] The same research suggests that the headscarf is neither perceived as a political opinion nor as a matter of identity.[38]

If law is supposed to reflect society's opinion on certain matters, then it is worth exploring the purpose of amendments passed by Parliament in February 2008 changing Articles 10 and 42 of the Constitution. Article 10 guarantees equality before the law, including equal access to all public services, as the new provision stipulates. Article 42, concerning the right to education, was amended to include a sentence preventing the denial of access to education, unless for a reason openly stated by law.[39]

Both amendments are clearly at odds with the previous judicial decisions. The suggested amendments pointed at the intention of Islamist political leaders to 'rethink' the Western political values and insist on a rights-centred understanding of the individual in society. The rights-based discourse is obviously related to their quest for legitimacy in Turkish politics.[40] The trend is confirmed by estimates that find only 22.6 per cent of the population to perceive secularism as under threat, leaving ample space for legal reforms.[41] Beyond this concern, however, it is difficult to question from a human rights perspective the protected right to religious self-determination. The balance between tolerance and diversity remains problematic, especially since on 5 June 2008 the Constitutional Court annulled amendments to both Articles 10 and 42 on the grounds that they were against the secular nature of the state. The battle appears to continue.

5.3.2 Religious and ethnic diversity in Turkey

There appears to be a clear dichotomy in social attitudes between those blatantly against 'otherness' and those openly and unambiguously in favour of diversity. The same duality is reflected at the legal level. To illustrate this division, the following example is relevant: in April 2006, the mandatory declaration of religion on identity cards was abolished. The state continues nevertheless to ask

36 Kuru (2007: 142).

37 Only 3.7 per cent of respondents to a 2006 survey indicated the headscarf issue as an important one for them (Çarkoğlu and Torpak, 2007: 26).

38 Ibid, at p. 29. Only 3.9 per cent consider covering headscarves to be an integral part of their identity.

39 The added text read: 'No one shall be deprived of the right to higher education because of their apparel.'

40 Dagi (2002: 41).

41 Çarkoğlu and Torpak (2007: 33).

citizens to declare their religious affiliation and beliefs, with repercussions for those leaving the section blank.[42]

Historically, minority status in Turkey is linked with religion, as defined in the 1923 Lausanne Treaty.[43] The restricted definition of Lausanne automatically excludes Turkey's ethnic, linguistic and cultural minorities. As there has been no legislative reference to the concept, it becomes difficult, if not impossible, to argue in favour of the recognition of diversity and fundamental rights protection in the current legal framework. The following categories of rights demonstrate that the exercise of devising yardsticks of tolerance, in its Western understanding, calls for additional measures.

5.3.2.1 Linguistic rights

The first language legislation measures were introduced in Turkey around 1839. Language awareness was the fruit of Western influence, and at the same time a reaction against the West.[44] A defining element of the process of nation-building in Turkey, it was intended as a means to enforce integration. As Virtanen pertinently points out, however, 'It is important to remember that, unlike assimilation, integration does not aim for absolute homogeneity.'[45] Article 42 of the Constitution is strict: 'No language other than Turkish shall be taught as a mother tongue to Turkish citizens at any institution of training or education.'[46] The Constitution does not recognize or afford any protection for minority languages or cultures. A partial exception to this rule is found in Article 40 of the Treaty of Lausanne that awards non-Muslims the 'right to establish, manage and control at their own expense, any charitable, religious and social institutions, any schools and other establishments for instruction and education, with the right to use their own language and to exercise their own religion freely therein.'

Recent legislation has reviewed the state's stance of cultural inflexibility. Laws of 2002 and 2003 allow the organization of classes teaching minority languages, yet at the participants' expense and only to the extent that they do not threaten the 'indivisible integrity of the state'.[47] Subsequently, private courses in Kurdish came into existence as of 2004,[48] but closed down soon thereafter due to

42 Ibid, at p. 3.

43 Treaty of Peace with Turkey, 24 July 1923, 28 *LNTS* 11.

44 Virtanen (2003: 6).

45 Virtanen (2003: 9).

46 For an English version of the Turkish Constitution, see Office of the Prime Minister/Directorate General of Press and Information, *The Constitution of the Republic of Turkey*, available at http://www.byegm.gov.tr/mevzuat/anayasa/anayasa-ing.htm.

47 Law on the Amendment of Certain Laws, No. 4771, 3/08/2002, *Official Gazette* No. 24841, 9 August 2002 (in particular Article 11) and Law on the Amendment of Certain Laws, No. 4963, 30/07/2003, *Official Gazette* no. 25192, 7 August 2003.

48 MRG Report 2007, at p. 16.

bureaucratic restriction and the reluctance of participants to pay to learn their mother tongue. In similar spirit, for non-Muslim minority schools, the state's interference is such that it denies the essence of Article 40 of the Treaty of Lausanne.[49]

Regarding media and broadcasting rights, the liberalization of broadcasting in minority languages has evolved positively, particularly for the Muslim ethnic groups. As a result of reforms, in 2004, broadcasts in five minority languages were initiated.[50] The legal framework for these activities is nevertheless heavily regulated and includes time limitations and prior authorization upon completion of audience profiles in order to approve such broadcastings.

Finally, regarding the use of minority languages in the individual's relations with public authorities, Article 39 of the Treaty of Lausanne grants to non-Muslims this right 'for the oral use of their own language before the Courts'. For Muslim minorities, there are only exceptional and marginal cases where the minority language can be used, despite bold local initiatives in line with international standards to the opposite direction. These efforts were sanctioned with prosecutorial investigations and administrative measures.[51] It is worth noting that Article 220(8) of the Penal Code punishes 'making propaganda of an organization of its goals' and indeed, this was the legal basis used in the case against Abdullah Demirbas for demanding the use of minority languages in public services, amongst a predominantly Kurdish local population.

5.3.2.2 *Religious beliefs*

Article 10 of the Constitution guarantees the principle of equality 'irrespective of ... philosophical belief, religion and sect'. Secularism is deeply rooted in that respect in the workings and processes of the republic. *De facto*, this freedom has encountered restrictions in two directions: for non-Muslim minority groups, despite Article 40 of the Treaty of Lausanne, the state denies legal personality to non-Muslim religious institutions, with repercussions to the status of their respective properties.[52] The 2008 Law on Foundations has mitigated the effects of restrictions, allowing religious foundations to apply for the restitution of their properties.[53] The law, nevertheless, has not addressed the issues of properties of foundations seized and sold to third parties, or properties of foundations merged

49 For example, the state appoints Turkish culture teachers as well as the deputy principals in each private minority school.

50 MRG Report 2007, at p. 17. These are the Zaza and Kurmanci dialects of Kurdish, together with Arabic, Bosnian and Circassian.

51 The case related to Kurdish spoken in Sur Municipality (MRG Report 2007, at p. 19).

52 European Commission, *2009 Progress Report on Turkey*, http://ec.europa.eu/enlargement/pdf/key_documents/2009/tr_rapport_2009_en.pdf at p. 21.

53 Ibid, at p. 27.

before the new legislation was adopted. Similarly, the ban on the training of clergy creates adverse effects to the exercise of the freedom of religion. For Muslims, the tight control of the state over religion also raises objections to the basic concept of secularism as guaranteed under the Constitution. A typical illustration of the controversy has been depicted in the headscarf issue.[54]

An equally controversial issue, in conjunction with the right to education, is the fact that religious culture classes remain compulsory. In the light of the recent ECtHR decision on an application lodged by a family who were followers of Alevism,[55] religious diversity requires further measures for its protection. This observation is enhanced by the puzzling arguments of the Turkish government in the case of *Zengin* sustaining that 'the teaching of religion in schools is an appropriate method of combating fanaticism....'[56] More constructive in the overall assessment of the issue was the acknowledgement of the Turkish government that 'in the religious culture and morals lessons, the religious diversity which prevails in Turkish society is not taken into account'.[57] Accordingly, but not surprisingly, the Court found a violation of Article 2 of Protocol 1 to the ECHR guaranteeing a right to education.

5.3.2.3 Freedom of expression and identity

Adoption of Turkish identity, in the discourse of fervent secularists, has been often elevated to an argument of cultural superiority and forced assimilation, imposing thus over time its linguistic as well as cultural characteristics on groups of different ethnic background.[58] On the occasion of a Constitutional Court decision suspending a political party in 1999, the Court did not hesitate to state that 'the only national culture in the country is the Turkish culture' and continued: 'the languages which remained local and underdeveloped cannot enable individuals to improve their spiritual beings',[59] although the expression of ethnic identity was not overall prohibited.[60]

Freedom of expression acquired special features in Turkey in the context of peaceful advocacy of minority protection. Despite the 2001 constitutional amendments that have alleviated Articles 26 and 28 of the Constitution from

54 See above.

55 *Hasan and Eylem Zengin v Turkey*, application no. 1448/04.

56 Para. 59 of the judgment.

57 Para. 67 of the judgment.

58 Van Bruinessen (1997) gives an account at p. 3 of his paper of Genral Ihasn Gökcel's views during the 1982 deliberations on the draft text of Article 66 of the Constitution. He is quoted as stating: 'If we wish to identify citizenship and Turkishness, we should definitely include the element of adoption of Turkish identity. The person who cannot call out from his heart the words "happy is he who calls himself a Turk" cannot be a Turk.'

59 Decision No. 1999/1 of 26 February 1999, at p. 78, as quoted in Virtanen (2003: 23–4).

60 Ibid, at p. 89 of the decision.

restrictions due to 'language prohibited by law', free speech remains conditional upon safeguarding 'the indivisible integrity of state with its territory and nation'. Articles 301[61] and 216[62] of the Penal Code have been the legal basis for a string of cases against intellectuals, writers and activists.

The prohibition against 'denigrating Turkishness' contained in Article 301 has been interpreted restrictively by public prosecutors. Both sociologically and legally, however, the concept of *Turkishness* remains to be defined.[63] Recent surveys hinted at the reluctance of respondents to address sensitive identity and tolerance issues for fear of the circumstances under Turkish law and its application contributing to the restriction of their freedom of expression on minority groups.[64] Such concern was not entirely unfounded, as the number of persons prosecuted under the provisions in question doubled in 2006, compared to 2005, with a further increase in 2007.[65] In April 2008, the Turkish Parliament adopted amendments to Article 301 changing the wording of the text, lowering the upper limit of the penalty and abolishing the higher penalty for insults in a foreign

61 Under Article 301:

> '1. Public denigration of Turkishness, the Republic or the Grand National Assembly of Turkey shall be punishable by imprisonment of between six months and three years.
> 2. Public denigration of the Government of the Republic of Turkey, the judicial institutions of the State, the military or security structures shall be punishable by imprisonment of between six months and two years.
> 3. In cases where denigration of Turkishness is committed by a Turkish citizen in another country the punishment shall be increased by one third.
> 4. Expressions of thought intended to criticize shall not constitute a crime.'

62 Article 216 stipulates:

> '(1) A person who openly incites groups of the population to breed enmity or hatred towards one another based on social class, race, religion, sect or regional difference in a manner which might constitute a clear and imminent danger to public order shall be sentenced to imprisonment for a term of one to three years.
> (2) A person who openly denigrates part of the population on grounds of social class, race, religion, sect, gender or regional differences shall be sentenced to imprisonment for a term of six months to one year.
> (3) A person who openly denigrates the religious values of a part of the population shall be sentenced to imprisonment for a term of six months to one year in case the act is likely to disturb public peace.'

63 The definition of Turkishness as put forward by the 1982 Constitution disposes in Article 66 that 'Everyone bound to the Turkish State with the bond of citizenship is a Turk' but does not provide any further substantial features of the concept. For a historical account of the connections between freedom of expression and identity in Turkey, see Van Bruinessen (1997).

64 Çarkoğlu and Torpak (2007: 32).

65 European Commission, *Turkey 2007 Progress Report*, COM (2007) 663 final, at 14.

country. In addition, the amendments introduced a requirement for prior authorization from the Justice Minister in order to launch criminal investigations.[66] Following the adjustments, however, the wording does not justify fundamental changes and the requirement of prior authorization opens the door for political considerations to enter into play.[67]

5.3.2.4 Right to political participation

The Constitution guarantees to all citizens the right to political participation and equal access to the political system (Article 68). More disputable is Article 33 of the Electoral Law[68] that requires parties to pass a national electoral threshold of 10 per cent in order to obtain representation in the national parliament. The July 2007 elections were the first instance of members of a minority group having been represented in parliament,[69] yet as independent candidates, in order to circumvent the threshold.

ECHR case law, as recently as 2007, dealt with precisely the question of the excessiveness of the 10 per cent threshold.[70] Article 67 paragraph 6 of the Constitution provides that 'electoral laws must strike a balance between fair representation and governmental stability'. The applicable threshold can indeed be considered excessive by international standards,[71] disproportionately affecting smaller parties and minority political formations. While it is difficult from a legal point of view to demonstrate that the electoral threshold was fixed to block the representation of voters of Kurdish ethnic origin,[72] Article 3 of Protocol No. 1, which Turkey has signed, includes the right to vote and to stand for election. When discussed and challenged before the ECtHR, the Court, based on the doctrine of the margin of appreciation and 'in the light of the political evolution of the country concerned',[73] accepted that the 10 per cent threshold did not violate Article 3 of Protocol 1 to the ECHR. What was at stake in this case, however, was not the choice of an appropriate electoral system. Instead, it was the unusually high percentage vote required to obtain representation in the Grand Assembly.

In the same direction, the Law on Political Parties[74] forbids parties from claiming the existence of minorities and from using minority languages at their meetings,

66 European Commission, *Turkey 2008 Progress Report*, COM (2008) 674 final, at 15.

67 Ibid, at 15–16.

68 Law No. 2839.

69 The media have covered in particular the case of Sebahat Tuncel who was imprisoned on a charge of PKK membership, but following her election was released, as she enjoyed parliamentary immunity. (See *The Economist*, 'General Displeasure', 4 August 2007, at p. 27.) Of the 26 independent candidates, 20 are of Kurdish ethnic origin.

70 *Yumak and Sadak v Turkey*, Application no. 10226/03, 20 January 2007.

71 Council of Europe, Parliamentary Assembly Resolution 1380 (2004).

72 See para. 45 of the judgment.

73 *Yumak and Sadak v Turkey* (2007), at para. 61.

74 Law on Political Parties, No. 2820, 22 April 1983, Article 81(a).

statutes and programmes.[75] Most importantly it sanctions the 'aiming of and engaging in activities towards disturbing the unity of the nation by creating minorities on the territory of the Republic of Turkey through protecting, advancing or spreading languages and cultures other than the Turkish language and culture'.[76] In December 2009, the judges of the Turkish Constitutional Court unanimously ruled in favour of closing down the Democratic Society Party (DTP) on the grounds that its activities conflicted with 'the independence of the state, its indivisible integrity within its territory and the nation'. The party was sanctioned for promoting the Kurdish identity and for maintaining links with the separatist militant group, PKK.[77]

5.4 EU MEMBERSHIP: A VALUE-DRIVEN PROCESS?

Turkey has traditionally accorded importance to its relations with Europe, despite the fact that 'many decades ago, Turks chose the West, but have sometimes felt the West rejected their very choice of the West'.[78] A salient component of Turkey's Westernization reverts around and relates to EU membership, as an incentive for change and reform. In 2006, only 37 per cent of EU nationals considered that Turkey could successfully join the Union by 2020.[79] At the same time, public support in Turkey for EU membership has already dropped below 50 per cent.[80] As the momentum for EU membership appears to be fading away, it is crucial to examine whether this mutual distancing is due to identity politics in Turkey that have surfaced yet again, and how the EU affects the process of the transfer of its fundamental principles and human rights values to Turkey.

5.4.1 Brief overview of recent EU–Turkish relations

In 1995, Turkey signed the EU Customs Agreement.[81] During the Helsinki Conference in 1999, Turkey was granted EU candidate status. The first Accession Partnership was signed in March 2001. In the 2003 Strategy Paper on *Continuing*

75 Article 81(c).

76 Article 81(b).

77 Amnesty International, 'Turkey criticized for closing Pro-Kurdish political party', www.amnesty.org, 14 December 2009.

78 Testimony of Elliott Abrams and James Spain in *Cyprus, Greece and Turkey*, Before the Subcommittee on Human Rights and International Organizations of the Committee on Affairs/House of Representatives, Washington DC, US Government Printing Office, 1983, at pp. 6 and 17–18.

79 *To Vima*, 24 September 2006, at p. 67/A35.

80 *The Economist*, 'Turkey and the European Union: The ever lengthening road', 9 December 2006, pp. 25–6.

81 For a chronology of the key dates on EU-Turkey relations as of their start see http://ec.europa.eu/cgi-bin/etal.pl.

Enlargement, the Commission acknowledged reforms that had been undertaken in the meanwhile, placing emphasis on freedom of expression, of peaceful assembly, cultural rights and civilian control of the military. It nevertheless insisted that the implementation of reforms required the collaboration of judges, prosecutors and executive organs that should avoid adopting narrow interpretation of rights guaranteed, depriving them of their essence.[82]

Following the 2004 annual report on Turkey's progress towards accession, in 2005, the Council adopted a negotiating framework setting out the principles governing the negotiations and formally opened accession negotiations with Turkey. A revised Accession Partnership was adopted in December 2005. Yet one year later, due to the Turkish failure to apply to Cyprus the Additional Protocol to the Ankara Agreement, the Council decided that the most crucial chapters would not be opened and no chapter would be provisionally closed until Turkey had fulfilled its commitments. In February 2008, the most recent revised Accession Partnership was adopted.

5.4.2 The mixed nature of EU membership in Turkey

The revival of the politics of tolerance coincides with the country's process for harmonization with the EU. It involves consideration of the Kurdish and Alevi questions, that of non-Muslim minorities and developments in the Middle East. It is beyond the scope of this paper to question the true intentions and political motivations of the AKP ruling party, which has claimed EU membership to be of primary importance to the country. It will be therefore accepted that EU accession represents a genuine target of Turkish foreign policy.

In this light, it is possible to conceive the EU integration process as the continuation of Kemal's modernization process and as a quintessentially Westernizing venture. If one therefore assumes that EU membership represents a form of Europeanization, then the internalization of Western legal principles is to be expected. But is the pronounced civil rights discourse demonstrated by AKP related to and dependent on the EU? In part, it is. The path to EU membership offers the first opportunity to develop modernization built on socio-economic trajectories. Previous instances of Westernization under Atatürk were viewed as 'a mechanism of the state to control people and to be an insurance of the internal regime'.[83] This 'new' form of Europeanization as Westernization cannot however be entirely justified as a project based on tolerance concerns or a political move based on preference.

82 http://europa.eu.int/comm/enlargement/report_2003/pdf/strategy_paper2003_full_en.pdf, at 15.
83 Inaç (2004: 38).

5.4.2.1 *The idiosyncratic nature of EU negotiations with Turkey*

The Turkish candidacy to the Union operates against a background of reducing support for further EU expansion as EU citizens seem to share the opinion that the 'aim of unifying the continent has largely been achieved'.[84] European institutions nevertheless embrace a different view.

According to the 2005 Negotiating Framework, EU negotiations would be based on the individual characteristics of the Turkish candidacy, without reference to the progress and speed of negotiations with other countries, unlike in some instances in 2004 in Central and Eastern Europe.[85] The EU's role in the Turkish context was declared as being to 'ensure the irreversibility of progress ... and [its] full and effective implementation with regard to fundamental freedoms and to respect of human rights'.[86] Through the use of periodically updated Accession Partnerships, first in 2001 and then in 2003, 2005 and 2008, the Union attempted to provide a concrete basis for political reforms and at the same time a yardstick for measuring future progress.[87] Short-term priorities in particular have included requirements that stem directly from so-called European values such as the rule of law and democracy, respect for human rights, civil and political rights as well as more specific points pertaining to the topical issues of freedom of expression, of religion, cultural rights and women's rights.[88] The issue of civilian oversight of the security forces, or put more simply, the quest for minimal military intervention in political issues, was also listed prominently as an item on the Council's list.[89]

The domestic reactions to the adaptation pressures for a different system of values were broadly two-fold. On one side, one part of the Turkish political world sustained a vision of the country based on national and social homogeneity where national sensitive issues should resist any type of reform. Socio-cultural rights for non-dominant ethnic communities, freedom of religion potentially undermining the secular regime and the role of the military in politics were such issues. A different segment of the political world and civil society more aligned to European integration, was more receptive to the post-modern character of the EU, and embraced the concepts of pluralist democracy and multi-tier governance with significantly fewer reservations.[90] The extent to which Kemal's Westernization

84 Yackley (2008: 7).

85 Negotiating Framework, at para. 1.

86 Negotiating Framework at para. 4.

87 Council Decision 2008/157/EC of 18 February 2008 on the principles, priorities, and conditions contained in the Accession Partnership with the Republic of Turkey and repealing Decisions 2006/35/EC, O.J. L051, 26/02/2008,4–18, Annex at para. 1.

88 Ibid, at para. 3.1.

89 Ibid.

90 For an analysis of the concerns, policy expectations from both sides see Piccoli (2005), in file with the author.

process was able to achieve internalization of European and global norms of tolerance and multiculturalism appears thus unclear.

The sweeping August 2002 reforms touched upon perceptions of Turkish identity, insofar as they embodied amendments in the direction of cultural diversity.[91] They even went further than EU membership requirements, questioning the ideological foundations of Turkish identity and its constant desire for Westernized modernity. The confusion of unity with uniformity prevailing pre-2002 stands separately from any 'reconciling' role with the Muslim world that we may want to assign to Turkey. In other words, while it is definitely undisputed that Turkey remains a Muslim country, it is also a secular one – despite the rule of a pro-Islamist government for the last few years – and as such, insisting on the paradigm of Turkey as a 'bridge between the Occident and the Orient' can only have limited effects.[92] Turkish identity, after all, is partly the consequence of Ottoman heritage, which historically has been treated as 'Europe's Other'.[93] Yet national feelings and identity cannot be always rationally justifiable. The value of Turkey's bid for accession lies precisely at this point: allowing the circulation of values between parties involved by gradually abolishing the strict demarcation between 'us' and 'them'.[94] Transformation can only occur under such circumstances. The Union is after all a social (and legal) construction that is based on unity in diversity.

At times of contentious relations between communities in Europe, modern understandings of Islam in our continent have been a prominent topic of religious, political, social and even legal debate. Clearly the question of Turkish EU membership has accentuated the broader issue once more, bringing fuzzy concepts such as Euro-Islam back to the fore. Mainstream literature distinguishes two 'variants' of Euro-Islam, relevant for this analysis: one that proposes the adoption of European liberal-democratic fundamental values as a remedy to emerge from a 'decaying' religion and its ensuing mental attitudes,[95] and another that seeks to embrace and re-surface the 'universally valid' fundamental values of Islam.[96]

In a way, the theological reform debate in Turkey is now entangled with EU membership and is no longer taking place in a vacuum.[97] Its repercussions are visible in the balancing of secularism and Islamism, in the light of AKP

91 The reforms included, *inter alia*, the abolition of the death penalty in peacetime, allowing broadcasting in other languages and dialects than the Turkish language, and authorized their learning as well. For an overview of the package, see ABGS, *Harmonization Laws: 57th Government*, Ankara, 2002.

92 Svensson (2008: 18).

93 Reference is made here to the sixteenth and seventeenth-century history of the Ottoman Empire. For more on the point see Svensson (2008: 19).

94 Stråth (2000).

95 Bassam Tibi is the main proponent of this interpretation of Euro-Islam. The main critique for this understanding of Islam within Europe regards it as a call for assimilation.

96 Tariq Ramadan is the most representative scholar in favour of this self-assertive conception of Euro-Islam that is nevertheless criticized for its lack of theological grounding.

97 See e.g. Stahr (2006).

governance. The modernization of pro-Islamic politics as evidenced by progressive and reformist law-making has fuelled the intellectual discussion about a secular Islamic alternative for Turkey within Europe. Can Islam as an essential defining value be compatible with the rule of law, democracy and human rights? The Turkish national goal of EU accession and the conditionality imposed by the Union in the form of the Copenhagen criteria constitute indeed one possible path in the direction of Islamic modernism. The position that 'an intellectual cannot be Islamist, and an Islamist cannot be an intellectual', is thus gradually losing ground.[98]

5.4.2.2 The domestic reactions to the 'import of values': options and paradox

Particularly, for Islamists, the European project disposes of added value: it operates as a guarantee of their democratic rights,[99] although doubts about the sincerity of the EU's intentions towards Turkey's membership subsist. The main argument put forward, in favour of Turkey's membership, will provide a strong and unquestioned guarantee of continuous stability and economic development. Particularly for the aspects that regard the democratic regime, this paradigm has been utilized in the past in the cases of Spain and Greece, for example, and has proven efficient. The real question, however, that is posed will be the extent to which the promised stability will affect the Europeanization process and the ensuing attitude of Turkish people towards the West. And if so, will a trend develop in favour of a rights-based understanding of democracy? As importantly, will the current divide between secularism and Islamism gradually subside?

Human and individual rights do not appear to be a firmly established idea in today's Turkey,[100] as the previous sections of this paper have argued. Indeed, the Commission is ambivalent in that respect: while it commends the primacy of the democratic process as it emerged through the spring 2007 elections, it criticizes the non-alignment of the Turkish practices in the areas of broader fundamental rights and cultural rights of minority groups.[101] It would be thus a desired side-effect to trigger a deeper and more coherent understanding of the individual's fundamental rights in society, regardless of his/her ethnic, linguistic or religious identity. Linked to that, some also argue in favour of EU membership as a solution to Turkey's cultural identity ambivalence. At this level of argumentation, it is quite important to consider the transformation from a collectivist culture into an

98 Ibid.

99 Nas, (2001: 186).

100 Inaç (2004: 51).

101 European Commission, Communication to the European Parliament and the Council – *EU Enlargement Strategy and Main Challenges 2006–2007*, including annexed special report on the EU's capacity to integrate new members, COM (2006) 649, at pp. 56, 57, 60.

individualist one.[102] From the legal perspective, this transition would tie up harmoniously with the above-mentioned clearer understanding of human and individual rights. It would also signify that recent constitutional amendments are heading in the direction of alignment with declared EU values and principles.

Moving away from the historically contradictory Turkish attempts to Westernize, whereby sovereignty rhymed with *limited* democracy,[103] it remains legally unorthodox that an incentive for change is provided by a (moderate) Islamist party. From the perspective of the EU, the value of Turkey's membership would constitute an important paradigm of a country in transition adhering to all the fundamental principle of liberty, democracy and the rule of law striking the right balance between secularism, Europeanization and Muslim identity.[104]

5.4.3 Enlargement and the 'train crash' factor

Previous political history suggests that the European Community (along with NATO and the UN) was hesitant to apply pressure and sanctions to Turkey in circumstances where levels of democracy were low in the country.[105] This policy choice was justified by Cold War concerns, especially as Turkey was strategically placed between the democratic nations of Western Europe and the Soviet Union, provided that it remained risk-free of an Islamic or leftist takeover. Both the Commission and the Council maintained the view that the (then) Community could only utilize conditionality on Turkey while maintaining political and economic links as stipulated in the Association Agreement.[106]

Yet there are at least two points of substantial differentiation between the 1980–83 period and the current conjuncture: at the time, Turkish membership was neither desired nor feasible from the EC side, as it could have introduced further instability with Greece, set to join in 1981. Second, today Turkey is ruled by a democratically elected government and the perception of a threat to democracy stems not from military rule but instead from Islamist ideology and policy.

In 1999, at the Helsinki Summit, Turkey was finally given a candidate status, despite the 'too big, too poor and too Muslim' line of argument.[107] In December 2006, negotiations came to a halt with the freezing of eight out of thirty-five negotiating chapters with the European Commission, as a reaction to the Turkish refusal to open their ports and airports to traffic from Cyprus. Commissioner Olli

102 Ibid, at 51.

103 Dagi (2002) pertinently describes it as 'a popular but limited democracy in which the tutelage of the state elite and the army was justified ... as republicanism'.

104 European Commission, *Communication to the Council and the European Parliament-Recommendation of the European Commission on Turkey's progress towards accession*, COM 2004 (0656) final, at point 3.

105 Düzgit and Gürsoy (2008: 16–17) for the 1980–83 period.

106 Ibid, at 33, in particular footnote 99.

107 Expression borrowed from Akçapar and Choubi (2006: 51).

Rehn's fears of the 'train crash' between Turkey and the EU were thus partially realized.[108] In the background of this slow-down, France and Austria view the candidacy unfavourably, while Germany insists on a 'privileged partnership', instead of a full membership.[109]

One of the greatest successes of the Union has been the spread of stability, security and democracy across the European continent. Clearly, enlargement has at the same time posed functional as well as ideological questions. In particular, recurring arguments against 'widening' include the question of geographical limit as well as that of the resistance of electorates in many countries, in particular with respect to the perspective of full Turkish membership.[110]

It should come as no surprise that both the EU in itself and its continuing enlargement are hard to 'sell' to domestic electorates, particularly in circumstances of widespread economic recession and high unemployment. To that effect, and drawing from experience with previous enlargements, the Commission made clear that it intends to inform and better prepare citizens for future enlargements. It has already identified the gap of the process which it aims to address by supporting a 'strong, deep and sustained dialogue between the societies of the candidate countries and in the EU Member States'.[111]

With Turkey, this dialogue is primarily aimed at tackling the prevailing perceptions regarding social and political issues for Turkish membership both within EU and Turkish public opinion. A significant part of the envisaged dialogue concerns values expressed by society and the state(s) on both sides. The activities projected cover the development of civil society, social affairs and education through targeted funding activities which are expected to foster further links between the two parties, mutual knowledge and understanding.[112] The crucial areas of gender equality, civil and human rights, social exclusion and discrimination have been singled out as points where dialogue in the form of cooperation, exchange of practices and direct financial contribution would encourage the transfer of values. Similarly, public debates on religious identity form part of the Commission's agenda, with the clear intention to carry across the diversity of perceptions and the *rapprochement* of values.

108 Olli Rehn said that, despite Turkey's refusal to accommodate the Additional Protocol: 'There is a slowing down because of works further down the tracks, however the train continues to move.' Akçakoca (2006: 14).

109 *The Economist*, 'The Turkish train crash', December 2, 2006 at p. 34.

110 The most recent Euro-Barometer poll on enlargement found that 69 per cent of Germans, 54 per cent of French and 81 per cent of Austrians were opposed to Turkish entry.

111 European Commission, Communication from the Commission to the Council, the European Parliament, the European Economic and Social Committee and the Committee of the Regions: Civil Dialogue between the EU and Candidate Countries, 29/06/2005, COM (2005) 290 final, at 2.

112 For a detailed list of activities see Communication COM (2005) 290 final at 6–13.

Within this framework, the implications for Turkey's Europeanization are twofold: in the case of future full membership, the process of internalization of Western values will remain unaffected, helping to stabilize the more unstable elements of democracy in the country. For the Islamist ruling party, it would entail guarantees against military interventions, and for the army it would offer the required assurances of the maintenance of the secular character of the republic. Ideally, for ethnic and religious minorities, it would also offer a breakthrough in the visibility and content of their rights. The May 2007 constitutional amendments, while not entirely attributed to EU candidacy, move towards the fulfilment of the Copenhagen political criterion, especially in relation to the introduction of election of the President by popular vote.[113] It is crucial that all reforms were subsequently endorsed by referendum on 21 October 2007.

In case of withdrawal of the membership bid, it should not be assumed that the process of Westernization will be automatically frozen. It is arguable however that it might be diverted and possibly acquire different characteristics. The direction of the process will largely depend on whether looking to the West is a question of *identity* or of *choice* for Turkey. To the extent that it is a matter of identity, the process has high chances of being salvaged. The role of conditionality as a soft law instrument will continue to be emphasized so as to create a legal and political environment conducive to adaptation to the values and principles of the *acquis communautaire*. In that direction, it appears likely that gaps in the current legal framework will be addressed. A similar line of argument maintains that Turkey's ties to the West are too strong[114] to be cut by a refusal to join the Union. Yet, in this case Turkey's Westernization will be conceived and construed as a defensive tool against Europe (i.e. Turkey as Europe's Other). To the extent that it is a matter of choice, the case will become one of seeking alternatives in the face of the United States, countries in the Middle East, the Caucasus or the former Soviet central Asian countries. Shared concerns over the creation of an independent Kurdish state create favourable conditions for a rapprochement with Iran and Syria.[115] In other words, Westernization will be adjusted to the current policy needs of the country, not necessarily resulting in further legislative changes or a genuine internalization of European norms.

From the EU perspective, Turkey offers specific assets valuable to the EU and its future fellow Member States. Yet its bid for membership along with the projected enlargement to the Balkans leads to potential forms of divergence in the Union.[116]

113 Other reforms included the shortening of the government's term of office from five to four years and the establishment of a quorum of one-third for all sessions and decisions of parliament. See European Commission, *Turkey 2007 Progress Report*, COM (2007) 663 final, at 6.

114 Yackley (2008: 11).

115 Ibid.

116 Emerson and Tocci (2004: 5).

One of the most ambiguous normative aspects of Turkey's membership strictly related to identity, lies in the potential for the contribution of European integration to conflict resolution, in particular the reconciliation between the Turkish state and its Kurdish population.[117] Multiculturalism would also clearly benefit both parties, provided that Turkey's democratic values become entirely consolidated. So far, Commission reporting has stressed the lack of progress in ensuring 'full civilian supervisory functions' over the activities of the military, including public comments on issues of domestic and foreign policy such as Cyprus, secularism and Kurdish matters.[118]

The question of Turkey's entry into the EU disposes of another, non-negligible dimension: it constitutes a test for Europe's discourse on the cosmopolitanism of diversity, multiculturalism and celebration of difference. If the Union still wishes to sustain itself as a world actor guided by ideology and not geography, it needs to streamline its enlargement policies in that direction.[119] Within the framework of lessons learned from previous enlargements, the Commission has proposed to improve the quality of the accession process with respect to *inter alia* more systematic use of benchmarks and a more individualized approach to negotiations with specific countries (i.e. avoiding further group-country enlargements).

5.5 CONCLUDING REMARKS: 'CATCHING THE TRAIN OF MODERN CIVILIZATION'[120]

Despite the deep roots of Atatürk's legacy, Turkish society has developed over the last few decades interest and concern over the identity of the state and of its nationals, while in the orbit of EU membership. A sectarian approach to identity and tolerance is reflected in Turkey's current legal framework. 'Otherness' is addressed through recent constitutional amendments, but 'otherness' in ethnic origin and its ensuing rights does not enjoy the same attention as religious 'otherness'.[121] Both aspects are nevertheless necessary in a Europeanized legal environment.

117 Ibid, at 10.

118 European Commission, 2007 Report on Turkey, at 9. The Turkish Parliament recently passed an amendment to the Code of Criminal Procedure allowing the trial of military personnel in civilian courts for forming gangs, committing acts of terror and crimes against the Constitution. It also brought an end to the trial of civilians in military courts (cf. Selçuk Gültaşli, 'European Union backs CMK amendment on military courts', *Today's Zaman*, 01/07/2009), www.todayszaman.com.

119 The European Commission has for example acknowledged the need for better communication on enlargement. See 'Commission proposes renewed consensus on enlargement', Press Release IP/06/1523, 8 November 2006.

120 Slogan used by the newspaper *Radikal* in one of its pro-EU campaigns.

121 Recent polls indicate that only 11.4 per cent of individuals support education in Kurdish for citizens of Kurdish origin and around 5.3 per cent support the financial contribution of the state to Alevi Cem houses (Çarkoğlu and Torpak, 2007: 31).

Aspirations to Westernize entail the transformation of the 'vicious circle' of EU membership into a 'virtuous' one.[122] There is no shortage of strategic arguments in favour of Turkey's membership: it is a large, secular Muslim democracy, relevant from the point of view of energy as it controls gas and oil pipeline routes, controls the Bosphorus and has a significant role to play in the EU's Common Foreign Security Policy. For Olli Rehn, Turkey's 'importance and membership are inseparable',[123] especially since Europeans are used to 'seeing enlargement as a charitable gift from a rich West to its poorer neighbours'.[124] It is not a gift in that sense, it remains a gift however for both sides when it operates as a stabilizing tool that creates new markets and free movement leading to interdependence and prosperity, not to mention the prospects for better protection of human rights.

Faced with the complexities of the circulation of arguably cosmopolitan values and norms, Eriksen argues that the solution to the issue are positivization and constitutionalization.[125] He cites and analyses the Charter of Fundamental Rights as an example, explaining how it adds to the fundamental rights of Union citizens in the quest for humanism and democracy.[126] The view that the constitutionalized Bill of Rights, at present with fully legally binding force since December 2009, provides the EU with the moral, political and legal competence to pursue human rights as its constitutive values both internally and externally is note entirely abstract any more. Yet it presupposes that the institutionalization of the values that relate to 'unity within diversity' is reflected in both internal and external activities, given the discrepancies observed during the 2004 and 2007 enlargements.[127] Concerns, however, over the degree of the EU's fair and rigorous conditionality, while legitimate, do not constitute a self-sufficient argument. In fact, the Commission appears to be entirely conscious of the effectiveness of conditionality as a crucial tool to 'overcome crisis, state weaknesses and challenges to democracy'.[128] In that sense, the transformation of Turkey into a pluralist democracy has become intrinsically linked with the EU's capacity to 'export' certain values such as tolerance and respect for diversity. Implementation of EU requirements will lead to the improvement of relations between the state and society, not only from a security perspective. The window of opportunity is not, however,

122 Akçakoca (2006: 26).

123 *The Economist*, 'Give and Take', May 29, 2008, Special Report 2008.

124 Ibid.

125 Eriksen (2005: 7).

126 Indeed, as he pertinently points out, the preamble of the Charter is revealing : '... conscious of its spiritual and moral heritage, the Union is founded on the indivisible, universal values of human dignity, freedom, equality and solidarity; it is based on the principles of democracy and the rule of law'. Ibid, at 9.

127 See indicatively in the area of minority rights, Topidi (2010).

128 European Commission, Communication from the Commission to the European Parliament and the Council on 'Enlargement Strategy and Main Challenges 2007–2008', COM (2006) 663, at 9, point 3.1.

limitless. In the words of a 2002 pro-EU campaign: 'Turk, be proud, work, trust and be quick'.[129]

Overall, it is not required to treat the issue of EU membership as a goal in itself but as an incentive for reform. At the same time, the Turkish legal system is evolving and changing in the direction of a more individualist format of protection of rights. The internal debate between anti-democratic secularism versus anti-Western democracy is a false dilemma in that respect, as it fails to account for change and reforms pursued under the current circumstances towards a Europeanized understanding of rights triggered by an albeit moderate Islamist leading party. Clearly, not all Islamic groups have a problematic relationship with secularism and democracy and at the end of the day the democratic process and EU conditionality contribute to the moderation of radical Islamic perspectives.[130] In that sense, the threat of diversion in the road Europeanization does not lie in the delusion of Turkey's perspective of EU membership but instead in the sectarian approach to the protection and fostering of diversity and tolerance. What if a 'non-Western form of modernity' should be the outcome of what started off as a pure 'Europeanization' venture?[131]

The evolution of the EU cannot avoid the re-examination of the characteristics of its public sphere as they have been shaped by enlargement(s), the institutionalization of human rights beyond the nation state or the development and implementation of a common Foreign Policy. According to Dworkin, the most significant aspect of law in a political community is the requirement that the state applies certain standards in its relation with individuals which are pre-set.[132] He moves on to label the process of setting standards according to some 'correct' procedure as legality. Transposing the paradigm to the EU, and more specifically to human rights protection at EU level, after five enlargements, it is worth reflecting further on how the Union addresses the wider issue of human rights protection, how it attempts to export it but more crucially how it manages to transform legal and political landscapes in its quest for more democracy and humanity.

Bibliography

Adelman, S. (2010) 'Cosmopolitanism Sovereignty', in Bailliet and Aas (eds), Chapter 1.

Akçakoca, A. (2006) 'EU-Turkey relations 43 years on: train crash or temporary derailment?', EPC Issue Paper No. 50.

Akçapar, B. and Choubi, D. (2006) 'Turkey's EU Accession: The Long Road from Ankara to Brussels', Roundtable, *Yale Journal of International Affairs* 50–57.

129 *Avrupa Hareketi 2002* slogan, paraphrasing a Kemalist motto ('*Türk, Övün, Çalis, Gülven ve Elini Çabuk Tut*').

130 Kuru (2007: 151).

131 Yilmaz (2008).

132 Ronald Dworkin, *Justice in Robes* (2006: 169–71), as quoted in Cali (2009: 809–10).

Akyol, M. (2007) 'Turkey's Liberal Ideology and How Came to Be', *Turkish Policy Quarterly*.
Aydin-Düzgit, S. and Gürsoy, Y. (2008) 'International Influences on the Turkish Transition to Democracy in 1983', *CDDRL Working Papers*, No. 87, available at http://cddrl.stanford.edu.
Baban, F. and Keyman, F. (2008) 'Turkey and Postnational Europe: Challenges for the Cosmopolitan Political Community', *European Journal of Social Theory* 11(1): 107–24.
Beck, U. (2005) *Power in the Global Age: A new global political economy*, Cambridge: Polity Press.
—— (2006) *Cosmopolitan Vision*, Cambridge: Polity Press.
—— (2009) 'Re-Inventing Europe: A Cosmopolitan Vision', *Quaderns de la Mediterrania* 10: 109–16.
Cali, B. (2009) 'On Interpretatism and International Law', *The European Journal of International Law* 20(3): 805–22.
Çarkoğlu and Torpak (2007) *Religion, Society and Politics in a Changing Turkey*, Istanbul: TESEV.
Dagi, I. (2002) 'Islamic Political Identity in Turkey: Rethinking the West and Westernization', Central European University/Open Society Institute, available at http://pdc.ceu.hu/archive/00001804/.
Delanty, G. (2005) 'The Idea of a Cosmopolitan Europe: On the Cultural Significance of Europeanization', *International Review of Sociology* 15(3): 405–21.
Delibas, K. (2000) 'Conceptualizing Islamic Movements: The Case of Turkey', *International Political Science Review* 30(1): 89–103.
Emerson, M. (2006) 'Dear Turkey, Play it Long and Cool', CEPS Commentary, available at http://enarpri.org/Article.php?article_id=551.
Emerson, M. and Tocci, N. (2004) 'Turkey as a Bridgehead and Spearhead: Integrating EU and Turkish Foreign Policy', Centre for European Policy Studies, No. 1.
Ende, W. (2008) 'Justice as a Political Principle in Islam', pp. 19–34, in Krawietz and Reifeld (eds), *Islam and the Rule of Law: Between Sharia and Secularization*, www.kas.de.
Erdogdu, E. (2002) 'Turkey and Europe: Undivided but Not United', *Middle East Review of International Affairs* 6(2).
Eriksen, E. O. (2005) 'Towards a Cosmopolitan EU?', Working Paper No. 9, available at http://www.arena.uio.no.
European Commission, Communication from the Commission to the Council, the European Parliament, the European Economic and Social Committee and the Committee of the Regions: *Civil Dialogue between the EU and Candidate Countries*, COM (2005) 290 final.
—— Communication to the European Parliament and the Council – *EU Enlargement Strategy and Main Challenges 2006–2007*, including annexed special report on the EU's capacity to integrate new members, COM (2006) 649.
—— Communication from the Commission to the European Parliament and the Council on 'Enlargement Strategy and main challenges 2007–2008', COM (2006) 663.
—— *Turkey 2007 Progress Report*, COM (2007) 663 final.
—— *Turkey 2008 Progress Report*, COM (2008) 674 final.
—— *2009 Progress Report on Turkey*, http://ec.europa.eu/enlargement/pdf/key_documents/2009/tr_rapport_2009_en.pdf.
Habermas, J. (2001a) 'Why Europe needs a Constitution', *New Left Review* 11: 5–26.

—— (2001b) in M. Pensky (ed.), *The Postnational Constellation: Political Essays*, Cambridge: MIT Press.
—— (2003) 'Toward a Cosmopolitan Europe', *Journal of Democracy* 14(4): 86–100.
Hale, W. (2000) *Turkish Foreign Policy 1774–2000*, London: Frank Cass Publishers.
Inaç, H. (2004) 'Identity Problems of Turkey during the European Union Integration Process', *Journal of Economic and Social Research* 6(2): 33–62.
Krawietz, B. (2008) 'Introduction' in Krawietz and Reifeld (eds), *Islam and the Rule of Law: Between Sharia and Secularization*, www.kas.de, 9–16.
Kuru, A. T. (2007) 'Changing Perspectives on Islamism and Secularism in Turkey: The Gülen Movement and the AK Party', available at http://www.gulenconference.org.uk/userfiles/file/Proceedings/Prcd%20-%20Kuru,%20AT.pdf.
Minority Rights Group (MRG) (2007) *A Quest for Equality: Minorities in Turkey*, 2007 Report, available at http://www.minorityrights.org/download.php?id=425.
Nas, Ç. (2001) 'Turkish Identity and the Perception of Europe', *Marmara Journal of European Studies* 9(1): 184.
Pamuk, O. (2005) 'On Trial', *New Yorker*.
Piccoli, W. (2005) 'Enhancing Turkey's EU Membership Prospects via Securitizing Moves: The Role of Turkish NGOs in the Country's Europeanization', 7th Annual Graduate Student Workshop, Harvard University.
Stahr, V. S. (2006) 'Synthesis of Islamic Thought, Secularism and Modernity: Turkey as a Laboratory of Islam?', available at www.qantara.de.
Stråth, B. (2000) 'Introduction: Europe as Discourse' in Stråth (ed.), *Europe and the Other and Europe as the Other*, Brussels: Presses Interuniversitaires Européennes.
Svensson, A. (2008) 'Turkey as the European Other: A Constructivist Account of Turkey's Accession Process to the EU', Lund University, available at http://theses.lub.lu.se/archive/2008/01/08/1199783717-29066-437/Turkey_as_the_European_other_080120.pdf.
Topidi, K. (2010) *EU Law, Minorities and Enlargement*, Antwerp: Intersentia.
Van Bruinessen, M. (1997) 'Race, culture, nation and identity politics in Turkey: some comments', Paper presented at the Mica Ertegrün Annual Turkish Studies Workshop on Continuity and Change, Department of Near Eastern Studies, Princeton University, available at http://www.let.uu.nl/□martin.vanbruinessen/personal/publications/identity_politics.htm.
Virtanen, E. O. (2003) 'Recent Changes in Turkey's Language Legislation', Ciemen/Mercator Working Paper 11, available at http://www.ciemen.org/mercator/pdf/wp11-def-ang.pdf.
Weiler, J. (2003) *Un Europa cristiana: Un saggio esplorativo*, Milan: BUR Saggi.
Yackley, J. (2008) 'Turkey, the EU and Democracy: How Public Opinion divides Ankara and Brussels', ETH Zurich, International Relations and Security Network.
Yilmaz, H. (2008) 'Conservatism in Turkey', *Turkish Policy Quarterly* 7(1).

Chapter 6

All the people in all the world

A cosmopolitan perspective on migration and torture

Barbara Hudson

6.1 INTRODUCTION

As this volume and the conference at which the papers were presented demonstrate, *cosmopolitan justice* is a term which is developing a wide range of meanings and connotations. In law and in international relations, it is sometimes used to refer to international laws, conventions and agreements covering a range of applications from transnational crime to trade; in political theory it can refer to blurring or pooling of sovereignty and citizenship, for example within the European Union, as well to international activism in 'humanitarian intervention'. Where these developments are concerned only with relations between states and not with the lives of individuals, they would not be regarded as cosmopolitan justice by its advocates: 'cosmopolitan' is more than simply a synonym for 'international'. Developments in international justice where nation-states are the actors but the rights and opportunities of individuals are the objectives may be regarded as 'cosmopolitanism from above'. 'Cosmopolitanism from below' is urged as necessary to mitigate the effects of globalization based on a neo-liberal political and economic model, on the powerless and impoverished people of the world (Santos and Rodriguez-Garavito, 2005).

Boaventura de Sousa Santos (2002) has become one of the leading proponents of 'cosmopolitanism from below', or as he terms it, 'subaltern cosmopolitanism', which he defines as a range of legal, political and social movements and practices which challenge the hegemony of neo-liberal globalization. Rather than cooperation between states, this cosmopolitanism from below typically involves the coming together of social groups and social movements who may start from different geographical positions, and often from different political positions, but who share or come to share a common cause.

One model of 'cosmopolitanism from above' is the 'cosmopolitan federalism' advocated by, for example, Jurgen Habermas (1999, 2003) and Seyla Benhabib (2004, 2006). Cosmopolitan federalism argues for the establishment of international organizations to mitigate global inequalities in resources, freedoms, and life chances that exist in today's world, and to regulate international contacts so as to avoid conflicts and disagreements between nation-states. These theorists draw on the 'Perpetual Peace' essays of Immanuel Kant, in which he called for the establishment of international organizations to govern relations between nations, avoiding war by removing or resolving its causes and providing rules and facilities for settling disputes (Kant, 1983).

Cosmopolitanism from above differs from orthodox international relations discourses in that it is concerned with the fates of individuals; its aim is to reduce inequalities in life-chances within and between nations, not only to regulate relationships between nations. This cosmopolitanism from above is inevitably confronted by the problem of the dissonance between the universalism of ethics and the particularity of law (Post, 2006). The idea of human rights demonstrates this dissonance clearly: tensions between national sovereignty and the universalism of rights, between rights that are privileges of citizenship of a particular nation-state and the rights that are due to all humans and should be honoured for non-citizens, and how these tensions may be resolved, are questions at the root of much thinking about cosmopolitanism from above.

Benhabib (2004, 2006) for example, sees developments such as the European Union, where member states give many of the privileges of citizenship to members of other states within the Union, as moving towards a lessening of the links between rights and nationhood. Kymlicka (2006), in a response to Benhabib, questions whether the extension of the right to work, to healthcare, to vote, and the European Court, where nation-state members can be held to account for breaches of their and other member states' citizens rights, represents a 'transcendence' of liberal nationalism – a move towards a single European state – or a 'taming' of it, so that the nations of the European Union retain their individuality and sovereignty but desist from conflictual and competitive relations, and lay down certain rights and standards that should apply to all citizens of member states.

The International Criminal Court is another example of at least partial cosmopolitanism from above. The Court was established to punish gross violations of human rights throughout the world, and it can be criticized for its accountability to the UN Security Council, dominated by its permanent member nations (USA, UK, France, Russia and China), from which it might be inferred, among other things, that violations by officials of these countries would be unlikely to be brought to trial (Matsueda, 2009). The International Criminal Court can also be criticized for its European legal culture of proceeding only if responsibility for genocide and other crimes against humanity can be established for specific individuals, doing nothing about the contexts and groupings relevant to violations (Hagan, 2003; Hagan and Rymond-Richmond, 2009). Although, then, there are valid criticisms to be made of the International Criminal Court, the question 'is it cosmopolitan?' can be answered at least partly in the affirmative (Pureza, 2005). The ICC may be a justice from above, but it is established to punish suffering inflicted on individuals and on social groups; it is acting in the name of victims of actions by governments and other powerful actors.

Cosmopolitan justice needs more than courts and conventions. Amartya Sen (2009) calls for international organizations, laws and processes to take account of the injustices and oppressions from which individuals and groups suffer, rather than focusing exclusively on relations between nation states. Sen is critical of the 'transcendental institutionalism' he finds in much international legal and political innovation which concentrates on the creation of treaties, legal frameworks and international organizations, and does nothing to remove injustice in the world. Sen shares Nagel's pessimism that the dominant tendency of interpreting 'global justice' as the creation of international institutions will not ameliorate injustices, whether between nations or among individuals:

> I believe that the most likely path toward global justice is the creation of patently unjust and illegitimate global structures of power that are tolerable to the interests of the most powerful current nation-states.
>
> (Nagel, 2005, quoted by Sen, 2009: 25)

While international relations theory in law and political science concentrates on institutions and processes to promote international/global justice, sociology and allied disciplines have been more concerned with cosmopolitan identity. Ulrich Beck (2006) has captured the commonplace understanding of cosmopolitan identity in his example of the Danish businessman encountered on a plane journey. Beck questions his fellow-traveller about when and where he feels particularly Danish or when he defines himself as European; when he feels his professional identity is most salient; when he is very conscious of his local or regional identity; when he feels Christian; when very much a husband and father. This 'pick-and-mix' identity, Beck shows, is not necessarily politically progressive or cosmopolitan: the businessman reveals himself to be a member of an anti-immigration group. The elite professional, the CNN target demographic, the person who is comfortable in hotel rooms all over the world, who enjoys the food, wine and music of many countries, the person who has friends across the world, who contrasts herself with the 'provincial', is the person most readily thought of as 'cosmopolitan'.

Paul Gilroy (2004) similarly argues for a 'planetary humanism' which sees identity as fluid, as having many aspects which have more or less salience in different circumstances and contexts. He calls for what he terms 'raciology' to be replaced by a cosmopolitan understanding of identity, arguing that culture, which includes religion, education, class, professional status and other elements of selfhood has become more significant than race.

These identity theorists join cosmopolitan justice theorists such as Iris Young (2002) in pointing out that binary constructions of identity – black/white, male/female, Western/oriental, for example – exaggerate differences between groups, and gloss over or disregard differences within groups. Understanding populations in terms of a dominant group that can be considered similar in all relevant respects, means that those who are different in significant respects from this dominant identity are likely to be excluded, marginalized, or to be responded to inappropriately. Calls for justice to accommodate excluded or marginalized groups have tended to be piecemeal, for justice to be more responsive to the circumstances of women, of ethnic minorities, of different sexual orientations or religions, for example. What has not happened to any significant extent is movement towards a justice that is based on the idea of diversity as a normal characteristic of populations (Hudson, 2008). Young (2002) suggests that diversity and difference should not be seen as a difficulty for doing justice, but as a resource, where voices that have been repressed can be heard and where the excluded can become participants in the justice discourse.

Emphasis on the inclusion of the marginalized, repressed and excluded within the community of justice moves away from the contemporary commonplace usage of cosmopolitan for the elite, worldly professional, turning instead to the older Greek meaning of 'all the people in all the world'. For cosmopolitan justice advocates, all the people in all the world have rights merely by virtue of being human, and we all have responsibilities to persons outside our immediate groupings of families, neighbours, associates and fellow citizens (Appiah, 2006). The word 'cosmopolitanism' is generally agreed to have been used first by Diogenes, thought to have lived from around 412 to 323 BC, who described himself not as a Greek, an Athenian or a Corinthian, but as a cosmopolitan, a 'citizen of the world'.

Diogenes is also said to have introduced the term 'cosmopolitics', which he defined as the demand of the outcast, the homeless, the stateless, the one without possessions, to be taken into account. For me, cosmopolitan justice is the counterpart of cosmopolitics, it is a justice which takes into account the outcast, the impoverished, the homeless and stateless, the person without possessions and without membership of a state or society. Cosmopolitan justice responds to the powerless, the non-citizen, to members of excluded and subordinated groups, to the deviant and the different.

6.1.1 The stranger and the camp

As well as Diogenes' figure of the outcast, writing on cosmopolitan justice has centred on the 'stranger'. While the word 'outcast' denotes someone who may have had membership of a state or city and has been banished because of some offence against fellow-citizens or some risk posed to them – the criminal, the scapegoat or the leper, for example – the stranger is someone who is unknown, someone who is encountered prior to understanding and prior to classification. Kant's theory of cosmopolitan justice is predicated on the idea of justice in encounters between strangers, encounters which are inevitable if one ventures beyond the narrow confines of the familiar and the local. The stranger Kant had in mind was the inhabitant of a foreign land, encountered through trade or colonization. The encounter may not just be with someone who is geographically outside the traveller's own community, but who is also a stranger in moral terms, because Kant did not conceive of non-Europeans, especially black non-Europeans (as Gilroy, 2004, points out) as sharing the same principles of justice as members of Enlightenment European societies. Trade and travel demanded, for Kant, that models of justice within a community of common values, developed through shared occupation of territory and shared experiences through the generations, needed to be complemented by models to establish relationships of justice between peoples who could not be anticipated to share similar values and understandings.

Kant's proposals for justice among strangers call for recognition of a right of *hospitality*, by which he means the right of a stranger to be received without violence when entering another's territory. The idea of a right of hospitality is central to contemporary formulations of cosmopolitan justice put forward by, for instance, Derrida (2000, 2001, 2003) and Bauman (2004). For them, Kant's principle of the right of the stranger to be received without violence gives a political dimension to Levinas's idea of the self's responsibility to the stranger simply because of her presence. Responsibility to the stranger, on this account, precedes any relationship of comprehension or of reciprocity; responsibility exists prior to any demands that may be made on the stranger. Bauman calls Levinas's demand for acceptance of responsibility towards the stranger merely because of her presence the 'great reversal' of the European tradition of moral philosophy which has seen responsibility towards others as deriving from recognition of the alikeness of the other to the self (Bauman, 1993). Casting responsibility to the stranger as a right – and therefore a duty upon the person/state in whose presence the stranger arrives – transposes it from the face-to-face sphere of ethics into the political sphere of social and legal relationships, thus establishing it as a principle of justice.

The stranger is not a guest, the encounter is unsought, we do not know if the stranger who comes into our presence will be hostile, or friendly: each encounter contains a threat (Bauman, 1991). The hospitality that is called for is, therefore, a hospitality of *visitation* rather than of *invitation* (Derrida, 2003: 128). This visitation might be dangerous, and therefore we may need to take some measures to protect ourselves, to give conditional or restricted rather than full hospitality. Conditions and restrictions must not, however, according to Derrida, Bauman and others who have embraced this idea of hospitality as a principle of justice, be such as to become an absence of hospitality; the response must not be violence, degradation, or refusal to meet the needs of the stranger.

Far too often, in the real rather than the theoretical world, the response to the presence of the stranger – the applicant for entry, the beggar, the disorderly and disreputable – is to confine them, to segregate them, or to exclude them altogether. Prisons, detention centres, ghettoes and gated estates demonstrate the refusal of hospitality and the desire to avoid encounters with strangers, rather than to respond to their claims and needs. As Kant explained, however, because we live on an earth which is spherical rather than a flat, infinite plane, it is impossible to avoid encounters with strangers, since one step away from anyone brings one closer to someone else. It is the predicament of being in shared possession of this earth that makes a principle of receiving the stranger without violence an essential response to the existential situation in which humanity finds itself.

Spaces of segregation of those who are excluded from justice or who are unacknowledged as having claims on justice are the *camps* that Agamben (1998: 123) suggests are 'the hidden paradigm of the political space of modernity'. Camps are where the person exists without rights, without citizenship; camps are the places where the stranger imagined by Derrida and Bauman, the outcast of Diogenes, is to be found. The inhabitants of the camps have, Agamben suggests, only 'bare life': they are allowed to exist only as long as those in power tolerate their presence; they can be expelled or even killed, he argues, and their disappearance or death will have no consequence for those in power.

The camp envisioned by Agamben is not just the tented city that arises to give shelter to those displaced by war or disaster; the camp is any place where the normal rules of law and the normal routines of orderly life are suspended. Agamben describes them as places of exception, where those contained within them cannot rely on the protection of law, or on any solidarity from those outside the camps; rather, the camp dwellers are at the whim of those in command. Drawing on Carl Schmitt's work on sovereignty and the power to decide exceptions, Agamben suggests that camps represent the power of the sovereign authority to reduce their inhabitants to *homo sacer*, 'bare life', the life which has no protections of citizenship or acceptance of their right to remain. The camp-dweller must protect herself as best she can, by removing her presence, or at least by rendering herself inconspicuous and undemanding.

Although the tented area outside the city, the encampment of strangers fleeing persecution from beyond the borders, or of persons internally displaced by wars or natural disasters, most readily comes to mind with the word 'camp', Agamben points out that the camp is also to be found inside the city or the state, and may take many forms. The shanty towns or 'favelas' which ring the sprawling cities of the south; the Roma districts throughout Europe; the 'first people' reservations in colonized lands; the ghettoes and also the 'sink estates' of north American and European cities and towns, are camps in Agamben's sense. These camps are neither temporary nor permanent. Camps for refugees can be long-lasting, their residents being neither itinerants nor locals, with 'shelters' the only homes known to second, third and even fourth generations, developing their own economies, health and social facilities, and their own systems of status and government. Shanty towns where workers drawn to the city from impoverished rural areas congregate become long-term slums, where people live precariously exposed to disease, fires and earthquakes through inadequate sanitation and insubstantial buildings (Davis, 2006). Such spaces receive little by way of protection from the state: building regulations are not applied, health, education and welfare facilities are meagre, and they are policed by way of occasional violent invasions, with police acting as border patrols, making sure that those occupying these spaces do not encroach on the 'respectable' areas (Hudson, 2010).

Santos and Rodriguez-Garavito ask 'Who needs cosmopolitanism?' and reply:

> The answer is straightforward: whoever is a victim of local intolerance and discrimination needs cross-border tolerance and support; whoever lives in misery in a world of wealth needs cosmopolitan solidarity; whoever is a non- or second-class citizen of a country or the world needs an alternative conception of national or global citizenship. In short, the large majority of the world's population, excluded from top-down cosmopolitanism, needs a different type of cosmopolitanism.
>
> (Santos and Garavita, 2005: 14)

Cosmopolitan justice, then, in the sense intended here, is justice which greets the stranger without violence and offers her hospitality, rather than confinement to the marginalized spaces of Agamben's camps and Davis's slums.

6.1.2 The camp and the border

The stranger at the border is a figure who tests the limits of hospitality; the stranger at the border embodies in her person the dilemma of the universality of ethics and the particularity of law. Article 13 of the Universal Declaration of Human Rights recognizes the right to leave one's country, and also establishes as universal and fundamental, rights to life, freedom from torture and freedom from slavery. The UN High Commissioner for Refugees has pointed out, however, that ever-tougher immigration policies in Europe which pursue narrowly conceived national interest rather than giving priority to protecting the human rights of migrants, violate the right to leave (Migreurop, 2010).

Most European and other Western countries have been highly critical of countries which make it difficult for their people to leave (Hudson, 2007). Although there was widespread celebration at the fall of the Berlin Wall in 1989, and although at the celebration to mark the twentieth anniversary of its destruction, European political leaders talked of the need to bring down other walls which divide cities, lands and peoples across the world, in fact there has been considerable activity in building walls – virtual and real walls – to protect their own borders. In Europe, the Spanish enclaves of Ceuta and Melila in Morocco are surrounded by six-metre high fencing; the patrol boats in the southern Mediterranean and the wall of passport control barriers at the Shengen Area border in Amsterdam's Schipol Airport demonstrate the building of walls. This wall-building is not only occurring at the borders of Europe: an actual wall has been built between Mexico and the USA, and destination countries such as Australia are also creating barriers by patrolling the seas around Indonesia and other places from which migrants are likely to come (Grewcock, 2007).

Europe has outsourced its migration control southwards to North Africa, and eastwards to Turkey and the Ukraine. The UK has also outsourced its migration control to countries such as India, Bangladesh and Pakistan. These contemporary borders are double walls, preventing both emigration and immigration. Rodier, in a report to the European Parliament, noted the use of the term 'illegal immigration' in a press release from a Conference of the Interior Ministers of the Western Mediterranean in May 2006, which welcomed 'the efforts of the countries of the southern Mediterranean to contain illegal emigration to Europe' (Rodier, 2006: 20). She also notes the arrest of 1,500 'potential emigrants' by Senegalese authorities. to prevent them leaving for the Canary Islands. There has been no legal challenge to restrictions on the right to leave, and the right of states to control their borders is not questioned.

Migreurop (a Euro-African network of forty organizations from thirteen countries working on migration policy, EU externalization policies and their impact within and beyond the EU borders) reports the establishment of camps, and other measures to strengthen anti-immigration controls (Migreurop, 2010). The network has counted 250 camps in the twenty-seven member states of the EU, notes the lengthening of permissible detention periods, and criticizes the conditions in which migrants (including children) are detained. Another Migreurop report examines three border areas (the Calais region in northern France, the Greek-Turkish border, and the Oujda region in Morocco) and they also report a case study of the Italian island of Lampedusa (Statewatch, 2009). The report states that although there are some differences in the immigration control policies in the various countries, experience on the ground is of appalling conditions in which the migrants live, whether in detention centres where they may be abused by guards, or in makeshift camps where they have little shelter and must scavenge for food while trying to avoid the police and immigration authorities, making themselves as invisible as possible. They are faced with risking death by climbing the walls of the Morocco enclaves, swimming across the River Evro between Turkey and Greece, crossing the Mediterranean or the Channel by whatever means they can. If caught, they may be forcibly returned either after reaching their destination or while en route.

Migreurop charge that thousands of people are facing terrible ordeals as they try to escape persecution or appalling conditions in poorer countries, and that European policies are forcing them to exist in semi-permanent states of invisibility or forced return. There appears to be little that could be defined as hospitality. The UN High Commissioner for Refugees has condemned these migration policies, and has commented that as well as the hardship and deaths in attempts to cross borders, these policies have driven more migrants into the hands of traffickers (Migreurop, 2010). In the destination countries of northern Europe, politicians announce their success in raising the number of deportations and the decreases in numbers of arrivals consequent on their tougher policies: repelling unwanted migrants is the policy goal, rather than providing a safe haven for those who need it.

One aspect of European migration policies which receives particular criticism from those adopting a cosmopolitan justice concern for the safety and well-being of migrants is the Dublin Regulation which establishes that the first country through which asylum-seekers enter the EU is responsible for assessing their applications. Although politicians and media in countries such as the UK, the

Netherlands and other northern European states constantly complain that they bear an 'unfair burden' of people wanting to settle there, a glance at map of Europe, Africa and Asia shows that for the poorest migrants who could not possibly afford to come to Europe by air, the southern and eastern-most countries of Italy and Greece are bound to be the ones with the most 'first arrival' migrants.

Conditions in detention centres in Greece have been strongly criticized, with centres in Patras and in Lesvos being closed after campaigning by migrant welfare groups. Acceptance of refugee status and recognition of a duty of protection is low in Greece compared to other EU countries. Help with translation and other assistance is minimal, so asylum-seekers from places such as Afghanistan, Iraq and Somalia (from where there are currently many arrivals) are often unable to make their applications at all, or in accordance with the regulations. The Office of the United Nations High Commissioner for Refugees (UNHCR, 2009) has argued that governments should 'refrain from returning asylum seekers under the Dublin Regulation or otherwise' to Greece.

Once inside the border, immigrants are still subjected to violence and refused the basics of hospitality. In January 2010, attacks on migrant workers were reported in Rosarno, Italy, with outbreaks of violence between them and local residents. The workers gave accounts of degrading and inhumane conditions of living and working and forced segregation from the citizens of Rosarno. This incident follows reports of violence against Roma in many parts of Italy, and against North African workers in Spain. Reports in the UK press revealed that migrant workers were living in makeshift camps outside the town of Boston, Lincolnshire, without access to healthcare or money to buy food, and that deaths had been reported of migrant workers in the harsh winter conditions in the nearby county of Norfolk (Barber, 2010).

Throughout the world, rich and professional people can go to work and live where they like; it is the poor who are unwanted. Loic Wacquant (2005) has described the repression and control of the poor through criminal justice as a major international trend, and this can clearly be seen in the detention and penalization of unwanted, impoverished migrants. As well as linking migration to pressures on resources, culture, and social solidarity, linking immigrants to crime has played a large part in producing support for tighter migration controls, increased use of detention, and accelerated deportations. Migration has been increasingly criminalized and penalized. Migration classification and control has produced a series of 'status offences' (illegal entry, overstaying of student or tourist visas, for example) which are dealt with by criminal justice measures. Mary Bosworth (2007) describes the similarity of immigration detention and removal centres to prisons; the link between immigration management and criminal justice is further demonstrated in the UK by the extension of the remit of the Prisons Inspectorate to immigration detention centres.

Not only have new criminalizations connected with migration itself been introduced, but migrants have become 'suspect populations' associated in the popular and political mind with 'real crime'. Even before the attacks on the London Underground by 'home grown' Islamic terrorists in July 2007, and the current focus on Pakistan as an almost 'failed state' that is the source of terrorists and that is not fighting terrorism in its remoter regions as robustly as it should, Pakistan was associated in the mind of many UK citizens with drug importation and with forced marriage, while East Europeans are thought to be responsible for most of the sex-trafficking and prostitution in our cities. In Greece, Bulgarians and Albanians are the 'prime suspects' for most crimes, in France and Spain this status is allotted to migrants from North Africa; in Italy, and throughout much of southern and eastern Europe, the Roma are persecuted because of their stereotyped construction as criminals.

Current policies in the rich destination countries of the global north clearly violate the basic principle of cosmopolitan justice, the right of the stranger to be received without violence. While there has always been migration, there has never previously been so much classification and regulation of migration as at present. The stranger at the border will be subject to interrogation and classification before receiving anything that could commonly be understood as hospitality. She may suffer the violence of detention or forced deportation; if she is not classified as a desirable, or legal immigrant, or fits the requirements of refugee status, in most Western countries today she will be denied rights to work, to welfare benefits, to housing and health care.

Cosmopolitan theorists argue against the dominance of nation-state thinking on migration (Carens, 1987; Unger, 2005). Moellendorf (2002) has taken issue with nation-state theorists, in particular John Rawls' *Law of Peoples* (2001). Rawls suggests that societies can be divided into the well-ordered and non-well-ordered, and argues that while there is some limited duty on well-ordered nations to assist others to become well-ordered, there is no general right of persons from non-well-ordered societies to enter into the well-ordered societies. As Rawls himself acknowledges, Mollendorf and other cosmopolitans argue, against this, that Rawls' own 'difference principle' should be applied when thinking of global justice, rather than only to justice in single states. This principle in his much admired *A Theory of Justice* (1971) proposes that inequalities should only be allowed to the extent that they benefit the least well-off in the society, but he does not extend this to global justice. Moellendorf argues, however, that the equal opportunity principle should operate globally as well as nationally. He advocates the strengthening of international organizations to regulate global inequalities as well as global relationships, but claims that because of the extreme state of global inequalities at present, everyone should have the right to move to where they can flourish, economically as well as in terms of freedom and self-recognition. Migreurop (2010) suggests that the latest United National Development Programme report appears to support this view, calling for a 'lifting' of migratory barriers.

6.1.3 The camp beyond the pale

Another figure who tests the limits of our commitment to justice and of our hospitality in the sense in which the term is used here, is the terrorist, or terrorist suspect. While the migrant may be unwanted, it is possible for most people to imagine that if they faced persecution, discrimination, starvation or other privations they might seek to live somewhere else. For those of us in democratic countries, where change by peaceful means is possible, it is impossible to imagine piloting planes into buildings full of ordinary workers, driving vehicles full of explosives into crowded market places, secreting explosive substances about our persons and bringing them onto aircraft, or doing any of the things with which terrorists and terrorist suspects in detention camps in Iraq, Afghanistan, and around the world are charged. Occupants of war-on-terror detention camps are 'beyond the pale' – they are in the spaces reserved for those who do not conform to the religious/moral ideas of the dominant community.

The usual presumptions of the rule of law in modern democratic societies – no detention without trial, for example, no penalty without conviction, and the universal, fundamental right not to be subject to torture – are challenged by the terrorist. Since 9/11, Western democracies (the USA and UK in particular) have increased pre-trial detention periods, have either not held trials or have held military trials rather than normal trials where juries weigh the evidence against a 'beyond reasonable doubt' standard, and have tortured detainees, or else 'rendered' them to countries where they are tortured.

Detention centres in Afghanistan, Iraq, and Guantanamo Bay are camps of the kind Agamben writes about: they are spaces where the rule of law does not obtain, where those held in them have no rights or protections, and where they are subject to the whims of their captors. Although some of the incidents of inhuman and degrading treatment that have come to light (such as at Abu Graib) have resulted in the prosecution of individuals who have ill-treated inmates, prosecution has been of officers of the lower ranks. There have (to date) been no prosecutions of commanding officers or government officials at the highest level who approved torture as an instrument of policy. Well-documented enquiries such as those by lawyer Philippe Sands (2008) have shown that escalating levels of 'intensive interrogation', with the top level certainly amounting to torture by any reasonable definition (simulated drowning, the technique that has come to be known as 'water boarding', for example) were authorized by White House legal officers, and by Secretary of Defense Donald Rumsfeld and Vice-President Dick Cheney (Hudson, 2009).

Detention facilities such as Guantanamo Bay are 'sites of exception', where the normal processes of law do not obtain, and where power can be exercised arbitrarily (Aradau and Munster, 2009). While Tony Blair, British Prime Minister at the time of the 9/11 attacks, is reported as saying that exceptional times call for exceptional measures, analysis of 'the state of exception' drawing on the work of Carl Schmitt points to the idea of the exception not as something unusual and temporary, but as a defining moment of law – the decision as to what, and most importantly who, is inside and who/what is outside the protection of law is demonstrative of sovereignty and constitutive of law (Agamben, 1998, 2005). While in *Homo Sacer* (1998) Agamben retains a sense of exception in the everyday sense of something unusual, unprecedented, outside the normal range of experience – it has a relationship with the normal, rather than being normal – by *The State of Exception* (2005), he is arguing that in today's political discourse, the state of exception is becoming the normal paradigm of governance. While the attacks of 9/11 were undoubtedly an enormous atrocity, the extending use of the paradigm of exception exemplified in terms such as the 'war on crime', the 'war on drugs', indeed attests to the growing 'normalcy' of the paradigm of exception. An increasing range of illiberal policies and practices which go beyond counter-terrorism are justified through claims of exceptional threats (Neal, 2006).

Just as the irregular, undocumented or rejected migrant is outside the protections of citizenship and permitted residence, so the terrorist suspect is outside the protections of due process and of 'cosmopolitanism from above'. The terrorist suspect is stripped of all the protections which might normally obtain in situations of war or of crime. The terrorist suspect is classified as 'not an enemy combatant', because s/he is not a member of the armed forces of a nation with whom the captor nation is at war and so is without the protections of the protocols on the treatment of prisoners of war; s/he is not a citizen of a state with whom the captor nation is at war, so is not protected by conventions on the avoidance of suffering of civilians; the camp is not in the USA so there no protection by the normal legal procedures.

In *The State of Exception* (2005) and *Remnants of Auschwitz* (2002), Agamben has drawn some comparisons between the war on terror policies and practices of the US government and policies of the Nazi regime towards its Jewish populations. Responding to some criticisms of these parallels, he explains that he is not talking of US policies towards minorities in general, only of the practices towards terrorists and terrorist suspects held in the detention camps:

> But I spoke rather of the prisoners in Guantanamo, and their situation is legally-speaking actually comparable with those in the Nazi camps. The detainees of Guantanamo do not have the status of Prisoners of War, they have absolutely no legal status. They are subject now only to raw power; they have no legal existence.
>
> (Raulff, 2004: 610)

The more common understanding of exception as something unusual or unprecedented has, however, been a prominent theme of justification for the use of strategies and techniques which do not accord with the usual practices of democratic societies, in responding to terrorism. The idea of the 'lesser evil', that it might be permissible, although regrettable, to use methods that would normally be considered unacceptable, to counteract the greater evil of death and injury to the citizens of liberal democracies by terrorist acts has gained widespread support. Michael Ignatieff (2004), a prominent liberal thinker, for example, defends the use, in an age of terror of what are, and should be acknowledged as, normally unacceptable methods to counteract the threat from terrorists. Ignatieff suggests that torture is the most morally and politically difficult case in arguing for the use of a lesser evil to defeat a greater. It is the very same liberal principles of respect for human dignity and avoidance of inflicting pain that urge both the prohibition of torture and the use of all possible measures to prevent the suffering of innocent victims of terrorism. Because of the ethical conflicts involved in thinking about torture, Ignatieff imagines that while there will be disagreement among people of conscience as to whether torture might be permissible in exceptional circumstances, there will be agreement that it can never be a general practice.

The 'ticking bomb' scenario is a common way of representing the lesser evil dilemma of whether torture is permissible in liberal democracies. The question that is asked of liberals is whether or not torture of someone who knows the location and time of detonation of a bomb planted in a public space is acceptable in order to avert the act and so prevent the suffering of many members of the public (Hudson, 2003, 2009; Harel and Sharon, 2008). It has been suggested that this lesser evil scenario is the only kind of circumstance in which torture can be accepted that is compatible with the liberal principle that cruelty must be avoided (Luban, 2005). Any other use of torture – to inflict pain and humiliation on an enemy, to demonstrate power over others, to eradicate the autonomy of the tortured – denies the basic tenets of liberalism's commitment to respect for the dignity and humanity of all. Torture, if used at all, must only be done, on this lesser evil argument, with bad conscience.

While the 'ticking bomb' scenario is the epitome of the permissible use of torture according to the lesser evil ideology, its correspondence with real situations in which torture is used, has been challenged. Sands (2008) dissects the case of Mohammed a-Qahtani, Guantanamo detainee 063, who was variously described as the twentieth 9/11 hijacker, and someone high in the al-Qaeda chain of command. He was subjected to 'intensive interrogation' techniques, but at the time the higher-level techniques began to be used he had been in captivity for almost a year, and had been kept apart from other detainees, so it is not credible to suggest that he was tortured because he had information on current and future planned atrocities. Luban also suggests that the ticking bomb scenario is seldom met in reality. He describes it as an 'ideology' of torture for democratic societies, which challenges liberals to say that governments and their agents should stop short of doing everything possible to save their citizens from harm; surely, the challenge suggests, we should accept the torture of one to save many lives (Luban, 2005). In an argument somewhat similar to that of Finnis (1980), Luban argues that the ticking bomb and other lesser evil scenarios deflect attention from the real pain of the person tortured to the imagined pain of those who may be injured by the (real or hypothetical) ticking bomb.

The 'lesser evil' arguments and the 'threat to democratic values' arguments with which they are countered, both reflect nation-state thinking. Lesser evil arguments for the use of torture and other restrictions on liberty and human rights in the response to terrorism are about the state's duty to protect its citizens. The most frequent counter-argument is that such developments undermine the values of the societies they seek to protect (Dworkin, 2002). These measures have been described as 'counter-law' – they threaten fundamental principles of the rule of law, such as due process and the presumption of innocence, and come from the 'precautionary logic' of contemporary societies which prioritize prevention at all costs of risks deemed to carry such terrible consequences that all measures are permissible in the name of security (Ericson, 2007). These mentalities of insecurity that Ericson describes have close affinities to Agamben's arguments for the exception as increasingly the normal paradigm of governance (Aradau and Munster, 2009).

A more cosmopolitan concern is expressed by Waldron in his critique of Dershowitz's suggestion that because, in the wake of 9/11, torture to prevent the greater evil is widely accepted and will inevitably take place, it should be legally regulated (Dershowitz, 2002; Waldron, 2005). Waldron's counter-argument is that a prohibition on torture is needed for exactly these lesser evil/greater evil circumstances: a torture ban is most needed against the circumstances in which and for the protection of the people against whom governments like our own are most likely to resort to torture, and where public approval is most likely to be forthcoming. If protocols and conventions against torture do not hold in the times and the spaces of exception, then, on this argument, they are of no use at all.

Waldron develops his critique of the use of torture in more usual terms of the protection of the values of democratic society. He argues that the prohibition of torture, in both national and international law, is an *archetypal* law: a law that is important not only for itself but also because it articulates and exemplifies principles of law and shared values that define the liberal democratic type of society. The ban on torture is archetypal of the move from law as a system of arbitrary brutality exercised through the prerogative of sovereignty, to a system of rules democratically agreed. The ban on torture represents the difference between rule by law and rule by terror, and thus its breach is a mark of decline in democratic society's adherence to its liberal principles.

Although Waldron develops his argument for the preservation of a total ban on torture in terms of the defence of the liberal values of democratic societies, he does at least direct our attention to the reality that the spaces of exception are populated by humans and that it is these humans, not the 'innocent victims' of hypothetical scenarios, who are vulnerable to torture. They may be moral strangers, but they are, nonetheless humans and therefore, from a cosmoplotian perspective, they are deserving of our concern and our protection. They may be, as Donald Rumsfeld is reported as saying, 'the worst of the worst' but nonetheless they are fellow humans (Otty, 2008: 447).

Much has been made of the innocence, or at least the absence of proven convictions of those on whose behalf campaigns against torture and captivity are raised, but for cosmopolitan justice of the Diogenes/Derridean tendency, the 'worst of the worst' are those most in need of its protection. Cosmopolitan justice's imperative of receiving the stranger without violence means that as well as concerning ourselves with those beyond our communities of family, neighbours and fellow-citizens as Appiah urges, we must receive without violence those who even after extensive and open dialogue, may fail to arouse our sympathy or understanding.

6.2 CONCLUSION

The terrorist/terrorist suspect and the unwanted migrant are among the categories of people who need cosmopolitan justice. Cosmopolitan justice is a discursive form of justice: it gives those who come before it the opportunity to tell their stories, to give an account of who they are, what they have or have not done, and what their needs are. It is a form of discursive justice that gives people the opportunity to tell their stories in their own way; a form of discursive justice that considers people as individuals, but also as members of groups who may experience disadvantage and discrimination; a form of discursive justice that looks not only to rules and precedents, but asks 'what would be justice in this case' (Hudson, 2008).

The terrorist and the unwanted migrant and other people who are dispossessed and despised need 'cosmopolitanism from above'. They need the UN Declarations prohibiting torture, prescribing correct and incorrect treatment of prisoners, allowing for the right to leave countries where they are being persecuted or have no opportunity to flourish and to enjoy their human capacities.

The poor, the powerless, the unwanted and the outcast also, however, need cosmopolitanism from below. It is through campaigns by individuals and groups on behalf of those being tortured or detained without trial, refused admittance or facing deportation, and those in the many other categories of those who need cosmopolitan justice, that the laws, treaties, conventions and protocols of cosmopolitanism from above can be made to hold in situations and for people where they are most likely to be disregarded. It is also through solidarity of individuals and groups that the provisions of cosmopolitanism from above can be expanded, for example so that asylum laws can cover forms of persecution that were not written into the Conventions, so that those awaiting decisions can be given assistance, given time, and given access to healthcare, money, and other elements of hospitality and so that the definitions of prisoners of war and of civilians in war zones, can cover those who are not members of state armies, or not citizens of states against whom war has been declared.

The identity cosmopolitanism of Beck and Gilroy directs attention to the diversity within groups. Cosmopolitanism from below, on the other hand, often develops through individuals and groups finding that they have things in common with those whom they thought of as different. One example of this is the way in which communities may campaign to stop the deportation of people they find to be good neighbours and cherished friends, even if on first meeting they seemed strange and irreconcilably different. Another example could be writers, musicians and academics who lobby for their counterparts in parts of the world under occupation, or under governments with harsh censorship.

The insights of cosmopolitan perspectives on identity and the principles of cosmopolitan justice are relevant to the risks and the opportunities of life in the contemporary world of diversity and globalization, where it is impossible to carry out our activities only among people like ourselves. Justice which is responsive to the stranger, to the inhabitants of the camps, calls for us to develop a more fluid sense of self, going beyond nationality and ethnicity to recognize being human as our first and most basic identity. The dominance of the idea of the nation-state in law and politics needs to be tempered so that it does not suppress the demands of the outsider, who needs protection and solidarity. Cosmopolitan justice, justice which can respond to the demands of cosmopolitics, needs its fundamental precept to be that of meeting the stranger with hospitality rather than with violence.

Bibliography

Agamben, G. (1998) *Homo Sacer: Sovereign Power and Bare Life*, trans. D. Heller-Roazen, Stanford, CA: Stanford University Press.

—— (2002) *Remnants of Auschwitz: The Witness and the Archive*, trans. D. Heller-Roazen, New York: Zone Books.

—— (2005) *State of Exception*, trans. K. Atell, Chicago: Chicago University Press.

Appiah, K.A. (2006) *Cosmopolitanism: Ethics in a World of Strangers*, London: Allen Lane.

Aradau, C. and Muster, R. van (2009) 'Exceptionalism and the "War on Terror": Criminology Meets International Relations', *British Journal of Criminology* 49(5): 686–701.

Barber, S. (2010) 'Jobless migrants living in shanty towns offered free flights home', *The Observer*, 7 February.

Bauman, Z. (1991) *Modernity and Ambivalence*, Cambridge: Polity Press.

—— (1993) *Postmodern Ethics*, Oxford: Blackwell.

—— (2004) *Europe: An Unfinished Adventure*, Cambridge: Polity Press.

Beck, U. (2006) *The Cosmopolitan Vision*, Cambridge: Polity Press.

Benhabib, S. (2004) *The Rights of Others: Aliens, Residents and Citizens*, Cambridge: Cambridge University Press.

—— (2006) *Another Cosmopolitanism*, ed. R. Post, Oxford: Oxford University Press.

Bosworth, M. (2007) 'Immigration detention in Britain', in M. Lee (ed.), *Human Trafficking*, Cullompton: Willan.

Carens, J. (1987) 'Aliens and Citizens: The Case for Open Borders', *Review of Politics*, 49(2): 251–73.

Davis, M. (2006) *Planet of Slums*, London/New York: Verso.

Derrida, J. (2000) *Of Hospitality: Anne Dufourmantelle Invites Jacques Derrida to Respond*, trans. R. Bowlby, Stanford, CA: Stanford University Press.

—— (2001) 'Cosmopolitanism', in S. Critchley and R. Kearney (eds), *Cosmopolitanism and Forgiveness*, London: Routledge.

—— (2003) 'Autoimmunity: Real and Symbolic Suicides', in G. Borradori (ed.), *Philosophy in a Time of Terror*, Chicago: University of Chicago Press.

Dershowitz, A.M. (2002) *Why Terrorism Works: Understanding the Threat, Responding to the Challenge*, New Haven, CT: Yale University Press.

Dworkin, R. (2002) 'The real threat to US values', *The Guardian*, Saturday Review, 9 March: 3.

Ericson, R.V. (2007) *Crime in an Insecure World*, Cambridge: Polity Press.
Finnis, J. (1980) *Natural Law and Natural Rights*, Oxford: Clarendon Press.
Gilroy, P. (2004) *Between Camps: Nations, Cultures and the Allure of Race*, Cambridge, MA: Harvard University Press.
Grewcock, M. (2007) 'Shooting the passenger: Australia's war on illicit migrants', in M. Lee (ed.), *Human Trafficking*, Cullompton: Willan.
Habermas, J. (1998) *The Inclusion of the Other*, eds C. Cronin and P. De Greiff, Cambridge: Polity Press.
—— (2003) 'Fundamentalism and Terror', in G. Borradori (ed.), *Philosophy in a Time of Terror*, Chicago: University of Chicago Press.
Hagan, J. (2003) *Justice in the Balkans: Prosecuting War Crimes in the Hague Tribunal*, Chicago: University of Chicago Press.
Hagan, J. and Rymond-Richardson, W. (2009) *Dafur and the Crime of Genocide*, Chicago: University of Chicago Press.
Harel, A. and Sharon, A. (2008) 'What is really wrong with torture?', *Journal of International Criminal Justice* 6(2): 241–59.
Hudson, B. (2003) *Justice in the Risk Society*, London: Sage.
—— (2007) 'The rights of strangers: Policies, theories, philosophies', in M. Lee (ed.), *Human Trafficking*, Cullompton: Willan.
—— (2008) 'Re-imagining justice: principles of justice for divided societies in a globalised world', in P. Carlen (ed.), *Imaginary Penalities*, Cullompton: Willan.
—— (2009) 'Justice in a Time of Terror', *British Journal of Criminology* 48(4): 702–17.
—— (2010) 'Regulating Democracy: justice, citizenship and inequality in Brazil', in H. Quirk, T. Seddon and G. Smith (eds), *Criminal Justice and Regulation*, Cambridge: Cambridge University Press.
Ignatieff, M. (2004) *The Lesser Evil: Political Ethics in an Age of Terror*, Edinburgh: Edinburgh University Press.
Kant, I. (1983) 'To Perpetual Peace', in *Perpetual Peace and Other Essays*, trans. T. Humphrey, Cambridge: Hackett Publishing.
Kymlicka, W. (2006) 'Liberal Nationalism and Cosmopolitan Justice', in S. Benhabib, *Another Cosmopolitanism*, Oxford: Oxford University Press.
Luban, D. (2005) 'Liberalism, Torture and the Ticking Bomb', *Virginia Law Review* 91: 1425–61.
Matsueda, R.L. (2009) 'Toward a New Criminology of Genocide', *Theoretical Criminology*, 13(4): 495–502.
Migreurop (2010) *2010, the year of the right to migrate?* http://www.migreurop.org/article1605.html downloaded 29/01/2010.
Moellendorf, D. (2002) *Cosmopolitan Justice*, Boulder, CO and Oxford: Westview Press.
Neal, A. (2006) 'Foucault in Guantanamo: Towards an Archaeology of the Exception', *Security Dialogue*, 37: 31–46.
Otty, T. (2006) 'Honour Bound to Defend Freedom? The Guantanamo Bay Litigation and the Fight for Fundamental Values in the War on Terror', *European Human Rights Law Review*, 2008(4): 433–53.
Post, R. (2006) 'Introduction', in S. Benhabib (ed.), *Another Cosmopolitanism*, Oxford: Oxford University Press.
Pureza, J.M. (2005) 'Defensive and oppositional counter-hegemonic uses of international law: From the International Criminal Court to the common heritage of mankind', in

B. de Sousa Santos and C.A. Rodriguez-Garavito (eds), *Law and Globalization from Below: Towards a Cosmopolitan Legality*, Cambridge: Cambridge University Press.
Raulff, U. (2004) 'An Interview with Giorgio Agamben', *German Law Journal* 5(5): 609–14.
Rawls, J. (1971) *A Theory of Justice*, Cambridge, MA: Harvard University Press.
—— (2001) *The Law of Peoples*, Cambridge, MA: Harvard University Press.
Rodier, C. (2006) *Analysis of the External Dimension of the EU's Asylum and Immigration Policies – Summary and Recommendations for the European Parliament*, Brussels: European Parliament.
Sands, P. (2008) *Torture Team: Deception, Cruelty and the Compromise of Law*, London: Allen Lane.
Santos, B. de Sousa (2002) *Toward a New Legal Common Sense*, London: Butterworths.
Santos, B. de Sousa and Rodriguez-Garavito, C.A. (2005) (eds), *Law and Cosmopolitanism from Below: Towards a Cosmopolitan Legality*, Cambridge: Cambridge University Press.
Sen, A. (2009) *The Idea of Justice*, London: Allen Lane.
Statewatch (2009) *The EU's murderous borders: four poles of suffering and denial of rights*, http://www.statewatch.org/news/2009/dec.02eu-migreurop-report.htm downloaded 31/01/2010.
Unger, R. (2005) *What Should the Left Propose?* London: Verso.
UNHCR (2009) *Observations on Greece as a country of asylum*, Office of the United Nations High Commissioner for Human Rights, December.
Wacquant, L. (2005) 'The great penal leap backward: incarceration in America from Nixon to Clinton', in J. Pratt et al. (eds), *The New Punitiveness: Trends, theories, perspectives*, London: Sage.
Waldron, J. (2005) 'Torture and Positive Law: Jurisprudence for the White House', *Columbia Law Review* 105(6): 1681–1750.
Young, I.M. (2002) *Inclusion and Democracy*, Oxford: Oxford University Press.

Chapter 7

A borderless world?

Cosmopolitanism, boundaries and frontiers

Katja Franko Aas

In June 2009, the following letter by sixteen NGOs was submitted to the European Commission and the UN Human Rights Commissioner:[1]

> On 7 May 2009, 227 people (including 40 women, three of whom were pregnant) on board three boats were rescued in the Maltese SAR area by Italian motorboats, 35 maritime miles away from the island of Lampedusa. As far as we know, following agreements with Libya, the captains of some Italian Navy ships received all the migrants on board to then take them immediately back to Libya, were they were handed over to the Libyan authorities. On 8 May there was a second refusal of entry after an Italian tow-boat in service on an ENI oil rig intercepted a boat carrying 77 people and led it back to Libya. Analogous operations were also carried out in the following days, as was stated before the press corps by the Italian interior minister, who, until 10 May, indicated that the migrants returned to Libya were around 500, describing the episodes as a 'historical result'. None of the people transported to Libya was officially identified, nor was their nationality recorded, there were no checks as to whether they were minors or not, the state of pregnancy of the women, the migrants' health conditions, nor was there any control of possible requests for international protection.... It is reasonable and plausible to believe that there may have also been refugees among the migrants returned to Libya, who would have had the right – inviolable – to have access to the procedure for the recognition of international protection in Italy.

According to the European Commission's own sources, approximately one-third of those arriving by sea to Italy in 2007 applied for asylum (ca. 7,000 people). On average, almost half of all asylum applicants in Italy are eventually recognized as refugees or granted some other form of protection. UNHCR has repeatedly expressed its serious concern to the Italian government about the events detailed

1 http://www.asgi.it/public/parser_download/save/respingimenti_libia_esposto_istituzioni_internazionali.pdf.

above, considering that the operations enacted by the Italian government 'contravene the non-refoulement principle sanctioned by the 1951 Geneva Convention that is also applicable in international waters. This fundamental principle, which does not have any geographical bounds, is also contained in European legislation and in the Italian judicial system.'[2]

The letter is by no means an isolated example when it comes to describing the many humanitarian and political controversies surrounding the European border control practices; including the questionable living conditions in Greek, UK and other detention centres and the large numbers of fatalities on the Mediterranean shores. The letter can therefore serve as an illustrative starting point for our discussion which aims to explore the geographies of inclusion and exclusion with the imaginary of cosmopolitan justice. The chapter examines the discursive and political development of cosmopolitanism against a seemingly contradictory trend: the growing border-consciousness and border-defensiveness of Western societies. Based on the nation-centric and territorial model of justice, borders seemingly run counter to the cosmopolitan project. However, this chapter offers a critique of the cosmopolitanism–nationalism dichotomy. Using the example of European borders and border policing, it argues that borders are not only a source of demarcation but also of pan-European solidarity and integration. At the same time, the coupling of universalistic ethics with the essence of Europeanness can, paradoxically, transform cosmopolitanism into a language of exclusion.

7.1 THE 'WHAT' AND THE 'WHERE' OF COSMOPOLITAN JUSTICE

The question of borders is quintessentially a question of justice and its limits. Borders demarcate belonging and non-belonging, as well as revealing specific conceptions of justice and its boundedness. Borders point to the continued importance of space and power relations inscribed in space. They serve as a potent reminder that in the abstract totality of the globe, the local and the national carry an enduring salience. The defence of the border is, in essence, a reiteration of the state's right to determine the right of entry. As such, the border is intrinsically connected to the nation-state and its attempts at controlling access to its territory. Borders demarcate the limits of sovereignty and reveal sovereign attempts to impose control, or at least a semblance of it. Borders are therefore, by their very nature, 'a tool of exclusion' of which the aim is to 'demarcate a coherent inside from a chaotic outside' (Rajaram and Grundy-Warr, 2007: x).

The border today, in its more or less wall-like features, represents an essential instrument for maining the stratified global order. The phenomenon of borders

2 UNHCR – press release of 15 May 2009.

today incorporates a variety of phenomena and practices. As Amore et al. (2008) point out:

> In addition to its traditional geophysical characteristics, the border has taken on virtual, de-territorialized attributes as well. Castles, walled cities, and extensive border battlements have been replaced by gated communities, expansive border zones, and management by 'remote control.' The contemporary border is constituted as much by data-flows, artificial zones and spaces of enclosure that seep into the city and the neighbourhood, as by older state and geographic boundaries.

Several observers have pointed out the tension at the heart of globalization and the emerging global order: between deterritorialization and re-territorialization; between global flows and the continued salience of local and national moorings (Aas, 2011, forthcoming). The phenomenon of borders and walling-up – of national and local variety – brings to our attention the fact that *what* and *where* it is to be human are two quite different questions (Rajaram and Grundy-Warr, 2007: xviii). It reveals the intensely territorial nature of humanity in which the *what* of humanity (as defined by human rights and cosmopolitan scholarship) is defined and redefined by the *where* of humanity – the geopolitical realities of a deeply stratified world order.

Cosmopolitanism, on the other hand, denotes a world view which seemingly aims to transcend national boundaries and achieve some form of 'planetary conviviality' (Mignolo, 2000); envisioning a borderless and united world in terms of moral obligation and solidarity, if not in terms of actual life circumstances. Much of cosmopolitan scholaship has been centred around the critique of the prerogatves of sovereignty and aimed at the unbounding of our ethical and legal imagination. Hence, as Hudson (this volume) points out, an important part of cosmopolitan scholarship has been addressed at the notion of hospitality and based on Kant's principle of the right of the stranger to be received without violence (Benhabib, 2004; Appiah, 2006). Yet, curiously, the proliferation in recent years of cosmopolitan discourse has gone hand in hand with the proliferation of the border as a strategy of governance. Nowhere is this disparity more evident than in the case of Europe. The European Union has been hailed by thinkers such as Beck and Habermas as a 'cosmopolitan laboratory' (see Adelman, this volume). A self-proclaimed 'area of freedom, security and justice' and an 'area of rights', it has been described by its pronents and representatives as a 'normative power', 'the peaceful continent', defined by a 'commitment to human rights, the empowerment of women, combating child labour, civil rights, freedom of speech, and the protection of natural resources' (Schüssel and Jagland, in *Time*, 2010). The border – which presupposes social division and exclusion – should therefore be deeply unsettling to the European cosmopolitan imagination. Nevertheless, in the past two decades, the EU has been, through progressive strengthening of its border controls, implementing practices of massive social exclusion, also of those who may potentially need its protection (see Hudson, this volume). Consequently, the (abstract) human right of asylum is, in practice, afforded only to a minority of migratnts who manage to penetrate its fortified borders.

Although the gap between the universalism of the European human rights discourse and the closure of the border may look like a classic distinction between ideals and realpolitik, the picture is far more complex. This chapter suggests that the progressive defence of European borders is, in official discourse and political documents, supported and justfied by a set of discursive practices which are essentially employing a cosmopolitan vocabulary. Cosmopolitanism thus represents not only an abstract discourse of justice, which is essentially played out at a different level from the more particularistic (national and local) arguments about the necessities of borders and walling-up. Rather, the fortification of the border, and its increasingly militant defense, is rooted in an imaginary in which the opposition between cosmopolitan ideals and nationalist border-defensive policies becomes blurred. Moreover, it will be suggested that the case of the EU's borders represents a development through which borders are transformed into frontiers and borderlands: not only in a geographic sense, but also in terms of the rule of law and its guiding principles.

7.2 AN 'AREA OF FREEDOM, SECURITY AND JUSTICE'

If we, for a moment, return to the deal between Libya and Italy, mentioned in the opening section of this paper, it clearly raises a series of humanitarian and legal issues. Libya is not a signatory of the 1951 Refugee Convention and its 1967 Protocol. Italy, on the other is, and is thus barred from returning people to unsafe places. 'The idea that preventing entry and forcibly returning them cancels the obligation to protect people from persecution stands the Refugee Convention on its head' (Frelick, 2009: 21), particularly since considerable numbers of those who eventually manage to enter end up getting some form of protection. Yet, even though the Italian agreement with Libya has created a considerable controversy on the EU level, we should be wary of interpreting it simply as an expression of particular (Italian) nationalist policies. Rather than being an anomly, the Italian policy can be seen as part of a continum of EU's immigration strategies which put priority on cooperation with neighbouring countries and systematic responsibilization of these to take a larger share of migratory flows. As revealed by the latest conclusions of the EU Council, the EU also plans actively to pursue:

> the dialogue on migration with Libya, with a view to setting up in the short term an effective cooperation. The Commission is invited to explore, *as a matter of urgency*, a cooperation agenda between the European Union and Libya with a view to including initiatives on maritime cooperation,

> border management (including possibilities for the development of an intergrated surveillance system), international protection, effective return and readmission of irregular migrants and issues of mobility of persons (emphasis added).[3]

In the past decade a large portion of the EU's border control efforts has been directed at 'getting ahead of the game' (Aas, 2005) and addressing unwanted migratory flows before they reach its geographic borders. The EU has developed a so-called four-tier model of border management[4] consisting of:

1 First-tier measures taken in third countries, especially in countries of origin and transit. These measures include advice and training from liaison officers and document experts.
2 The second tier consists of cooperation and agreements with neighbouring countries in the field of border management.
3 Measures at the external borders and border checks for every person entering or exiting the Schengen area.
4 The fourth tier comprises control measures within the area of free movement, including return.

The objective of these strategies has been clearly to shift the flows of unwanted migrants to so-called 'buffer zones' outside the EU territory (see also Hudson, this volume). Unfortunately these zones consist mostly of countries which have considerably poorer resources and human rights records than the EU itself. In the case of North Africa, this means that migratory flows are diverted to countries, which although (except for Libya) signatories of the Refugee Convention, nevertheless lack national asylum systems (UNHCR, 2010).

The strategy of enlisting the cooperation of third countries in the task of border policing furthermore highlights the blurring of boundaries between internal and external spheres of policing and security policies, and the progressive merging of foreign policy, migration management and development aid. The strategy has in recent years been branded as a 'Global Approach to Migration' and can be read as a testimony of political awareness of global interconnectedness. According to its wording:

> The Global Approach aims to formulate comprehensive and coherent policies that address the broad range of migration-related issues, bringing together different policy areas – development, social affairs and employment, external relations and justice and home affairs – and taking both short term actions as

3 Council of the European Union (2010) *Council conclusions on 29 measures for reinforcing the protection of the external borders and combating illegal immigration*, 25 and 26 February 2010.
4 COE (2008) *Schengen Catalogue*. 15250/2/08 REV 2.

> well as a longer term vision to address the root causes of migration and forced migration. The Global Approach has a strong theme of working in partnership with countries of origin and transit: its key concepts are partnership, solidarity and shared responsibility.[5]

Since its adoption in 2005 this approach has managed to achieve an extraordinary amount of highest level political activity, particularly with African countries, including Libya. And although it clearly contains elements of 'arm twisting', it is essentially a strategy for transferring responsibility for unwanted migratory flows to third countries. As Liz Fekete puts it, '[EU policies] have turned Third World governments into immigration police for Western Europe' (in Weber and Bowling, 2008).

> The policy framework includes funding for immigration controls (so-called 'migration management') in cooperating states, a preference for 'regional protection' (i.e. outside Europe) of refugees headed for Europe, and the deployment of EU 'border management' agencies to third countries.
>
> (Hayes, 2009: 33)

The objective is particularly visible in the recent Stockholm Programme which, while toning down the development aspect of the Global Approach, asserts the need to make migration an integral part of EU's external relations. As pointed out by a recent EU Council (2010) resolution, the objective is to use 'the full political weight of the EU' to secure return and readmission of irregular migrants to third countries as well as to improve their border management and surveillance capacities.

One of the central institutional components in the structures of the Area of Freedom, Security and Justice has been the recent establishment of the European Border Control Agency, Frontex. Frontex represents an example of transnational governance and of 'pooling of sovereignty', where the 'transnational system developed its own bureaucracy existing 'above' that of the apparatuses of nation states' (Sheptycki, 2002: 216). The agency was established with a Council regulation[6] in October 2004 and became operational a year later. As an international policing force Frontex obviously has several relatives, most notably Europol. However, it can also be distinguished by a relatively quick build-up of its capacity and, not least, coercive powers in the three years since its inception. There is much that indicates that this is a prioritized area of otherwise often halting European integration. Although Frontex aims to be an intelligence-driven agency, responsible for risk analysis and coordination, it also has considerable possibilities for direct use of force. Its 'armada' – listed in a centralized catalogue or

5 http://europa.eu/rapid/pressReleasesAction.do?reference=MEMO/07/549.

6 Council Regulation (EC) No. 2007/2004 of 26 October 2004 (Frontex Regulation).

record of available technical equipment (CRATE)[7] – consists of, among other things, a considerable number of helicopters, aeroplanes, maritime vessels, vehicles, mobile radar units, thermal/infrared cameras, etc. As such, Frontex represents a hybrid between a military and a police organization.

Frontex has, despite its relative youth, organized a series of so-called joint operations, particularly on the Southern Maritime borders of Europe. Their objective has been among others to fortify the border and to divert migrant flows back to the 'buffer zones' from which they came. These actions have been criticized for not complying with the principle of non-refoulment, grounded in the European Convention of Human Rights, the Geneva Refugee Convention and EU fundamental rights. The principle not only prohibits the return, rejection and diversion of persons to countries where they face serious human rights violations, but also obliges states to identify protection-seekers and offer them access to procedures for examination of an application for protection (Weinzerl, 2008: 4).

We can therefore see that the Italian–Libyan cooperation is by no means an anomaly when it comes to European migration control practices; rather the edges and borderlands of Northern Africa reveal the costs of common EU policies. The field of European border policing is a thoroughly internationalized activity and represents a typical example of transnationalization of law – a case of 'disembedding of law from its national encasement' (Sassen, 2007). Most notably since the signing of the Schengen Agreement in 1985, it became apparent that migration is increasingly subject to legal and institutional regulation and decision-making processes at the international level. Migration has been constituted as a challenge that requires trans-border, macro-regional and international responses. Policing of migratory flows has become one of the central elements of transnational and European policing and its emerging structures of the 'Area of Freedom, Security and Justice'. The Tampare Summit in 1999, in particular, and the current mobilizations against terrorism, have moved the issues of European police cooperation from their relative periphery to be one of the main motors of European cooperation and integration.

Through these processes of integration, European societies are today no longer (if they ever were) clearly delineated entities. This is true also of their justice systems, which are increasingly enmeshed with each other. When a system works as an integrated entity, some of its parts may be different than others, yet they produce effects together. For example, Norwegian borders are being defended not only in Norway, but also in Poland, Greece, Italy and Spain. These countries receive the lion's share of the migratory flows and as such contribute to the relative stability of the Norwegian asylum system, while their own resources are stretched to the limits, and consequently are more coercive and punitive. Similarly, Italian and Spanish border guard vessels in the Mediterranean protect not only Spanish and Italian but also German, French, Norwegian and other borders from

7 The 'catalogue' refers to a list of equipment that member states are willing to make available at Frontex's disposal.

unwanted migrants. Because of international agreements, the 'duty to guard what were previously only national borders becomes a duty owed to all the Schengen states' (House of Lords, 2008: 12). Simply comparing these national systems in terms of their human rights standards may be inadequate since they, although qualitatively different, support each other. Looking at the EU as a whole, the same task is performed by its neighbouring countries.

The relative humanity of European institutions thus needs to be seen in relation to the realpolitik towards the EU's Eastern and North African neighbours. As Hayes (2009: 33) observes:

> The EU's border controls have spread outwards as the EU has refined its attempt to prevent the arrival and entry of 'illegal migrants'. Since the member states often make no meaningful distinction in practice, this inevitably includes refugees fleeing war and poverty. This has allowed European states to claim to continue to uphold the Geneva Conventions on the protection of refugees and the right to asylum, while simultaneously denying increasing numbers of would-be refugees access to EU territory.

By employing the above-described anti-migration strategies, the EU has been actively pushing the boundaries of legality and what can be in terms of human rights considered as legitimate practice. As mentioned above, critics have raised the question about the legality of Frontex search and recue missions, which frequently dispose of the rescued migrants at the nearest port in a third country.[8] According to Brown (2009), the extrajuridical practices, which are not bound by legality, are surrounding borders throughout the world, exemplified by the activities of vigilantes on the US–Mexico border and the building of Israel's border fence. Rather than a distinct boundary and clear legal regimes, these practices turn the border area into a 'frontier', marked by ambiguity and absences of law and the shifting terrain between legality and illegality.

However, it may be important to note that the extra-legal and militarized nature of the southern border should by no means be seen as a representative image of the overall boundaries of Europe. By contrast, the EU's eastern peripheries are marked by greater fluidity, openness and cross-border cooperation (Marin, 2010). Borders can thus become facilitators of social exchange between the EU and its neighbours who, one should add, often enjoy the status of potential new members. The difference indicates that we may need to take a closer look at notions of

8 On 25 January 2010 the Council adopted a draft decision on the rules guiding rescue operations at sea conducted by Frontex. The rules clearly stipulate the primacy of non-refoulement and the moral duty of border patrols to recue migrants, they nevertheless suggest that priority should be given to disembarkation in the third country where the persons rescued started their journey. If this is not possible, disembarkation should take place in the country hosting the Frontex operation. The decision has already provoked objections from Malta and Italy which frequently host Frontex missions as they fear that the new rules will put even more pressure on them.

membership and belonging in order to fully understand the development and the shaping the southern frontier and its humanitarian challenges.

7.3 THE BORDER PARADOX

If the EU – with its structure of human rights legislation and institutions, as well as a history of humanitarian intervention by its members – represents a space of humanitarian self-identity, a question arises as to how it can be reconciled with the humanitarian anarchy at its southern fringes. The examples above reveal the contrast between the abstract (humanitarian) subject of law and the concrete practices of surveillance and exclusion which underpin the law's applicability in practice (see also Douzinas, 2007). There are today few, if any, possibilities for those in need of protection to access the EU's asylum system by legal means. Their journey to reach the EU's territory thus, by necessity, results in a complex involvement with illegality. This connection between migration and illegality takes place on two levels:

(a) by attempting to access EU territory in an unauthorized manner, migrants become labelled as 'illegals';[9] and
(b) in order to reach the territory, they need to employ services of more or less organized illegal networks of smugglers and other travel facilitators. Rather then reducing migration, control measures can thus 'produce a vicious cycle when more effective control leads to new smuggling strategies rather than a reduction in migration' (Carling and Hernandez-Carretero, forthcoming).

I argue that it is precisely this entanglement – political, discursive and practical – between migration and illegality which sustains the humanitarian anarchy on Europe's borderlands. The deployment of various border control strategies described above has been underpinned by a particular discursive turn which has been described elsewhere as the *securitization* of migration (Huysmans, 2006). The securitization of migration consists of a set of practical and interpretative measures which cast migration as a problem of security. It is 'a political technique of framing policy questions in logics of survival with a capacity to mobilize politics of fear in which social relations are structured on the basis of distrust' (Huysmans, 2006: xi). Securitization is therefore not only a set of bureaucratic, legal and technological practices but also a discursive phenomenon which frames migration, and immigrant populations, as a problem of security, rather than, for example, a humanitarian, developmental or economic issue.

9 See for example the wording of the Stockholm Programme. For a recent critique of the concept of illegal migration, see Commissioner for Human Rights (2009).

In the following section I shall suggest that the terminology of combating transnational criminal networks plays a crucial role in the progressive securitization of migration. In EU policy documents, migration control is regularly addressed together with issues of terrorism and organized crime, thus justifying the merging of policing and anti-migration measures.[10] Building on Jonathan Simon's concept of 'governing through crime', Walters (2004: 247) observes the tendency to 'govern central aspects of global migration by strategies of criminalization and illegalization'. According to Simon (2007), 'governing through crime' represents an attempt at solving social problems through strategies of criminalization and aggressive law enforcement, often through the use of war-making analogies. In numerous settings – institutions are seen as acting legitimately when they act to prevent crimes or other behaviour analogous to crimes – even though these interventions may have other motivations.

The figure of what Melossi (2003) terms the 'deviant immigrant' seems to embody the dangers and insecurities resulting from the rapid pace of social change and the intensity of glocal transformations. Discourses about human trafficking, transnational organized crime and terrorism symbolically represents popular concerns about global movements of people, and the perceived dangers of the foreign 'contaminating' the local. Melossi (2003) points out that allusions to a safe, mythical 'golden age', before the arrival of immigrants, have become an important aspect of contemporary European politics and identity. According to Bourdieu (1999) the opposition between 'natives' and 'immigrants' is gradually obscuring traditional class divisions within societies. The inequalities produced by the neo-liberal economic order are translated into political struggles about 'who has the right to claim all the advantages attached to membership in the national community' (1999: 188). Crime control thus becomes a central vehicle through which Western societies discuss membership and a method for keeping people at the borderlands of citizenship.

The securitization discourse may at first appear as the precise opposite of the cosmopolitan ambition: a discourse permeated by fear of the other and supportive of the exclusion of difference. Some of the most salient critiques of borders have come from writers, such as Seyla Benhabib (2004), who have argued for the systematic protection of the rights of immigrant others (see also Hudson, this volume). However, on closer examination the picture becomes far more complex and the opposition between cosmopolitanism and othering becomes at some points rather blurred.

10 It is a telling example that about 80 per cent of the entries in the Schengen Information System are recorded under article 96 and relate to illegal aliens, while article 95 (persons wanted for arrest and extradition) represents the smallest group of entries. The second-generation Schengen Information System (SIS II) is designed to become not only a reporting system but also an investigation system with open access for a series of EU authorities, such as Europol, Eurojust, security forces, etc. Information stored in what is essentially an administrative visa information system will be also be available to police and security agencies.

If we take a look at the discursive framing of the proposed European Border Surveillance System – EUROSUR – the system is publicly justified by three objectives: a) reduce the number of illegal immigrants entering the EU undetected, b) reduce the death toll of illegal immigrants by rescuing more lives at sea, and c) increase internal security of the EU as a whole by contributing to the prevention of cross-border crime.[11] We can see that the security objectives of migration control and crime control are carefully intertwined with the language of human security and the saving of lives. As a press release by the European Commission argued (ibid.):

> Many illegal immigrants and persons in need of international protection are traveling in conditions of extreme hardship and are taking great personal risks in their attempts to enter the EU illegally by hiding in vehicles, on cargo vessels, etc. The recent practice of traveling on board of unseaworthy and overcrowded boats, has multiplied the number of unfortunate migrants who continue to lose their lives by drowning in the Atlantic Ocean between Africa and the Canary Islands and in the Mediterranean Sea.
>
> The tragic death toll resulting from this kind of illegal immigration is unacceptable and must therefore be significantly reduced. The capacity to detect small boats in the open sea must be enhanced, contributing to greater chances of search and rescue and thereby saving more lives at sea. However, long-term solutions to the challenges posed by migration management can only be achieved through a comprehensive strategy that includes cooperation with third countries, also on border surveillance.

A look at the Frontex' account of their own activities reveals a similar mixture of a language of help and control.[12] The lives diverted back are therefore seen as lives that have been saved. As the following report on operation HERA, conducted near the Canary Islands, reveals:

> Total Intercepted in African Coast and diverted during HERA II Operational Phase – 3,887 illegal immigrants (57 cayucos or pateras) till 15/12/2006.
>
> This means that these people were stopped from setting off for a dangerous journey that might have cost their lives.[13]

The operations are thus framed in the language of humanitarianism, although critics have pointed out the reasons behind the dangerousness of migrants'

11 http://europa.eu/rapid/pressReleasesAction.do?reference=MEMO/08/86andformat=HTMLandaged=0andlanguage=EN.

12 A similar argument has been advanced recently by the Norwegian government proposing increased use of detention of asylum seekers in order to protect asylum as an institution (restraining freedom in order to protect freedom).

13 Source: http://www.frontex.eu.int/gfx/frontex/files/hera-statistics.pdf.

journeys can be also found in the progressive militarization of borders, thus forcing them to depart from geographically remote areas and employing help of organized smugglers. Moreover, as pointed out by the discussion above, the operations clearly push the burden of migratory flows on EU neighbouring countries with poor resources and human rights records, a fact that Frontex seems to be aware of.

> In Kufra the delegation visited the detention camp for illegal immigrants where 130 sub-Saharan citizens were detained. The condition of this structure can be described as rudimentary and lacking in basic amenities.
>
> The mission was informed that, during 2006, the Libyan authorities had apprehended 32,164 illegal immigrants and had repatriated 53,842 during the same period. Furthermore, some 60,000 illegal migrants were currently detained.
>
> (Report on the Frontex-led mission to Libya 28 May–5 June 2007[14])

If we look at two concepts, which more than any others have contributed to the securitization of migration and have constituted the border as an entity to be defended, the ambiguity becomes even clearer. Human trafficking and international terrorism are the two threats that have guided much of European border policy, as is evident from the Eurosur press release mentioned above:

> Border surveillance has not only the purpose to prevent unauthorised border crossings, but also to counter cross-border crime such as the prevention of terrorism, trafficking in human beings, drug smuggling, illicit arms trafficking etc. To counter these threats is first and foremost a task for the police forces and intelligence services of Member States. However, an effective border management system both at national and European level will provide a valuable tool for fighting cross-border crime.

The anti-immigration and anti-trafficking measures have in some documents merged to an extent which makes the two policies almost indistinguishable.[15] The following passage is from the Stockholm programme,[16] where the top of the section on 'policies to combat illegal immigration', thus reiterates:

> The fight against trafficking in human beings and smuggling of persons, integrated border management and cooperation with countries of origin and transit, supported by police and judicial cooperation, in particular must

14 http://www.statewatch.org/news/2007/oct/eu-libya-frontex-report.pdf.

15 See also the recent *Action-Oriented Paper on strengthening the EU external dimensions on action against trafficking in human beings* (2009), which follows in all its major traits the general lines of EU's border control strategies and its Global Approach to Migration: responsibilizing third countries, pre-border controls, enhanced role of Frontex and Europol, etc.

16 http://www.se2009.eu/en/the_presidency/about_the_eu/justice_and_home_affairs/1.1965.

> remain a key priority for this purpose. Our aim must be to prevent the human tragedies which the activities of human traffickers expose persons to.

Morrison and Crosland (2001: 40) thus suggest that despite the 'obvious concern to protect victims and to prevent the abuses of trafficking the overall debate is still dominated by the desire to seal Europe's borders which as it has been shown can have detrimental effects on refugee protection'.

The figure of the 'deviant immigrant' has moreover important gender dimensions, representing the case of what Pratt Ewing (2008) terms 'stigmatized masculinity' and its opposite – victimized femininity – where women are cast into the role of innocent victims of male brutality. Here, the discourse of cosmopolitan justice, particularly as promoted by various NGOs – guided as it may be by noble and important goals – enters a terrain which is by no means antithetic to othering. Consequently, several scholars have criticized the human trafficking and 'modern slavery' discourse as too black and white and unrealistic.

> The beauty of trafficking, constructed as a problem of organized transnational crime within which the 'mafia' of various countries purportedly make billions of dollars by kidnapping or luring passive and 'innocent' young women and children into sexual slavery, is that it apparently represents a form of forced migration that simultaneously involves the violation of the human rights of the 'trafficked' person *and* a threat to national sovereignty and security. With trafficking understood as such, governments can present more restrictive immigration controls as if they were measures designed to protect and promote human rights.
>
> (O'Connell Davidson, 2005: 69)

The issue brings to our attention the borders within the cosmopolitan imaginary. The figure of the deviant (male) immigrant thus performs a certain kind of 'boundary work'; it creates and reinforces divisions with the seemingly universal notion of humanity where exclusion is possible precisely on humanitarian grounds. The EU's borders are defended by a language of exclusion which in central aspects evokes the discourse of justice: women's rights and the protection of innocent life. Thus the ethically problematic aspects of 'illegality' of migration, become less so, when fused with the moral depravity of its purported organizers. The 'otherness' which is excluded from the EU's Area of Freedom, Security and Justice is thus to a large extent criminalized and securitized – presented either as a threat to morality, or security, or both.

7.4 CONCLUSION: USES OF THE OTHER

Borders are techniques for managing global inequality. They, however, are not natural entities but social, political and cultural constructs. They are both spatial and non-spatial techniques of exclusion. A question can be asked though whether a society – with cosmopolitan or any other self-identity – can exist without boundaries. At least since Durkheim, the importance of outsiders for the self-constitution of society and for development of national forms of governance has not been lost on social theory. Foucault's (1977) sceptical voice has pointed out the othering of the criminal as a practice that underpinned the universalistic discourse of humanistic Enlightenment penal theory. A question may be asked whether, in order for the universal humanity to become a governable entity in terms of global governance, there needs to be an outside. This raises a question about the relevance of borders for contemporary Western notions of subjectivity. Borders not only bound but also *invent* the societies they delimit (Brown, 2009). Melossi (2003) thus suggests that the deviant immigrant discourse serves as a vehicle for a debate about the contested nature of European identity. Similarly Pratt Ewing (2008: 20) argues that 'the stigmatization of Muslim and Turkish masculinities has been used as a strategy to manage immigrants and consolidate [German] national identity'.

One of the critiques raised by Calhoun (2003: 532) has been that cosmopolitanism tends to be, falsely, presented 'as freedom from social belonging rather than a special sort of belonging'. The freedom of movement awarded to most cosmopolitan actors stands in stark contrast to the immobility regimes to which a large part of the world's population are subjected. There is no doubt that the fight against 'illegal immigration' and organized crime is accelerating the speed and complexity of European integration. As Walker (2003: 121) aptly puts it, the so-called justice and home affairs have moved from being a 'poor cousin of European integration' to a position of a mature member of the family, in some regards, 'vying for the mantle of head of the family'. In addition to being an area of freedom of movement, a cosmopolitan 'borderless world', the EU is also, in Beck's (1999) term, a world risk society, united by fear and common security concerns. It is no coincidence that the cosmopolitan businessman described by Beck is also an avid supporter of anti-immigration policies (see Hudson, this volume).

The 'axiom of unity' which underpins so much of writing on cosmopolitan democracy and globalization thus creates a certain illusion of universality which to a large extent overlooks what Tsing (2005) terms *friction* – 'the messy materiality and awkward engagements'. Friction, resistance and global divisions need to be taken into account when examining the global and the universal. This chapter has argued that borders are not antithetic to the cosmopolitan imaginary. Proliferation of borders has been an essential aspect of globalization, constituting what might be termed its underside. In a similar manner also cosmopolitan aspirations to universality mask important divisions within its imaginary.

By exploring global divisions, borders and boundaries (real and symbolic), one enters the terrain where the global and the universal is still in the making and where globalization creates its frontier lands. This is a territory covered with what Sassen (2008: 67) terms 'third spaces', which 'are not exclusively national or global but are assemblages of elements of each'. Frontiers are marked by the shifting terrain between legality and illegality. They are the 'meeting point between savagery and civilization'; 'zones of not yet – not yet mapped, not yet regulated' (Tsing, 2005: 28). These types of spaces make possible 'kinds of engagements for which there are no clear rules' (Sassen: ibid.) that open for collaborations among legitimate and illegitimate partners (Tsing, 2005: 27). European border police forces can divert thousands of migrants to Libya and other countries with poor human rights records; Western police and intelligence agencies can cooperate with disreputable partners and dictatorial regimes in the global wars on drugs and terror, and Western humanitarian intervention can become a fertilizer for organized crime in the Balkans (Andreas 2008). Here, we can witness the paradoxical and contradictory nature of global connections, where often the objective of their globality is precisely to keep the world divided, rather than connected and unified.

Bibliography

Aas, K. F. (2005) 'Getting Ahead of the Game: Border Technologies and the Changing Space of Governance' in M. Salter and E. Zureik (eds), *Global Policing and Surveillance: Borders, Security, Identity*, Cullompton: Willan Publishing.

—— (2011, forthcoming) 'Victimhood of the National?: Denationalizing Sovereignty in Crime Control' in A. Crawford (ed.), *International and Comparative Criminal Justice and Urban Governance: Convergences and Divergences in Global, National and Local Settings*, Cambridge: Cambridge University Press.

Amoore, L., Marmura S. and Salter, M. B. (2008) 'Smart B 110 Orders and Mobilities: Spaces, Zones, Enclosures', *Surveillance and Society* 5(2), available at: http://www.surveillance-and-society.org/journalv5i2.html.

Andreas, P. (2008) *Blue Helmets and Black Markets: The Business of Survival in the Siege of Sarajevo*, Ithaca and London: Cornell University Press.

Appiah, K. A. (2006) *Cosmopolitanism: Ethics in a World of Strangers*, London: Penguin Books.

Beck, U. (1999) *World Risk Society*, Cambridge: Polity Press.

Benhabib, S. (2004) *The Rights of Others: Aliens, Residents, and Citizens*, Cambridge: Cambridge University Press.

Bourdieu, P. (1999) 'The Abdication of the State' in P. Bourdieu et al. (eds), *The Weight of the World: Social Suffering in Contemporary Society*, Cambridge: Polity Press.

Brown, W. (2009) 'Walled States and Waning Sovereignty', CCIG Keynote lecture, 16 December 2009, available at: http://www.open.ac.uk/ccig/media/walled-states.

Calhoun, C. (2001) 'The Necessity and Limits of Cosmopolitanism: Local democracy in a global context', Paper presented to UNESCO/ISSC conference, 'Identity and Difference in the Global Era', Candido Mendes University, Rio de Janeiro, 20–23 May 2001.

—— (2003) 'Belonging in the Cosmopolitan Imaginary', *Ethnicities* 3(4): 531–68.

Commissioner for Human Rights (2009) 'Criminalisation of Migration in Europe: Human rights implications'. Issue paper, available at: https://wcd.coe.int/ViewDoc.jsp?id=1579605andSite=CommDH.

Council of the European Union (2010) Council conclusions on 29 measures for reinforcing the protection of the external borders and combating illegal immigration. 2998th Justice and Home Affairs Council meeting Brussels, 25 and 26 February 2010.

Douzinas, C. (2007) *Human Rights and Empire: The political philosophy of cosmopolitanism.* Abingdon: Routledge-Cavendish.

Foucault, M. (1977) *Discipline and Punish; The Birth of the Prison*, trans. by A. Sheridan, New York: Vintage Books.

Frelick, B. (2009) 'Don't treat refugees as refuse', *The Guardian Weekly*, 19.06.09: p. 21.

Hayes, B. (2009) *Neoconopticon: the EU security-industrial complex.* Transnational Institute in association with Statewatch: http://www.statewatch.org/analyses/neoconopticon-report.pdf.

House of Lords (2008) *FRONTEX: The EU external borders agency.* Report with evidence, at: http://www.publications.parliament.uk/pa/ld200708/ldselect/ldeucom/60/60.pdf.

Huysmans, J. (2006) *The Politics of Insecurity: Fear, Migration and Asylum in the EU*, Milton Park: Routledge.

Melossi, D. (2003) 'In a Peaceful Life: Migration and the Crime of Modernity in Europe/Italy', *Punishment and Society* 5(4): 371–97.

Mignolo, W. D. (2000) 'The Many Faces of Cosmopolis: Border Thinking and Critical Cosmopolitanism', *Public Culture* 12(3): 721–48.

Morrison, J. and Crosland, B. (2001) 'The trafficking and smuggling of refugees: the end game in European asylum policy?' UNCHR Working Paper No. 39, at: http://www.arena.uio.no/sources/jpa/dublin/unhcr/morrison.pdf.

O'Connell Davidson, J. (2005) *Children in the Global Sex Trade*, Cambridge: Polity Press.

Pratt Ewing, K. (2008) *Stolen Honor: Stigmatising Muslim Men in Berlin*, Stanford, CA: Stanford University Press.

Rajaram, P. K. and C. Grundy-Warr (2007) *Borderscapes: Hidden Geographies and Politics at Territory's Edge*, St. Paul, MN: University of Minnesota Press.

Sassen, S. (2007) *A Sociology of Globalization*, New York and London: W.W. Norton.

—— (2008) 'Neither Global nor National: Novel Assemblages of Territory, Authority and Rights', *Ethics and Global Politics* 1(1–2): 61–79.

Sheptycki, J. (2002) 'Accountability Across the Policing Field: Towards a General Cartography of Accountability for Post-modern Policing', *Policing and Society* 12(4): 323–38.

Simon, J. (2007) *Governing through Crime: How the war on crime transformed America and created a culture of fear.* Oxford: Oxford University Press.

Sousa Santos, B. d' (1999) 'Towards a Multicultural Conception of Human Rights' in M. Featherstone and S. lash (eds), *Spaces of Culture: City – Nation – World*, London: Sage, pp. 214–29.

Time (2010) 'Europe speaks back', 29 March 2010, available at: http://www.time.com/time/magazine/article/0,9171,1973214,00.html.

Tsing, A. L. (2005) *Friction: An Ethnography of Global Connection.* Princeton, NJ: Princeton University Press.

UNHCR (2010) '2010 Regional Operations Profile – North Africa', viewed at: http://www.unhcr.org/pages/49e485f36.html.

Walker, N. (2003) 'The pattern of transnational policing' in T. Newburn (ed.), *Handbook of Policing*, Cullompton: Willan Publishing.

Walters, W. (2004) 'Secure Borders, Safe Haven, Domopolitics', *Citizenship Studies* 8(3): 237–60.

Weber, L. and Bowling, B. (2008) 'Valiant beggars and global vagabonds: Select, eject, immobilize' in *Theoretical Criminology* 12(3): 355–75.

Weinzerl, R. (2008) 'Human rights at the EU's common external maritime border: Recommendations to the EU legislature'. Policy Paper No 11. Berlin: German Institute of Human Rights.

Part IV

Chapter 8

The cosmopolitanism of transnational economic law

*Robert Wai**

8.1 COSMOPOLITAN JUSTICE AND TRANSNATIONAL ECONOMIC LAW

Cosmopolitanism seems an obvious frame for discussion of the laws of the global market. A cosmopolitan social theory that analyses the contemporary reality of 'mutual interdependence on a world scale' (Fine, 2007: 2) must account for the economic relations that now straddle sovereign boundaries in myriad ways.

Beyond sociology, the ethical project of cosmopolitanism comprises the effort to view questions of justice from the lens of the world, of nature and of humanity (Pogge 1992). In particular, cosmopolitan justice challenges the framework of the nation-state and posits that our moral obligations to others extend well beyond those to whom 'we are related by ties of kith and kind' (Appiah, 2006: xv). If the distinct concern of cosmopolitan justice is to examine the normative import of the sociological reality of transnational connections of various kinds (Fine, 2007: 2), then surely this must include the economic relations that now straddle sovereign boundaries in myriad ways.

Too often, however, the ethical significance of cross-border economic relations reduces to one of two standard forms. On one side, economic globalization certainly has its boosters, often moving from an acceptance of global markets as an unavoidable feature of contemporary society, a slippage from description to acceptance to celebration (e.g. Friedman, 1999). In contrast, progressive theorists see limited normative potential for cross-border economic activity, seeing such activity mainly as the source of ethical problems, the causes or symptoms of an unjust world order. Critical scholarship often sees little real possibility of cross-border commercial activity ever being described in the language of cosmopolitan justice, any such framing suspect as a form of apology for global capitalism. So, a cosmopolitan market sensibility is associated with the interests

* Associate Professor, Osgoode Hall Law School, York University, Toronto. Research funding for this chapter is partially provided by a grant from the Social Sciences and Humanities Research Council of Canada. My thanks to the Council for that funding and to Ian Medcalf (Osgoode JD 2010) for research assistance.

and consciousness of the transnational capitalist class (Sklair, 2000) or the class consciousness of the frequent traveller (Calhoun, 2003). In turn, exploration of critical cosmopolitan politics is mostly situated as the turn to options outside the market, to 'transnational solidarities' among workers or other groups (Calhoun, 2003: 108), or to global civil society and human rights (Baubock, 2003: 115–16). Even while there is some interest in the potential role in cosmopolitan justice of public international law, this does not generally extend to any of the existing economic laws of the international system. For example, Baubock (2003: 115) observes that 'nobody can seriously believe that economic globalization and its current regulatory regime contribute to the emergence of a global sense of political community, except by way of triggering resistance of the type we recently witnessed at the 1999 WTO summit in Seattle'.

This chapter explores whether there is another register in which to discuss these questions. Markets, including transnational markets, involve social relations with potential ethical content. Furthermore, the range of transnational economic relations is varied and complex, and therefore it make no sense to categorically refuse to explore whether the cosmopolitanism of the global economy can be something more than capitalist apology.

This chapter argues that the lens of transnational law provides an appropriately complex frame for a consideration of cosmopolitan justice in the context of global markets. Although the basic distinction of ethical and institutional cosmopolitanism is respected (Pogge, 1992), theorists often draw on examples from legal regimes since any account of cosmopolitan justice must still look at such institutional forms to give some sense of ethical possibilities. For example, Benhabib's work on cosmopolitan justice has looked to the 'jurisgenerative' element immanent to current practice in European and international law. Her examples focus on European jurisprudence on citizenship and international humanitarian law, such as the post-Nuremberg development of crimes against humanity and the Rome Treaty establishing the International Criminal Court. Benhabib develops the interests of Arendt (1965 [1977]) in the nascent laws related to international human rights, war crimes and crimes against humanity; looking at those regimes four decades later, Benhabib sees an international human rights regime that she believes does demonstrate the institutionalization of Kantian cosmopolitan norms. Benhabib observes that the combined effect of these developing European and international regimes is that in some areas the existing laws outstrip the limited content of the Kantian texts (2006: 36). The resulting spread of cosmopolitan norms has 'yielded a new political condition: the local, the national and the global are all imbricated in one another. Future democratic iterations will make their interconnections and interdependence deeper and wider' (Benhabib, 2006: 74).

What is the place of the proliferating and plural regimes of transnational economic law in this developing world of cosmopolitan norms? Economic law is not a source of law that the cosmopolitan justice literature has tended to look at, yet it seems crucial to any discussion of the nature of cosmopolitanism in the global legal order now. In a comment on Benhabib's work, Waldron specifically notes that political theorists of cosmopolitanism have tended to focus on public law topics like international human rights and crimes against humanity, rather than the 'dense thicket of rule' around more quotidian topics like postal service and telephone, time zones, or currencies and banking (Waldron, 2006: 83–4). The norms of cross-border commercial life may be the better substantive test for the extension of cosmopolitan norms into the 'dense detail of ordinary life' (2006: 97). A consideration of commercial topics also reveals a more challenging array of sources of cosmopolitan norms. This includes the customary development of social practice in addition to the more obvious and spectacular formal juridical sources such as international human rights treaties or international criminal law trials (2006: 93–4).

While accepting the significance of public international law and institutions that theorists such as Benhabib and Fine (2007) examine, this chapter attempts to relate concerns of cosmopolitan justice to the quotidian heart of transnational economic law, which includes international law, but also a multiplicity of often overlapping forms of cross-border and sub-national norms, including both state and non-state forms, which create governance beyond traditional state models but short of world government. Attention to this broader range of norms also highlights the significant role of transnational private actors (such as civil society actors or multinational corporations) in influencing the governing norms of contemporary globalization (Keck and Sikkink, 1998).

An examination of the normative aspects of transnational economic activity also complements projects such as Habermas's effort to identify new forms of solidarity that would help to achieve material and security goals, but also secure legitimacy, in a global era (Habermas, 2006: 176). Habermas observes that potential new forms of solidarity are created in the lifeworld by the conditions of interdependence associated with globalization, which 'imperceptibly alters the self-image of nation-states and their citizens' (2006: 177). He notes that unlike the flow of goods, this 'process of consciousness formation' is not easily dictated from above or by elites or by administrative decision. Habermas recognizes that any emergent form of solidarity extending across borders must build from the role of the state, which retains significantly greater capacity for law and legitimate power than private forms of governance. However, solidarity must also become cosmopolitan in the sense of moving beyond traditional nation-state forms. With respect to law, like Benhabib, Habermas has focused on the formal realm of international law and institutions, including a variety of constitutional forms in the European context, rather than transnational law.[1] But Habermas also sees that there must emerge an 'intermediate level' of transnational regulation and fair policies between nation-states and the world organization (2006: 178–9).

1 Habermas occasionally and confusingly uses the term 'transnational' to refer to standard international relations among sovereign states (Habermas, 2006: 136).

It is perhaps a stark juxtaposition to move from the legitimacy concerns of Habermas in the postnational constellation to the realm of transactional economic law, but this latter is a primary example of the kind of intermediate level regulation that must form part of any exploration of legitimate contemporary governance. Hardt and Negri, for example, identify such forms of transnational law as both examples of the kind of empire that now governs world society (Hardt and Negri, 2004: 167–76) and models for the kind of subversive resistance of the multitude and 'the ever greater power of the common' against the empire (e.g. Hardt and Negri, 2009: 372–4).

A cosmopolitan perspective on the global economy must recognize that while the nation-state is clearly one venue for norm-generation, the forms of community are multiple and so likewise are sources of relevant norms of conduct. Normative communities are complicated and dynamic, and exist at many levels, from the local – including private or exclusive worlds like the family – through to the world public affairs of states (Singer, 1989: 86–7). Consequently, a consideration of transnational economic law may in some respects offer a better model for the simultaneous consideration of both state and non-state normative orders, and their interrelationship.[2] If the particular contribution of law comes from its synthesis of practical relevance and normative promise, then it is all the more important to consider the full range of normative practice in the global society.

8.2 COSMOPOLITANISM AND THE PLURALISM OF TRANSNATIONAL ECONOMIC LAW

Because of its close connection to ethics, the cosmopolitan frame seems particularly important for assessing the legal norms related to cross-border relations. However, the cosmopolitan frame also poses a challenge for legal scholarship, which still works from foundations originated within the frame of the modern nation-state, whether through domestic public law or public international law generated by the shared custom or negotiated treaties of nation-states. In contrast, 'cosmopolitan norms of justice, whatever the conditions of their legal origination, accrue to person as moral and legal persons in a worldwide civil society' (Benhabib, 2006: 16). A critical perspective such as cosmopolitanism that requires critical analysis beyond the nation-state seems essential for lawyers confronted with the complexity of instruments and actors and the variety of norms present in contemporary global society.

Nowhere is this challenge more clear than in the area of the laws of international economic relations. The multiplicity of relevant forms of regulation is

2 In earlier work, Habermas entertains the particular potential in private law in the domestic context to achieve the blend of public and private concerns needed for legitimate governance (Habermas, 1996: 407–11).

widely recognized by scholars working on the law and regulation of international business (e.g. Braithwaite and Drahos, 2000; Goode et al., 2007). The frame of legal pluralism has been required because neither traditional domestic public law nor public international law have responded well to the task of providing a meaningful institutional or conceptual frame for the role of law in transnational economic governance. A substantial amount of global regulatory activity falls outside of the zone of classic state regulation or inter-state regulation through international institutions or public international law. Two examples, one facilitative and one regulatory, illustrate the challenge to of an approach to global business regulation based on a public law perspective.

First is the spread of private ordering through the use of the *lex mercatoria* and through the use of international commercial arbitration. The *lex mercatoria* coupled with arbitration exemplifies what theorists have identified as the growth of private authority in global relations (Cutler, 2005). Important norms regulating international transactions are frequently not derived from domestic commercial laws or international law sources such as the Uruguay Round Agreements associated with the World Trade Organization, but rather from non-state sources such as the various codes of the International Chamber of Commerce,[3] or through the self-governance of international contracts, including through repeated iterations of standard contracts. The *lex mercatoria* has fascinated theorists of global law as well as theorists of contemporary governance more generally. Celebrants and critics equally are intrigued by the way in which transnational norms, shared by merchants or traders in a particular sector, such as among bankers with respect to bills of exchange or letters of credit, provided a seemingly stable base on which transnational practice develops, often without or to the side of state law (Sassen, 1996; Hardt and Negri, 2004: 169–71; Dalhuisen, 2006). Teubner identifies these as exemplary of the emergent global law without the state (Teubner, 1997).

A second example, but from the regulatory perspective, is the growth of voluntary norms of corporate social responsibility and their increased relevance for social regulation in many areas of traditional concern for public law, such as human rights, corruption, and environmental protection. Norms of corporate social responsibility are often seen as emerging from the recognition by transnational business actors of their enlightened self-interest to act in a responsible fashion with respect to social regulation such as environmental or labour practices, such that they voluntarily set and follow norms that go beyond formal domestic or international law requirements (Ruggie, 2007). Examples include soft law or self-regulatory standards set by individual companies or by groups of businesses, with or without the involvement of public institutions. The standards are often developed in particular trades, such as the toy industry (Snyder, 1999) or the extraction industries, such as the Kimberly Process Certification Scheme to

3 For example, the Incoterms in international sales, the Uniform Customs and Practice for Documentary Credits, and the ICC Rules of Arbitration (Goode et al., 2007: 208, 219–20).

regulate trade in conflict diamonds. The potential configurations of actors influenced by voluntary standards can extend to third parties, such as the Equator Principles followed by banks in determining, assessing and managing social and environmental risk in international project finance lending. From a still broader governance standard, the normative instruments relevant to transnational economic activity include a variety of forms of benchmarks and indices (Davis, Kingsbury and Merry, 2010).

In the examples of *lex mercatoria* and corporate social responsibility, concerns about compliance with state law, whether domestic or international, seem to fade into the background. Some soft law initiatives such as the United Nations Global Compact or the OECD Guidelines for Multinational Enterprises do involve traditional intergovernmental organizations; however, adoption remains voluntary, and compliance is rarely a requirement of public law. Accounts of the rise and effectiveness of such private norms refer to pressure from other private actors such as civil society groups, or emphasize an almost spontaneous private ordering. Voluntary private standards may be imposed by powerful multinationals, such as clothing manufacturers, on their own production and on sub-contractors in their global networks (Snyder, 1999: 338, 362). Motivations for compliance with private norms can be generated by direct action such as consumer or shareholder boycotts. The pressure can arise as well from the investment decisions of large institutional investors, as well as the internal reports supporting and publicity surrounding such decisions, by such mixed public-private funds as the Government Pension Fund of Norway deciding on appropriate investments under its Ethical Guidelines. The pressure also includes forms of direct action by civil society groups, such as environmental or church groups, for example through media campaigns pressuring the reputation and valuable brands of multinational businesses (Klein, 2000). Monitoring of voluntary standards can require elaborate participation of other non-governmental actors in an ongoing fashion (Barenberg, 2008).

The system of economic governance that includes such instruments as *lex mercatoria* and voluntary standards is recognized to be a complex plural regime of national laws, international law, and non-state normative systems. (Braithwaite and Drahos, 2000). Like sophisticated cosmopolitanism, the analysis of plural legal orders looks to normative regimes below, above and across state legal orders, while also recognizing that state sources remain highly relevant, not only to governance within in any single state, but also through extraterritorial effects beyond the border.

A nuanced account of the role of state law in transnational economic governance requires recognition of the combined cross-border and extraterritorial effect of the full range of national laws, whether public regulatory laws (such as banking regulation or competition laws), public facilitative laws (such as securities regulation, incorporation statutes, or intellectual property legislation), or private laws (such as property, tort and contract law). The combined effect occurs even when those national laws sit uneasily together, often overlapping or even conflicting. Moreover, the mutual effectiveness of such domestic regulation sometimes depends not just on traditional international law or diplomacy, but on new forms of transgovernmental cooperation (Slaughter, 2004). In the private law context, traditional state law can now involve complex transnational private action, such as transnational tort litigation, initiated by private plaintiffs, whether under regular domestic tort rules or under special legislation such as the Alien Tort Statute in the United States (Scott and Wai, 2004). Such private litigation may have as its goal not just money judgments, but also publicity and settlement, such as in the *Saro Wiwa* litigation in United States courts involving alleged human rights abuses by the Shell oil company in its Nigerian oil operations (Wuerth, 2009).

Similarly, while states remain central as the originators of international law, attention must be also paid to added complexity in the content and form of international law. Certainly, the number of specialized international regimes is proliferating,[4] including into new areas of particular relevance to international economic activity, such as the OECD Convention on Combating Bribery of Foreign Public Officials. Increasingly, it seems that the focus of such international treaties and institutions is directed less to inter-state disputes involving sovereign conduct (such as imposition of tariffs or quotas) and more to the regulation of transnational problems generated by private party actions. Efforts during the current financial crisis to strengthen the roles of the International Monetary Fund and the Basel Committee on Banking Supervision in the effective supervision of private financial institutions have this character, as does the expansion of concern of international human rights laws or international criminal law to include transnational business conduct that might violate humanitarian norms (Ruggie, 2007). Even in the deployment of public international law norms, the role of private actors, such as transnational advocacy networks, has become an established feature of global society (Keck and Sikkink, 1998).

The pluralism at play in the laws related to the international economy can lead to powerful and controversial hybrids. For example, international investment treaties such as NAFTA Chapter 11 clearly constitute transnational governance by empowering private actors through substantive and procedural innovations that provide for compensation claims through arbitral proceedings against sovereign authorities for sovereign acts that harm foreign investments. However, this advance in international law can be criticized as asymmetric with respect to transnational governance in that new rights are granted to private economic actors without adding any responsibilities and without enabling any rights or procedures for other private actors who might be affected by the conduct of foreign business actors. Moreover investment treaties may weaken local sovereign processes to which private actors such as citizen groups can otherwise turn to respond to and pressure

4 Report of the Study Group of the International Law Commission, finalized by Professor Martti Koskenniemi, Fragmentation of International Law: Difficulties Arising from the Diversification and Expansion of International Law, 13 April 2006, UN Doc. A/CN.4/L.682.

powerful transnational business actors, processes such as municipal governments or state environmental regulation in Mexico,[5] or civil litigation in Mississippi.[6] Such treaties have clearly generated political controversy and ethical concern (see Langford, this volume), but state-investor international arbitration also exemplifies the complexity of the normative venues of global economic relations.

In response to such complexity, scholarship on economic law has turned to transnational law. Transnational law frameworks challenge any traditional account based on an exclusive focus on traditional state-based sources of domestic and international law (Jessup, 1956; Cotterrell, 2009). Transnationalism recognizes that cross-border legal relations are not simply framed by traditional forms of domestic public law and public international law, but rather include substantial forms of private ordering (Zumbansen, 2006). Likewise, transnational law anticipates a varied terrain of private and public actors engaged in cooperation, but also in competition and contestation (Wai, 2006).

Transnationalism offers a promising description of the current norms of cross-border economic governance, and should be of interest to those interested in cosmopolitanism. But beyond sociology, what is the moral significance of the plural blend of orders of transnational economic governance? Cosmopolitanism would seem to provide an excellent potential critical perspective on this question. If we define transnational economic law as the full range of laws and norms that could be said to 'govern' cross-border economic relations, then a number of shared concerns with cosmopolitan analysis become clear. The field is clearly cosmopolitan in the sense of having cross-border objects of concern and cross-border sources of norms. But is this complex form consistent with any sense of justice appropriate for the global society? As noted above, it has been less easy to discuss the global economy from the perspective of cosmopolitan justice without a deep sense of unease. However, a consideration of transnational economic law from the perspective of cosmopolitan justice may be one way to provide helpful critical insights that are neither merely apologetic nor hopelessly utopian (Koskenniemi, 1989 [2005]).

8.3 THE KANTIAN VISION OF COSMOPOLITAN JUSTICE AND TRANSNATIONAL ECONOMIC RELATIONS

The potential connections between cosmopolitan justice and the world of transnational economic law will be explored in this section by a consideration of Kant's texts, in particular the essay *Perpetual Peace*, which have been the starting point

5 *Metalclad Corp. v Mexico*, ICSID Case No. ARB(AF)/97/1, Award, 30 August 2000.

6 *The Loewen Group, Inc. and Raymond L. Loewen v United States of America*, ICSID Case No. ARB(AF)/98/3, Award, 26 June 2003.

for many contemporary discussions of cosmopolitan justice. Kant's texts have not been used actively in consideration of economic relations. It will be argued, however, that the Kantian texts provide very useful insights as to the critical evaluation of emergent transnational economic law regimes.

This section will examine three key points that the *Perpetual Peace* essay suggests about the analysis of transnational economic law from a cosmopolitan perspective. First, the analysis of cosmopolitan right together with international right provides a powerful reminder of why any account of cosmopolitan justice must find a role for states, but also be able to account for other tiers of cross-border relations. Second, Kant's emphasis on the cosmopolitan right of hospitality has particular significance for international economic relations, especially as the conditions for economic contact between persons across borders expand. Third, Kant's emphasis on the limits of cosmopolitan right highlights the value of sovereign states for protecting cosmopolitan goals, and the result that cosmopolitan justice is only achieved when both states and individuals consent to set up transnational economic relations. Neither individuals nor states can be obliged to trade. The resulting framework is a powerful one for thinking about the relation between ideal theory and the actual practices of transnational economic law.

8.3.1 Both cosmopolitan right and international right

Kant's discussion of international affairs is especially important for assessing transnational relations because it combines a focus in cosmopolitan right on the treatment of individuals with a discussion of the ethics of the nation-state and the international system. Indeed, the *Perpetual Peace* essay is most renowned for its discussion of inter-state ethics, most clearly stated in his discussion of international right. In the Second Definitive Article, Kant argues for the importance of a federation of free states. This is a prescription not for a single world or global government, but rather for the pacific co-existence of states. This confederation would require that its members renounce the right of war against each other (Kant, 1795 [1970]: 104–5), and would require a number of preliminary conditions, including the renunciation of forcible intervention in the constitution and government of other states (1795 [1970]: 96). This Kantian version of the peaceful federation has remained an influential vision for the international order through to our time.

The discussion of international right through the pacific inter-state system is also linked to a discussion of the ethics of the republican form of state government. Indeed, attention to the internal government of sovereign states is a key element of analysis of the international system is the concern of the First Definitive Article in *Perpetual Peace*: that 'the Civil Constitution of Every State shall be Republican' (1795 [1970]: 99). Kant's account of the just inter-state system therefore includes an account of the state units of that system. In the language of international relations theory, Kant combines a second-image analysis of the sovereign state that is combined with a third-image analysis of the international system (Waltz, 1954). Attention to the impact on inter-state relations of the internal governmental form of the state units has inspired much of the interesting literature on the 'liberal peace' (Doyle, 1983) and on liberal theories international relations that connect the nature of inter-state relations to the domestic structure of sovereign states involved (Moravscik, 1997).

Even more impressively for analysis of contemporary transnational relations, Kant's account of international right is paired with an account of cosmopolitan right, in which he attends to the moral obligations due to individuals. This cosmopolitan analysis is a powerful reminder that obligations of right are not limited to those of, or owed by, states, but also by and to the individuals who are affected by social relations in an inter-connected world. The *Perpetual Peace* essay moves immediately and strikingly from the discussion of the high politics of the inter-state order in the Second Definitive Article, to a discussion at a seemingly humble scale of the right of hospitality in the Third Definitive Article. Thus the discussion moves dramatically from a discussion of issues of war and peace, to issues of proper treatment of strangers and foreigners.

8.3.2 The cosmopolitan right of hospitality

The juxtaposition of issues of hospitality with respect to strangers with issues of the republican form of states and pacific inter-state relations is almost startling. The cosmopolitan right clearly is a form of ethical constraint and limit on nation-states, even republican ones. As a matter of justice, a society is not free to treat foreigners as the enemy.

In addressing cosmopolitan right, Kant wrote within a long, rich tradition of thinking about hospitality, including Greek, Roman, Hebraic, and Christian traditions (Derrida, 2001: 16–20). The Third Definitive Article entitled 'Cosmopolitan Right shall be limited to conditions of Universal Hospitality' (Kant, 1795 [1970]: 105) provides for the 'right not be treated with hostility when he arrives on someone else's territory' (1795 [1970]: 105). The stranger can be turned away, so long as this does not cause his or her death, and the stranger cannot claim the 'right of a guest to be entertained'. But the stranger, so long as he or she is acting peaceably, can claim a 'right of resort'. What is anticipated here is the simple consequence of a limited terrestrial surface of the globe, a condition that dictates that humans must 'necessarily tolerate one another's company'. The result is a limited right:

> ...this natural right of hospitality, i.e. the right of strangers, does not extend beyond those conditions which make it possible to *attempt* to enter into relations with the native inhabitants. In this way, continents distant from each

> other can enter into peaceful mutual relations which may eventually be regulated by public laws, thus bringing the human race nearer and nearer to a cosmopolitan constitution.
>
> (Kant, 1795 [1970]: 106, emphasis in original)

The limited content of such a cosmopolitan right of hospitality might seem a very poor one. These rights of foreigners would not seem to include any rights of positive assistance let alone anything like rights of citizenship. Similarly, a limited conception of justice might limit the extent of obligations owed to foreigners or to foreign societies, such as claims for distributive justice. However, especially as the number of situations increase in which 'strangers' are presented in foreign lands, for example by globalization in which physical movements of peoples (migrants, travellers, merchants) increase and other forms of social connection across borders intensify (communication, shared ecological concerns), what might seem like modest rights and obligations, may take on much broader import (Beitz, 1979).

Kant's discussion of cosmopolitan right of hospitality through the presence of the stranger in foreign lands anticipates the basis for a significant number of transnational economic transactions of today, whether sale or purchase of goods by a merchant, offering of services (including employment), or the foundation for more sustained business relations, such as investment relations. This is an especially important point for thinking about transnational economic relations, and we will return to it below. Before doing so, though, it is important to see that the ethical limits on the cosmopolitan right of hospitality that Kant describes structure the kind of transnational economic relations that can be considered just.

8.3.3 The justice of limits on the cosmopolitan right of hospitality

Before focusing further on the connection of cosmopolitan right of hospitality and transnational economic law, it is important to note that the limits placed by Kant on the cosmopolitan right of hospitality have a distinct ethical justification.

The frame of international and cosmopolitan right is a reflection of the sociological reality for Kant in which the contemporary sovereign state system was already well established. To use the influential frame provided by Derrida, the discussion of hospitality is one of conditional rather than unconditional hospitality (Derrida, 2001: 20–3). As Derrida observes, Kant immediately imposed a careful limit on the universal right of hospitality, in recognition of the sociological reality that 'All this, even the Soil upon which it lies, is no longer soil pure and simple, and, even if founded upon the earth, must not be unconditionally accessible to all comers.' (Derrida, 2001: 21.) As a consequence, the right of hospitality is restricted to a right of visitation and not a right of residence. Furthermore, hospitality is interpreted to be about the nature of public space, and so 'hospitality, whether public or private, is dependent on and controlled by the law and the state police' (2001: 22). Elsewhere, Derrida sees Kant's analysis of a conditional right as the almost inevitable result of the 'juridicality of his discourse, to the inscription in the law of this principle of hospitality whose infinite idea should resist the last itself' (Derrida, 2000: 71). Other than in a 'pure subjective morality' (2000: 69), the law will always require something less. At best,

> It is a question of knowing how to transform and improve the law, and of knowing whether this improvement is possible in a historical space which takes place *between* the Law of an unconditional hospitality, offered *à priori* to every other, to all newcomers *whoever they may be*, and *the* conditional laws of a right to hospitality, without which *The* unconditional Law of hospitality would be in danger of remaining a pious and irresponsible desire, without form and without potency, and of even being perverted at any moment.
> (Derrida, 2001: 22–3, emphasis in original)

The limits partly result from the recognition that the system of sovereign states now frames the possibilities for sociability of world humanity; in particular Kant sees the republican form as a form of politics consistent with principles of justice. But there also are separate ethical justifications for the limits on cosmopolitan rights. First, the system of republican sovereign states can be understood as superior to a unified world government whose expanded range would lose its dynamism and potentially lapse into 'soulless despotism' (Kant, 1795 [1970]: 113). In contrast, a peaceful international system will avoid universal despotism through 'an equilibrium of forces and a most vigorous rivalry' (1795 [1970]: 114).

More impressive in the economic context, the limited cosmopolitan right is expressly justified in light of the abuse of alleged cosmopolitan and international rights that is found in earlier writings on international law and ethics. In particular, Kant clearly rejected the expansive interpretation of a cosmopolitan right of hospitality as a right to trade or a right to occupation. Kant accepted that a host society could have ethical reasons for refusing to trade with a foreigner. In contrast, the leading imperial states identified the unwillingness of foreign societies to permit free commerce into a just cause upon which a state could impose violence.

In this respect, Kant strongly distinguishes his views from the existing tradition of European international lawyers, Grotius, Pufendorf, Vattel, and the other 'sorry comforters' already having been dismissed as at best providing apologetic justification for military aggression (Kant, 1795 [1970], 103). Kant's conception of cosmopolitan right can be contrasted, for example, with how Vitoria moves from a nominal respect for the rights of the Indians to the right to impose violence and occupation. From a basic proposed duty to 'behave hospitably to strangers', Vitoria (1991: 278) moves to rights of strangers to trade and to proselytize, which in turn become substantive components of the law of nations. From there, Vitoria reasons that:

> [I]f the barbarians attempt to deny the Spaniards in these matters which I have described as belonging to the law of nations (*ius gentium*), that is to say from trading and the rest, the Spaniards ought to first remove any cause of provocation by reasoning and persuasion.... But if reasoning fails to win the acquiescence of the barbarians, and they insist on replying with violence, the Spaniards may defend themselves, and do everything needful for their own safety. It is lawful to meet force with force.
>
> (Vitoria, 1991: 281–2)

The alleged violations of the law of nations involved when a society refuses to be open to trade and other contact with the representatives of Spain become the basis for the application of the full force of sovereign sanctions, including war and occupation (Anghie, 2005: 21, 23).

Kant expressly contrasts his concept of cosmopolitan right with such expansive claims:

> If we compare with this ultimate end the *inhospitable* conduct of the civilised states of our continent, especially the commercial states, the injustice which they display in *visiting* foreign countries and peoples (which in their case is the same as *conquering* them) seems appallingly great.
>
> (Kant, 1795 [1970]: 106, emphasis in original)

Kant rejects such conquest, as for example in the Americas, and notes that countries such as China and Japan, 'having experience of such guests, have wisely placed restrictions on them' (1795 [1970]: 106–7).

Claims of a more expansive cosmopolitan right could be used as the ethical justification for disproportionate and self-serving interference in the affairs of other societies, the most obvious of which are found in the history of imperialism. A similar concern lies behind the principle of non-intervention in public international law, and also forms the basis for international right in Kant's pacific federation of republican states. The Fifth Preliminary Article of the *Perpetual Peace* provides that: 'No state shall forcibly interfere in the constitution and government of another state' (1795 [1970]: 96). The principle of non-intervention would become central to internationalist schemes for international order (e.g. Mill, 1859), and in contemporary international law instruments such as Article 2(4) of the United Nations Charter.

A similar respect for the legitimate sovereign authority of republican and pacific states is paired with the limits in *Perpetual Peace* on the content of cosmopolitan right of strangers with respect to host states. The resulting conditional right is subject to the reality but also the legitimate authority of the nation-state. The result is to create a consensual frame, in which the host state's consent is needed for anything beyond not treating the stranger as an enemy. In Kant's work, and in many later cosmopolitan texts, we can see that this consensual foundation can be the basis for extensive transnational economic relations.

8.4 THE COSMOPOLITAN VISION OF INTERNATIONAL COMMERCIAL RELATIONS

The Kantian account of cosmopolitan and international right provides the basis for ethical consideration of foreigners while still acknowledging the social reality of the state and its centrality to advancing concerns of justice. As a matter of justice, Kant accepts that sovereignty is foundational to social life, and yet the stranger need not be viewed as a Schmittian enemy. This is a cosmopolitan vision attentive to the ethical import of sovereign states, but also attentive to values and possibilities beyond the nation-state frame. Moreover, by attending to the individual as bearer of cosmopolitan rights, Kant's text draws attention to the potential ethical significance of more varieties of individual interaction across borders, a more positive sense of the possible social interaction below and across the state level.

The Kantian conception of a limited cosmopolitan right of hospitality is particularly useful for conceiving a vision of cosmopolitan economic relations based on consent. In particular, it suggests that international trade and investment does not occur as a matter of right, but rather as the voluntary recognition of societies that there are potential conditions of mutual and cooperative benefit that are possible through economic interaction. Such relations also depend on individual choices to enter into such cross-border economic relations. No trade or investment is mandated by Kant's description of cosmopolitan justice, but rather it is enabled by an openness to the benefits of cosmopolitan interaction. Kant's text anticipates that the benefits of cosmopolitan ties need not be mandated because such benefits would be transparently clear to both individuals and states in a global society.

8.4.1 Cooperative benefit among societies and among individuals

First, individual parties can benefit because of the distinct strengths or comparative virtues of different parties and different parts of the world. For Kant, the variety and diversity of peoples and production is both the condition of division but also one of the main vehicles of peaceful relations among peoples through which peace will be ultimately achieved (e.g. Kant, 1795 [1970]: 111). This is an old concept, for example, associated with Seneca, and cited in Grotius (1609 [2004]: 11).

The notion of productive differences among peoples also is the basis for the concepts of mutual benefit underlying key concepts of international trade theory such as theories of absolute or comparative advantage (e.g. Irwin, 1996: 75–98; Trebilcock and Howse, 2005: 1–4). Theories of comparative advantage are premised on the mutual benefits that arise from the efficient specialization of each party on the production in which it has the comparative advantage allowing for an increase in overall total production then available for international trade. The liberal trade prescription for removing national barriers to international trade, such as tariffs, quotas, or discriminatory regulations, is premised on the recognition by national societies that what could be beneficial to individuals from trade is also beneficial for societies overall. The consented to restrictions on such national barriers to open trade and full specialization and exchange are the subject of the core commitments of international trade treaties such as the General Agreement on Tariffs and Trade.

The benefits of a vigorous competition in the economic realm can be seen as a further justification for liberal cosmopolitan trade. Exposure to the widest market competition will push producers to provide the most efficient range of products and forms of production. The competitive market becomes a tool for limiting, at least to some extent, private power and private monopolies by exposure to competition from other private producers. Of course, achieving such benefits from competition require careful institutionalization – in both the domestic and international contexts – something that we will need to return to below.

From a perspective that emphasizes the cooperative benefits of economic relations of foreign markets and parties, some state measures appear to be disadvantageous constraints. In particular, measures such as border tariffs or quantitative restrictions can be viewed as arbitrary restraints on otherwise mutually beneficial transactions, done for distinctly parochial reasons. The defence of such restrictions consistent with cosmopolitanism can be made, e.g. to raise necessary national revenue for valuable social programmes, but the cosmopolitan perspective requires that these justifications be provided.

The economic benefits of consensual trade are further augmented for Kant and liberal internationalists by the potential contribution of such trade to reducing the threat of armed international conflict. Partly, the arguments of cooperative benefit from open trade replace conceptions of trade as a zero-sum game, in which one's state's gain must necessarily be another state's loss. More optimistically, cross-border economic interests in trade would be a force to avoid the disruptive impact of war; in Kant's text, indeed, the spirit of commerce, 'which cannot exist side by side with war' is identified as the most important social cause of peace (1795 [1970]:114). This optimism about the potential pacific effects of international trade persists through a variety of liberal internationalist traditions (Nye, 1988: 245–7). For example, Mill (1909 [1987]: 582), a sophisticated economist including with respect to international trade theory, observes in his leading text of political economy that:

> commerce first taught nations to see with good will the wealth and prosperity of one another. Before, the patriot, unless sufficiently advanced in culture to feel the world his country, wished all countries weak, poor, and ill-governed, but his own: he now sees in their wealth and progress a direct source of wealth and progress to his own country. It is commerce which is rapidly rendering war obsolete, by strengthening and multiplying the personal interests which are in natural opposition to it. And it may be said without exaggeration that the great extent and rapid increase of international trade, in

> being the principal guarantee of the peace of the world, is the great permanent security for the uninterrupted progress of the ideas, the institutions, and the character of the human race.

This connection to broader issues of international order is an important part of the rhetorical power of liberal trade for international lawyers, for international law is a discipline for which the inter-war period's failures are linked very much to inter-state competition in both the political and economic order, leading to linked problems of war and depression (Wai, 2001a: 155–78).

8.4.2 Commercial cosmopolitanism as a cooperative benefit for individuals

While the mutual benefits of open trade are typically cast in terms of the benefits to social welfare in each trading state, the mutual benefits of economic relations arise out of individual transactions in which individual parties, even if from different societies, realize it is in their self-interest to look beyond a parochial frame, and appreciate that the cosmopolitan society offers an expanded range of productive possibilities.

Beyond the cooperative but instrumental benefits of cosmopolitan trade, the positive conception of cosmopolitan relations in Kant can also be related to a kind of transnational transactional ideal. Economic and social engagement with foreigners can be viewed as an important expression of human freedom and choice. Sen's influential framework of development as freedom, for example, argues that the denial of economic opportunities through arbitrary controls can be a source of injustice in itself, including barriers created by religion, caste, status institutions of slavery, or, the state (Sen, 1999: chapter 1). Sen notes that this defence of the market 'does not depend on the efficiency or other consequential analysis of the market mechanism; it turns simply on the importance of freedom of exchange or transaction without let or hindrance' (1999: 25–6).

The negative critique of national restrictions on international transactions can also be joined to something more positive, a reaching out towards the stranger and the creation of transnational relations. Economic cooperation with foreigners, especially when a longer-term relation is formed, can be celebrated as an exemplary cosmopolitanism that overcomes parochial prejudices. Such transnational economic relations can have a creatively transgressive element: a curiosity and openness to other national traditions, a refusal of local customs or regulations, the effort to create relations in spite of cultural or political barriers. Of course, this kind of transgression can generate the backlash that has been the basis for many kinds of reaction against the rootless cosmopolitan, from productively conservative to genocidal (Appiah, 2006: xvi–xvii). But perhaps for that very reason, transnational relations can be viewed as a creative contribution to overcoming national or local prejudices. The spirit of exploration and genuine curiosity in other cultures often travels with the spirit of commercial self-interest. Even if Kant himself was not free of civilizational prejudices of his time that would limit his capacity to appreciate the full benefits of such cultural interaction (Harvey, 2000), the cosmopolitan framework that he sets out is consistent with a more positive view of inter-cultural contact.

The celebration of such cultural cosmopolitanism in transnational economic relations has expanded to new economic benefits that arise not just from the embrace of the foreign, but rather the creation of a transnational relation – whether one-off or more durable – in which there is positive mixing of influences. 'Mighty is the mongrel' proclaims not just the novelist Rushdie, but business writers attributing to cosmopolitanism the source of competitive advantage in the contemporary global economy (Zachary, 2000: ix). Foreign direct investment of various kinds has as one motivation this effort to benefit from the mixing of expertise and resources of different national systems. International business writers identify that such ongoing cosmopolitan contact can lead to creative forms of business organization. For example, one leading text of economic globalization emphasized the productive benefits of the mixing of global expertise and of genuine collaborative global strategic alliances, rather than complete takeover and control by one national partner (Ohmae, 1990 [1999]: 121).

8.4.3 International contract as an exemplary cosmopolitan legal instrument

In transnational economic law, the creative, positive vision of commercial cosmopolitanism is perhaps best represented by the international contract. Contracts are the key practical instrument through which parties to international economic transactions not only make sense out of, but also creatively construct, the complex multiplicity of laws and norms of transnational economic law (Vagts, 1998). Whether a one-off sale of goods or a longer-term investment transaction, parties can set out customized norms to govern their relationship, and in so doing they can be understood to be engaged in a creative and constitutive act of transnational self-regulation and governance. Although contracts mostly contain specific substantive terms, contract can also be more broadly viewed as concerned with the self-government of the relations between parties (Collins, 1999). For example, contracts can include a wide variety of clauses that can be viewed as procedural regulation of a relationship, including provisions to deal with deposits, inspections, repairs, external monitoring, and dispute settlement. Such provision are contained in many contracts for the international sale of goods (for example, the ICC Model Sales Contract) and in the contracts that support the many surrounding kinds of transactions that facilitate international sales, such as payment (for example, a letter of credit agreement), carriage (for example, a carriage contract as evidenced in a bill of lading) or insurance (for example, the marine insurance policy). Contract also plays this role in the regulation and governance of international investment relationships, such as in the voting, management, and dispute settlement provisions of a joint venture agreement.

In settling on these norms, parties to international business contracts can draw on a wide array of different norms to construct special, hybrid regulatory orders for their relationships. The contract can include specifically negotiated and customized provisions covering the particulars of the relationship of the parties, in as much detail as they choose. This customization can also extend to the incorporation and use of a wide variety of established norms. For example, international contracts can incorporate particular state norms (e.g. sale of goods legislation) or adapt them as they see fit. Parties can also bring into their relation sets of background or default norms developed by non-governmental associations, such as the norms of various shipping associations with respect to maritime insurance, or the International Chamber of Commerce's Incoterms for delivery terms in international sales of goods or its Uniform Customs and Practice for Documentary Credits. Through contractual choice, parties can also choose provisions of international treaties, such as the Vienna Convention on Contracts for the International Sale of Goods, even when such provisions might not otherwise apply to the business relationship. Finally, parties to a contract now increasingly have the authority to exercise their party autonomy over the governing law and the mechanism for authoritative dispute settlement of their international relationship (Nygh, 1999). Choice of law clauses, forum selection clauses, and arbitration clauses all highlight the extent to which acceptance of party autonomy through international contract may have expanded such that contract can provide the basis for a kind of autonomous, distinct legal order, perhaps even a form of global law without a state (Teubner, 1997).

8.4.4 Commercial cosmopolitanism and the challenge of transnational regulation

What can be hidden in the exemplary form of the international contract is the mutually constitutive interaction between private ordering and other legal orders, in particular the delicate balance between private ordering and state legal systems, particularly systems of private law (Wai, 2008: 120–1). The degree and nature of state oversight of private ordering has varied across time and jurisdiction (Cutler, 2005). In the past, transnational arrangements existed without, and often in spite of, state laws. The rise of the modern state and attendant formal legal orders involved the incorporation and integration of many private customary norms into state laws. In the contemporary context, however, this linkage seems to be loosening again as the delicate balance struck by state laws with respect to international commercial transactions increasingly includes an approach to sustaining party choice with respect to governance by foreign state norms and certain non-state social orders (Nygh, 1999).

Although states may have good cosmopolitan policy reasons for increasing support for party autonomy in international transactions, this trend should not disguise the fact that the cosmopolitan virtues of the contract depend on a broader institutional setting. If contract can be viewed as private parties constructing a customized form of self-governance that could blend and mix, while adapting, plural forms of public and private norms, one should nonetheless attend to the relationship of such private ordering through contracts to the institutional support and background rules of state systems. The observance of contractual obligations depends on the expectation of parties that state systems will not block and indeed will support enforcement of obligations in contracts.

The central role of law in constituting the terrain for private ordering is that it seeks to balance the promotion of the advantages of private ordering, while also structuring the ground rules for this ordering. Furthermore, such background state supports also are in place to defend policy values that go beyond party autonomy to concerns about regulatory goals in relation to third parties (and the public interest). Such considerations are well understood in the standard framework of contract law, that provides the underpinnings for both the support for but also the limits on freedom of contract (Trebilcock, 1993).

The need for law both to protect one or other party to a transaction, as well as third party interests, is surely one of the lessons of the current financial crisis and its aftermath. Markets such as derivatives markets are not self-regulating, especially when parties are able to externalize costs or risks to third parties (Stiglitz, 2010). Even savvy investors, such as the financial institutions that were counterparties on derivatives transactions, seemed unable or unwilling to protect themselves adequately, whether because of failed forecasting models, bad incentives, or faulty information.

8.4.4.1 As between the parties

State contract laws that support both domestic and international contract traditionally include limits on freedom of contract intended to better protect potential parties to contract. For example, contract law considers as problematic situations of incorrect or asymmetric information (mistake or misrepresentation), and situations of unequal power (such as duress, undue influence, or unconscionabilty) (Trebilcock, 1993). Social psychology and behavioural economics have suggested that, even with adequate information and without duress, parties sometimes make decisions other than in their own interest (Ramsay, 2007: chapter 2). From an efficiency perspective as between the parties, these are situations that are of concern for all contractual provisions including the situation of jurisdiction, choice of law, and arbitration clauses (Miller, 1999: 359–60).

For example, forum selection clauses, arbitration clauses, and choice of laws clauses may need to be subject to special scrutiny with respect to concerns about poor information, unequal bargaining power, or irrational choice (Nygh, 1999). Such clauses are too often hidden in agreements, and not carefully considered by all parties to contracts. They are often found in standard form contracts or often in the boiler-plate section of agreements. And yet their significance is potentially great, dramatically changing the dispute-settlement procedures and the set of applicable laws. These are clauses that may not accord with the normal expectations of parties with respect to the relative roles of domestic law and courts, foreign law and courts, and non-state norms and dispute settlement. In that context, the scrutiny to be applied to such clauses might be similar to contractual doctrines related to limitation of liability and exclusion clauses, such as interpretation *contra proferentum* or with particular requirements to draw the clauses to the attention of the other party. Limits on contractual autonomy can also be applied across-the-board to certain kinds of transnational relations. For example, labour and consumer contracts are excluded from the rules otherwise emphasizing party autonomy over applicable law in contracts in the European Union.[7]

8.4.4.2 Third party interests

In addition to the role of law in providing protective pre-conditions for parties to transactions, the contractual ideal also only makes sense in relation to an institutional configuration that attends to the protection of third parties and the public interest when considered in the context of the broader institutional setting of other forms of public law and other forms of private law (such as tort or fiduciary obligations). It is this side of transnational economic law that most clearly needs development in order to achieve ideals of cosmopolitan justice.

Contract law has not traditionally dealt with such interests, leaving the primary tools for such regulation with other institutions, or other kinds of law. The potentially harmful effects of behaviour enabled by contractual relations are often left to other areas of private law, in particular tort law, and to public law, in such obvious fields as competition policy, environmental regulation, or tax regulation. Traditional doctrines of contract law are concerned that contractual agreements are not themselves a tool of illegality or undermining of these other kinds of regulatory law. In the context of international contracts, this important limiting context for party autonomy is most evident in the basic principle that no domestic private laws will support party autonomy that seeks to ignore the mandatory laws of other relevant jurisdictions (Nygh, 1999: chapter 9).

But more may be needed in the transnational context. Particular risks associated with problems of transnational regulatory cooperation include regulatory gaps and regulatory competition in a sovereign state order in which there is no paramount authority and where collective action problems can arise among sovereign regulatory authorities (Ruggie, 2007: para. 82; Wai, 2002: 250–8). In the absence of such protections, individual cosmopolitan freedoms can be abused. For

7 Regulation (EC) No 593/2008 of the European Parliament and of the Council of 1 June 2008 on the law applicable to contractual obligations (Rome I).

example, Aihwa Ong documents some of the negative aspects of contemporary 'flexible citizenship' involving 'strategies and effects of mobile managers, technocrats, and professionals who seek to both circumvent *and* benefit from different nation-state regimes by selecting different sites for investments, work, and family relation' (Ong, 1998: 136). Ong understands that this is not all for the good, for some overseas elites demonstrate a lack of concern for any particular community, and the complex flexible networks also occasion injustice such as gender subordination and labour violence. In this respect, she notes that flexible citizenship may rather simply be an 'expression of habitus that is finely tuned to the turbulence of late capitalism' (Ong, 1998: 157).

The goal then for those working on transnational economic law is to encourage the development of plural systems of transnational economic regulation that parallel the growth in the institutional supports for facilitation of economic transactions. The growth of private ordering devices – such as consumer campaigns, investor pressure or reputational campaigns by civil society groups – exemplifies this kind of transnational regulation. However, the tools needed to address the regulatory goals may also require state action that will assist in such private ordering to protect third parties. Facilitative substantive and procedural reform in private law to enable transnational tort litigation is a good example of the kind of institutional supports that can strengthen transnational private ordering, and increase incentives for businesses to undertake and comply with voluntary corporate standards. The goals of cosmopolitan justice may also require the most traditional kinds of state public laws and regulations, as well as international treaties and diplomatic cooperation.

The complicated interaction among normative orders may also mean that limits in facilitative private laws would have to be considered in order to best protect against spillover harms on transnational regulatory concerns. One example is that allowing party autonomy to move contractual litigation to designated jurisdictions, and especially to confidential commercial arbitration, reduces the public knowledge of the nature of those contractual disputes (Wai, 2002: 262–3). The result might be a loss of the public information that is useful to regulators responsible for enforcement of public laws or regulations. Likewise, private law litigation can often produce information that is helpful to activists or advocates seeking to influence corporate behaviour in other contexts. Perhaps more serious, it may be that simply facilitating the sense among transnational economic actors of being outside or separate from any particular national legal regime may create a consciousness among those business actors that invites the loss of the public values associated with thicker identification with a well-developed set of national institutions (Wai, 2002: 263). In this respect, Teubner's account of global law without a state can act as a cautionary warning. As normative systems, such as merchant relations, separate from state systems, system-specific assumptions and biases can frame, for example, adjudication in the context of uncertainty or the exercise of administrative discretion. For example, private dispute resolution may be less inclined to consider matters of either domestic or transnational public policy.[8] A business law dispute heard in a state court with state laws in the background might be more attentive than an arbitration tribunal with *lex mercatoria* in the background as to how a contractual relation was related to human rights or consumer concerns.

Therefore, while public and private laws of various kinds can be used to protect third party interests, the tools to deal with such kinds of impact on third party and public interests may also require restraints on contractual autonomy in transnational contracts. What seems clear is that trade-offs involve real conflicts among important cosmopolitan policy values, and the element of transnational self-governance remains a significant, but not the sole, ideal for transnational contract law.

8.5 COSMOPOLITAN JUSTICE THROUGH PLURAL INSTITUTIONAL FORMS

There are good reasons consistent with cosmopolitan justice for individuals to choose to engage in cross-border economic connections. But it is also clear that the perspective of cosmopolitan justice recognizes the crucial role of the legitimate state in defining and delimiting the cosmopolitan rights of individuals to form or benefit from such connections. States may act consistently with cosmopolitan justice when they restrict such cosmopolitan right in order to protect the rights of others or the general social interest. The cosmopolitan ideal of voluntary self-regulation and customized governance is situated in a broader context of institutional forms that address policy goals equally consistent with cosmopolitan justice such as protecting third party interests and regulating relations between the parties themselves.

The pluralism of transnational economic law is therefore not inconsistent with the goals of cosmopolitan justice, and will likely be required to achieve the full benefits of cosmopolitanism. The mix of laws that could achieve cosmopolitan justice clearly includes the laws of states, which continue to have legitimacy for the social purposes of various citizens. It also includes public international law treaties intended to constrain some of the excesses of sovereign measures and provide for inter-state cooperation with respect to shared objects of regulatory concern, including the transnational behaviour of private actors. The mix will also include various forms of transnational private ordering, whether of the facilitative kind, such as norms of the *lex mercatoria* or of international contracts, or of the regulatory kind, such as voluntary codes or standards developed by transnational civil society groups. The institutional form to achieve cosmopolitan justice in the global economy will therefore be a blend of traditional and novel, of individual, state, and international sources, but all attentive to both facilitation and regulation of cosmopolitan connections.

8 For a good example of the sceptical and narrow approach to transnational public policy among arbitrators, see Pryles (2007).

Bibliography

Anghie, A. (2005) *Imperialism, Sovereignty, and the Making of International Law*, Cambridge: Cambridge University Press.

Appiah, K. A. (2006) *Cosmopolitanism: Ethics in a World of Strangers*, London: Penguin Books.

Arendt, H. (1965 [1977]) *Eichmann in Jerusalem: A Report on the Banality of Evil*, revised and enlarged edition, New York: Penguin.

Barenberg, M. (2008) 'Toward A Democratic Model of Transnational Labour Monitoring', in B. Bercusson and C. Estlund (eds), *Regulating Labour in the Wake of Globalisation: New challenges, new institutions*, Oxford: Hart.

Baubock, R. (2003) 'Political Community Beyond the Sovereign State, Supranational Federalism, and Transnational Minorities', in S. Vertovec and R. Cohen (eds), *Conceiving Cosmopolitanism: Theory, Context, and Practice*, Oxford: Oxford University Press.

Beitz, C. (1979) *Political Theory and International Relations*, Princeton, NJ: Princeton University Press.

Benhabib, S. (2006) *Another Cosmopolitanism*, ed. Robert Post with commentaries by J. Waldron, B. Honig and W. Kymlicka, Oxford: Oxford University Press.

Braithwaite, J. and Drahos, P. (2000) *Global Business Regulation*, Cambridge: Cambridge University Press.

Calhoun, C. (2003) 'The Class Consciousness of Frequent Travellers: Towards a Critique of Actually Existing Cosmopolitanism', in S. Vertovec and R. Cohen (eds), *Conceiving Cosmopolitanism: Theory, Context, and Practice*, Oxford: Oxford University Press.

Collins, H. (1999) *Regulating Contracts*, Oxford: Oxford University Press.

Cotterrell, R. (2009) 'Spectres of Transnationalism: Changing Terrains of Sociology of Law', *Journal of Law and Society* 36: 481–500.

Cutler, C. (2005) *Private Power and Global Authority*, Cambridge: Cambridge University Press.

Dalhuisen, J. H. (2006) 'Legal Orders and their Manifestation: The Operation of the International Commercial and Financial Legal Order and its Lex Mercatoria', *Berkeley Journal of International Law* 24: 129–91.

Davis, K., Kingsbury, B., and Merry, S. E. (2010) 'Indicators as a Technology of Global Governance', NYU Institute for International Law and Justice, Global Administrative Law Working Paper 10/2.

Derrida, J. (2000) *Of Hospitality: Anne Dufourmantelle Invites Jacques Derrida to Respond*, Stanford, CA: Stanford University Press.

—— (2001) *On Cosmopolitanism and Forgiveness*, London: Routledge.

Doyle, M. (1983) 'Kant, Liberal Legacies, and Foreign Affairs', Parts One and Two, *Philosophy and Public Affairs* 12: 205–35 and 323–53.

Fine, R. (2007) *Cosmopolitanism*, London: Routledge.

Friedman, T. (1999) *The Lexus and the Olive Tree*, New York: Farrar, Straus Giroux.

Goode, R., Kronke, H. and McKendrick, E. (eds) (2007) *Transnational Commercial Law: Text, Cases, and Materials*, Oxford: Oxford University Press.

Grotius, H. (1609 [2004]) *The Free Sea*, trans. R. Hakluyt, ed. D. Armitage, Indianapolis: Liberty Fund.

Habermas, J. (1996) *Between Facts and Norms*, trans. W. Regh, Cambridge MA: MIT Press.

—— (2006) *The Divided West*, Oxford: Polity.

Hardt, M. and Negri, A. (2000) *Empire*, Cambridge MA: Harvard University Press.
—— (2004) *Multitude: War and Democracy in an Age of Empire*, New York: Penguin Books.
—— (2009) *Commonwealth*, Cambridge MA: Harvard University Press.
Harvey, D. (2000) 'Cosmopolitanism and the Banality of Geographical Evils', *Public Culture*, 12: 529–64.
Irwin, D. A. (1996) *Against the Tide: An Intellectual History of Free Trade*, Princeton, NJ: Princeton University Press.
Kant, I. (1795 [1970]) 'Perpetual Peace: A Philosophical Sketch', in *Kant's Political Writings* (ed. and intro. Hans Reiss), Cambridge: Cambridge University Press.
Keck, M. and Sikkink, K. (1998) *Activists Beyond Borders: Advocacy Networks in International Politics*, Ithaca: Cornell University Press.
Klein, N. (2000) *No Logo: Taking Aim at the Brand Bullies*, Toronto: Knopf Canada.
Koskenniemmi, M. (1989 [2005]) *From Apology to Utopia: The Structure of International Legal Argument*, reissued with new epilogue, Cambridge: Cambridge University Press.
Mill, J. S. (1859 [1984]) 'A Few Words on Non-Intervention', in J. M. Robson (ed.), *Collected Works of John Stuart Mill*, vol. XXI, Toronto: University of Toronto Press.
—— (1909 [1987]) *Principles of Political Economy*, London: Longmans, reprinted 1987 by London: Augustus Kelley.
Miller, G. (1999) 'Choice of Law as a Precommitment Device', in F. H. Buckley (ed.), *The Fall and Rise of Freedom of Contract*, Durham: Duke University Press.
Moravscik, A. (1997) 'Taking Preferences Seriously: A Liberal Theory of International Politics', *International Organization* 51: 513–53.
Murray, C. et al. (eds) (2007) *Schmitthoff's Export Trade: The Law and Practice of International Trade* (11th edn), London: Thomson Reuters.
Nye, J. (1988) 'Neorealism and Neoliberalism', *World Politics* 40: 235–51.
Nygh, P. (1999) *Autonomy in International Contracts*, Oxford: Oxford University Press.
Ohmae, K. (1990 [1999]) *The Borderless World: Power and Strategy in the Interlinked Economy*, revised edn, New York: Harper.
Ong, A. (1998) 'Flexible Citizenship among Chinese Cosmopolitans', in P. Cheah and B. Robbins (eds), *Cosmopolitics: Thinking and Feeling beyond the Nation*, Minneapolis, MN: University of Minnesota Press.
Pogge, T. (1992) 'Cosmopolitanism and Sovereignty', *Ethics* 103: 48–75.
Pryles, M. (2007) 'Reflections on Transnational Public Policy', *Journal of International Arbitration* 24: 1–8.
Ramsay, I. (2007) *Consumer Law and Policy: Text and Materials on Regulating Consumer Markets* (2nd edn), Oxford: Hart.
Ruggie, J. (2007) Report of the Special Representative of the Secretary-General on the issue of human rights and transnational corporations and other business enterprises, 'Business and Human Rights: Mapping International Standards of Responsibility and Accountability for Corporate Acts', UN Doc. A/HRC/035 (9 February 2007).
Sassen, S. (1996) *Losing Control? Sovereignty in an Age of Globalization*, New York: Columbia University Press.
Scott, C. and Wai, R. (2004) 'Transnational Governance of Corporate Conduct through the Migration of Human Rights Norms: The Potential Contribution of Transnational Private Litigation', in C. Joerges, I-J. Sand and G. Teubner (eds), *Transnational Governance and Constitutionalism*, Oxford: Hart.
Sen, A. (1999) *Development as Freedom*, New York: Knopf.

Singer, J. (1989) 'Real Conflicts', *Boston University Law Review* 69: 1–129.
Sklair, L. (2000) *The Transnational Capitalist Class*, Oxford: Blackwell.
Slaughter, A. M. (2004) *A New World Order*, Princeton, NJ: Princeton University Press.
Snyder, F. (1999) 'Governing Economic Globalisation: Global Legal Pluralism and European Law', *European Law Journal* 5: 334–74.
Stiglitz, J. (2010) *Freefall: America, free markets, and the sinking of the world economy*, New York: Norton.
Teubner, G. (ed.) (1997) *Global Law without a State*, Aldershot: Dartmouth.
Trebilcock, M. (1993) *The Limits of Freedom of Contract*, Cambridge MA: Harvard University Press.
Trebilcock, M. and Howse, R. (2005) *The Regulation of International Trade* (3rd edn), London: Routledge.
Vagts, D. (1998) *Transnational Business Problems* (2nd edn), Boston: Foundation Press.
Vertovec, S. and Cohen, R. (eds) (2003) *Conceiving Cosmopolitanism: Theory, Context, and Practice*, Oxford: Oxford University Press.
Vitoria, F. de (1991) 'On the American Indians (De Indis)', in A. R. Pagden and Jeremy Lawrence (eds), *Political Writings*, Cambridge: Cambridge University Press.
Wai, R. (2001a) 'In the Name of the International: The Supreme Court of Canada and the Internationalist Transformation of Canadian Private International Law', *Canadian Yearbook of International Law* 39: 117–209.
—— (2001b) 'The Commercial Activity Exception to Sovereign Immunity and the Boundaries of Contemporary International Legalism', in C. Scott (ed.), *Torture as Tort: Comparative Perspectives on the Development of Transnational Human Rights Litigation*, Oxford: Hart.
—— (2002) 'Transnational Liftoff and Juridical Touchdown: The Regulatory Function of Private International Law in an Era of Globalization', *Columbia Journal of Transnational Law* 40: 209–74.
—— (2006) 'Conflicts and Comity in Transnational Governance: Private International Law as Mechanism and Metaphor for the Relationship among the Plural Orders of Transnational Social Regulation', in C. Joerges and E-U. Petersmann (eds), *Constitutionalism, Multilevel Trade Governance and Social Regulation*, Oxford: Hart.
—— (2008) 'The Interlegality of Transnational Private Law', *Law and Contemporary Problems* 71: 107–27.
Waldron, J. (2006) 'Cosmopolitan Norms', in Benhabib, S., *Another Cosmopolitanism*, ed. R. Post, Oxford: Oxford University Press.
Waltz, K. (1954) *Man, the State, and War: A Theoretical Analysis*, New York: Columbia University Press.
Wuerth, I. (2009) '*Wiwa v. Shell*: The $15.5 Million Settlement', *ASIL Insight* 13(14).
Zachary, G. P. (2000) *The Global Me: New Cosmopolitans and the Competitive Edge: Picking Globalism's Winners and Losers*, New York: Public Affairs.
Zumbansen, P. (2006) 'Transational Law', in J. Smits (ed.), *Encyclopedia of Comparative Law*, London: Elgar.

Chapter 9

Cosmopolitan competition

The case of international investment

Malcolm Langford[*]

9.1 INTRODUCTION: COSMOPOLITAN ARCHETYPES

The contemporary international investment legal regime represents the perfect embodiment of commercial cosmopolitanism. Foreign investors are protected by a thickening web of bilateral (and trilateral) investment and trade treaties that provide for expansive property rights backed by secluded, fragmented but powerful and growing international arbitration. The appropriation of human rights standards and jurisprudence to disproportionately protect foreign investors plays into the critique of legal cosmopolitanism by authors such as Douzinas (2007), Kennedy (2001) and Adelman in this volume. Paradoxically, the current patchwork is partially the result of a successful 'cosmopolitanism from below' archetype championed by these critics. The world's first global internet and street campaign helped scupper the development of a multilateral investment treaty in the late 1990s, but left in place a decentred and fragmented system that seems to defy transformation.

The first half of this paper examines the problematique of the investment regime, resistance to it from below, and why it nonetheless endures. The second half asks where do we go from here, by examining four roads to reform. At its core, the paper asks whether the theologies of resistance and liberation evoked by Douzinas (2007) in his 'cosmopolitanism to come' provide a way forward for reforming the international investment regime. Or, do we need to accept, or perhaps even celebrate, the realities of political economy, and tread a more pragmatic, state-centric and transnational legal path, taming the excesses of commercial cosmopolitanism, as suggested by Wai in the previous chapter?

* Research Fellow and Director of the Socio-Economic Rights Programme, Norwegian Centre for Human Rights (NCHR), Faculty of Law, University of Oslo. The author would like to thank Khulekani Moyo for research assistance and the South Africa Programme (NCHR) for the funding of earlier research. The author is grateful to Robert Wai and Costas Douzinas for feedback after the initial presentation of this paper.

9.2 THE RISE OF THE BILATERAL INVESTMENT REGIME

In his searching critique of scholarly cosmopolitanism ambitions, Douzinas (2007: 231) decries the neo-liberal and imperial visions that continue to shape the global security, economic and political architecture. He could look no further than the sprawling and expanding pantheon of the international investment regime that protects foreign investors and permits them to directly take disputes against host states to powerful and opaque international arbitration panels. With more than 2,676 bilateral investment treaties and 279 other agreements (mostly free trade) with investment chapters (UNCTAD, 2009), it represents the perfect embodiment of capitalist or commercial cosmopolitanism. By the mid-1990s, the regime was characterized as a transnational legal order (Leubuscher, 2003) while Schneidermann (2008) describes it as international constitutionalism.[1]

Moreover, this investment regime fits the bill of being thoroughly appropriationist in terms of human rights. In the drafting of investment treaties and the development by arbitrators of legal and remedial principles, human rights are more often called upon to 'buttress' the rights of foreign investors, rather than the rights of individuals and communities affected by investor practices (see discussion in Peterson, 2009: 23–6). At the same time, duties are rarely, if ever, placed on corporations, despite the fact that their economic and political power can often exceed that of their host state.

In order to give a sense of the dizzying dimensions of this commercial cosmopolitan order, consider the recent arbitration of *Foresti and Ors v Republic of South Africa*.[2] The case was launched in 2006 by Italian shareholders of a Luxembourg-based granite-mining corporation, against the South African government for contravention of two bilateral investment treaties signed between that state and Italy and Belgium and Luxemburg in 1993 and 1995. Two arbitrators from the United States and one from the United Kingdom were appointed to conduct oral hearings in London, but the relevant legal jurisdiction for the arbitration was the Netherlands, and the arbitration secretariat operates from the World Bank's International Centre for the Settlement of Investment Disputes (ICSID) in Washington. And the arbitrators might or might not have followed legal principles developed in hundreds of publicly or confidential arbitral awards generated by

1 After making the customary point that BITs were based on the export of US property rights and takings doctrines, he interestingly suggests that these were developed within the United States only once the government-led economic development of the nineteenth century US petered out and capital-holders demanded greater protection for their new-found wealth.

2 (ICSID Case No. ARB(AF)/07/01). Marlin and R.E.D. Graniti filed their request for arbitration with the International Centre for the Settlement of Investment Disputes (ICSID) on 1 November 2006 in accordance with Article 2(1) of the Arbitration (Additional Facility) Rules of ICSID's Additional Facility. The claim was recently withdrawn: Award of 4 August 2010.

ICSID, UNCITRAL,[3] Stockholm Chamber of Commerce, the International Chamber of Commerce, the Cairo Regional Centre for International Commercial Arbitration or other arbitration centre agreed to by party consent. The supposedly fragmented international human rights system looks positively humdrum and unitarian in comparison.

Some defenders of investment treaties acknowledge the legitimacy critique (David Collier, 2009), particularly when arbitrators exhibit activism in their procedural and substantive interpretations. Some arbitration panel decisions have taken the US doctrine of takings to its elastic limits. If investments are directly or indirectly affected, the relevant international human rights and environmental duties of states are of no consequence. In *St Elena v Costa Rica*, which concerned a claim for damages for expropriation for purposes of erecting an environmental conservation area, the panel stated:

> While an expropriation or taking for environmental reasons may be classified as a taking for a public purpose, and thus may be legitimate, the fact that the property was taken for that reason does not affect either the nature of the measure of compensation to be paid for the taking. That is the purpose for protecting the environment for which the property was taken does not alter the legal character of the taking for which adequate compensation must be paid. *The international source of the obligation to protect the environment does make no difference.*[4]

Procedurally, investors have been permitted at times to invoke the substantive 'most favoured nation' principles to gain the best procedural advantages that exist in any investment treaty ratified by a host state.[5] Other arbitrators have refused to pierce the corporate veil when nationals of a country use foreign incorporation to pursue a case against their own state, and human rights principles have been surprisingly used to justify this reticence.[6] Critics (such as Leubuscher, 2003: 15) have thus maintained that the current system is 'unworkable', since:

> The settling of disputes which involve serious issues of public interest in a purely commercial, closed forum, under whatever rules the dominant party wishes to set, with no access to justice for affected populations – who are thereby deprived of any possible remedy – is not merely inequitable but also dangerous.... By narrowing disputes in such a way that entire

3 United Nations Commission on International Trade Law.

4 *Compania del Desarollo de Santa Elena S.A. v Rep. of Costa Rica*, ICSID Case No. ARB/96/1 (17 Feb 2000) (emphasis added).

5 See discussion of conflicting case law in *Investment Arbitration Reporter*, 22 January, 2009 (Vol. 2, No. 2).

6 *Micula and Ors v Romania*, ICSID Case No. ARB/05/20, Decision on Jurisdiction, 24 September 2008.

> countries are transformed into the equivalent of a private company, ICA [international commercial arbitration] reformulates public discourse as between private parties, thereby removing from discussion major public interest issues affected by contracts while at the same time making it impossible for concerned groups, or even legal professionals, to find a 'handle' to approach the problem of such contracts and to put their arguments forward.

The investment regime nonetheless maintains its steady share of defenders and is largely championed on contractualist, instrumentalist, and partly human rights grounds. Collier (2009a: 231) argues that: 'The central premise that international investment treaties are hostile to the signatory state's regulatory autonomy is vitiated by the inescapable reality that BITs [bilateral investment treaties] are voluntary exchanges between states each of which seeks to gain advantage economically for the benefit of its citizens.' Moreover, it is possible to find rulings by the tribunals that have been sympathetic to human rights concerns. In *Continental Casualty Company v Argentina*,[7] the tribunal found that a state of necessity existed (most tribunals and courts dealing with the Argentine financial crisis of 2001 at first instance have not) and acknowledged that the state needed to act to protect constitutional guarantees and fundamental liberties. In some cases, tribunals have potentially sought to defend a wider set of rights when protecting investor's rights. In *Toikios v Ukraine*, the tribunal invoked freedom of expression when it indicated that the investment treaty would be breached by the government if it sought to silence a foreign media owner.[8] Taking up such examples, Fry (2007) eagerly highlights cases where investment tribunals have referenced international human rights. However, Fry's highly selective approach to the choice of cases undermines his broader claims. He fails to engage with case law where human rights have been dismissed or ignored; and he clearly does not understand the critique of appropriationism as he lists multiple cases where investors have used human rights norms to their advantage.

The defenders of the system can however justifiably point to some movement towards a fairer equilibrium. For example, the ICSID tribunal in *Tecmed v Mexico* endorsed the use of the state's regulatory power on the basis that 'the principles that the state's exercise of its sovereign powers within the framework of its police power may cause economic damage to those subject to its powers as an administrator without entitling them to any compensation whatsoever is undisputable'.[9] It went on to shift the indirect expropriation test away from a simple consideration of the effect on investors towards a balancing test that includes the public purpose

7 ICSID Case No. ARB/03/9, Award of 5 Sept., 2008. Discussed in Peterson (2009: 30).

8 See *Toikios v Ukraine*, ICSID Case No. ARB/02/18, Award of 26 July 2007, para. 123.

9 Case No. ARB (AF)/00/2, Award of 29 May 2003, para. 119.

of the regulation, an approach which has been picked up in some recent cases (Waincymer, 2009). Moreover, some states have also acted to change the rules of the game in response to controversial decisions. UNCTAD has pointed out that the texts of recently concluded investment treaties have partly responded to the critiques (Unctad, 2007). The three NAFTA countries, which seem to have been stung by investment decisions in that domain, have amended their BITs to more precisely define 'investment', restrict the reach of indirect expropriation and fair and equitable treatment standards and include transparency in dispute settlement procedures. Critics such as Alvarez (2009: 834) similarly acknowledge that the new 2004 US Model BIT 'recalibrates the balance between the rights accorded investors and a nation's right to regulate in the public interest'.

The extent of this shift is difficult to gauge, and Alvarez (2009) concedes that it may just be tinkering at the edges. If one examines the recent stream of jurisprudence, it is clear that the anarchic eclecticism persists. For instance, some tribunals are quite critical of the deferential *Tecmed* position (Waincymer, 2009). In *Siemens AG v Argentina*, the arbitrators stated that intention behind a state's regulatory act is irrelevant for determining whether expropriation has occurred.[10] Moreover, a closer examination of the US Model BIT of 2004 does not reveal substantial or transformatory change. Extensive restrictions of performance requirements remain, while the expropriation test is simply tweaked to reflect the form of European-driven investment treaties with no clarification over whether it covers indirect expropriation.[11] Moreover, there is no move to amend earlier ratified treaties. We are thus witnessing a significant but not major shift in treaty-making and jurisprudence. If a recent publication on investment and human rights by European-based international lawyers is a guide, the mood amongst the majority of authors is one of rhetorical receptiveness to human rights as long as investors' interests are not significantly affected (Dupuy et al., 2009).

9.3 RESISTANCE AND RESIGNATION

Critique of the regime is one thing; solutions are quite another. The resulting fragmentation of the international investment agreements is partly and paradoxically the result of a successful transnational civil society struggle against the development of a *multilateral* investment agreement. Representing the world's first viral global email campaign, that culminated in the 'Battle of Seattle' outside the WTO conference, it remains the leading and seminal cosmopolitan ideal of resistance

10 ICSID Case No. ARB/No 2/08, Award, 6 February 2007.

11 Although, Schwebel (2009) is outraged over the restriction of the fair and equitable treatment standard to a test of due process.

for the anti-globalization movement and beyond. Tarrow (2005) opens his book on *The New Transnational Activism* with: 'From the "battle of Seattle" to movement against the Iraq war, the extraordinary international protests of the late 1990s and the early years of the new century suggest that something is new on this planet of ours.'

The unified draft MAI (Multilateral Agreement on Investment), first launched within the OECD in the mid-1990s and later resuscitated in the WTO, provided a catalyst for social action. The content and potential impact of international investment principles became clear once they were reduced to a single over-arching agreement. Activists were surprised and shocked to find the MAI would prevent restrictions on foreign investment in sensitive domestic sectors, prohibit performance requirements that would for example support local employment (often the justification for foreign investment) and allow companies the automatic right to confidential and international arbitration of disputes (Vallianatos, 1997). In 1999, the agreement eventually died in the embers of the street protests that raged outside the 1990 WTO Ministerial Meeting (Cohn, 2005). Developing countries blocked further progress on the draft, and continue to do so in the context of the Doha negotiations.

The Lalumière Report (1998), drawn up by MEP Lalumière for the French Prime Minister on the state of the OECD negotiations, summarizes the roots of this success:

> For the first time, one is seeing the emergence of a global civil society represented by NGOs which are often based in several states and communicate beyond their frontiers. This evolution is doubtless irreversible. On one hand, organisations representing civil society have become aware of the consequences of international economic negotiations. They are determined to leave their mark on them.
>
> Furthermore, the development of the internet has shaken up the environment of the negotiations. It allows the instant diffusion of the texts under discussion, whose confidentiality becomes more and more theoretical. It permits, beyond national boundaries, the sharing of knowledge and expertise. On a subject which is highly technical, the representatives of civil society seemed to us perfectly well informed, and their criticisms well argued on a legal level.

However, one unintended consequence of this global civil society campaign, or more accurately its later dissipation, distraction or possibly sense of self-satisfaction, was the acceleration of the fragmented bilateral investment regime. While the current network of treaties has not reached the global pretension of the MAI, it is not that far off in terms of coverage of real economic activity. The deeper irony is that many of today's bilateral investment treaties (BITs) contain even stronger protection for investors than would ever have been achieved or imagined had a multilateral agreement been drafted in the WTO. In that forum, developing states are more organized and civil society keep check from the sidelines (Suda, 2006). It should not be forgotten that part of the original justification for developing the MAI was to unify the then 1,300 BITs into a more manageable investment regime (Marchi, 2007).

This post-1999 growth of the BITs regime has not been accompanied by anything faintly resembling the earlier transnational activism. The NGO Europe Centre acknowledged the stark reality that 'Bilateral treaties are … not very visible to public opinion, many of them have been reached on the sly and [they] are even more harmful to rights of people than international or regional treaties.'[12] The only time that the investment regime has generated significant 'resistance' and 'struggle' by broader social movements was in Bolivia in the wake of the 'water wars' (Peterson, 2011). The American corporation Bechtel retreated from the country, after popular protest forced the Bolivian government to cancel the water concession contract. Bechtel subsequently launched an arbitration claim against Bolivia for $25 million under a generous BIT between Bolivia and the Netherlands (where Bechtel was conveniently headquartered).[13] The ICSID tribunal rejected a civil society petition to present an amicus intervention[14] but a second round of protests directed at the arbitration itself, constituted by a part-Bolivian/part-transnational campaign, embarrassed Bechtel into withdrawing the arbitration claim.[15]

The other notable exception is Argentina, which by 2007 had encountered 42 arbitration claims, many of them concerning multinationals in the water and energy utilities sector. Domestic mobilization and consumer payment boycotts in the Province of Tucuman led to the authorities cancelling the water concession contract with the French multinational Vivendi, triggering a BITs claim in 1997. Although not the centre of protest like Bolivia, it formed a shadow over the myriad of domestic court cases, struggles and negotiations (Morgan, 2006). Eventually, in 2007, Vivendi prevailed in international arbitration but Argentina has sought the annulment of the $105 million award.[16] A similar pattern emerged in the *Suez* litigation against Buenos Aires (Fairstein, 2006). A regulatory freeze on increasing utility prices in the wake of the 2001 economic crisis led to a cancellation of the

12 *Written Statement submitted by the Europe Centre to the UN Commission on Human Rights*, UN Doc. E/CN.4/Sub.2/2004/NGO/10.

13 *Aguas del Tunari S.A. v Republic of Bolivia* (ICSID Case No. ARB/02/3).

14 See *Petition of La Coordinadora para La Defensa del Agua y Vida, et al.*, 29 August 2002 available at: http://www.ciel.org/Publications/Petition_Revised_Aug02.pdf and Letter of Response from President of ICSID Tribunal, David Carson, to Earth Justice, 29 January 2003, available at http://ita.law.uvic.ca/documents/Aguas-BoliviaResponse.pdf.

15 Decision on Jurisdiction, 21 October 2005, available at http://ita.law.uvic.ca/documents/AguasdelTunari-jurisdiction-eng_000.pdf.

16 Award of 20 August 2007, available at http://ita.law.uvic.ca/documents/VivendiAwardEnglish.pdf. The first arbitral decision in *Compañía de Aguas del Aconquija S.A. and Vivendi Universal v Argentine Republic* (ICSID Case No. ARB/97/3), Award of 21 November 2000 was annulled in 2002: Decision on Annulment, 3 July 2002; 'http://ita.law.uvic.ca/documents/vivendi_annulEN.pdf.

concession agreement and triggered investment arbitration. Unlike their Bolivian counterparts, a network of consumer associations together with local and international human rights and environmental NGOs broke new ground and obtained the right from the tribunal to submit an amicus submission concerning the human rights dimensions of the case. Nonetheless, the majority of the tribunal ruled in 2010 that Argentina had violated the fair and equitable treatment standard.[17] But no significant transnational advocacy campaign has resulted, although this is possibly because the Argentinean government shifted leftwards in 2001 and has taken a hard-line with both international institutions and investors (Ciblis, 2003).

9.4 EXPLAINING THE LANDSCAPE

This short vignette on the MAI struggle and its aftermath is proffered for three reasons. The first is that the international investment regimes possess a remarkable vitality in the face of well organized campaigns. Indeed, one can find the forebears of BITs in the first period of 'globalization', which had matured by the late nineteenth century, in the form of 'capitulations' which were concluded with countries not under colonial occupation, such as the Ottoman Empire and China. While the practice had scattered origins in the Middle Ages in various parts of the world, it was in 1536 that the first capitulation (and in effect model) treaty was signed between Francis I of France and Süleyman I of Turkey as part of a political alliance. It allowed French investors extensive privileges within the country, with disputes settled by the French consul in Istanbul. These privileges:

> were later extended to other European states, and which had the effect of placing Europeans in the Ottoman Empire outside local jurisdiction. Freely given as a means of fostering trade, the capiltulations were later resented by the Ottomans, while Europeans insisted on them as a defence of their nationals against the arbitrariness of a backward Asiatic state.
>
> (Mango, 1999: 6)

However, from 1917 to 1989, the commonplace acceptance of the international protection of foreign investors withered in the face of post-imperialism, communism, nationalization drives, post-colonialism and the Latin American Calvo doctrine, which rejected foreigners acquiring greater substantive or dispute settlement rights

17 *Suez, Sociedad General de Aguas de Barcelona S.A., and Vivendi Universal S.A. (Claimants) v The Argentine Republic (Respondent); AWG Group (Claimant) v The Argentine Republic (Respondent)*, ICSID Case No. ARB/03/19, Decision on Liability, 30 July 2010 and *Suez, Sociedad General de Aguas de Barcelona S.A., and InterAgua Servicios Integrales del Agua S.A. (Claimants) v The Argentine Republic (Respondent)*, ICSID Case No. ARB/03/17, Decision on Liability, 30 July 2010.

than local citizens (see overview in Lowenfield, 2008: 469–94)). Attempts by Western states to entrench the pro-investor Hull rule on 'prompt, effective and adequate compensation' in international law met with little success. Developing and particularly Latin American countries championed the idea of the social function of property. Compensation did not axiomatically follow an order of expropriation and when it did, there was no duty on a host state to pay promptly or without regard to its financial capacity. This division prompted the US Supreme Court in 1964 to conclude that 'There are few if any issues in international law today on which opinion seems to be so divided as the limitation on a state's power to expropriate the property of aliens.'[18]

In this sense, the normalcy of pro-investor international treaties and arbitration is relatively fresh and logically followed the emergence of the market-friendly ideological landscape of the post-Cold War period. Vandevelde (1998: 628) characterizes BITs negotiations in the 1960s and 1970s as a Western ideological campaign, since the treaties 'symbolize[d] a commitment to economic liberalism'. It is also economically predictable. From as early as Marx, burgeoning domestic capital (from the US to China to South Africa to Qatar to Spain to Norway) has been in search of more and more foreign receptacles. The demand for a handmaiden in the form of an investment treaty is thus unlikely to disappear quickly.

Curiously, this elevated role of BITs in the global economy persists even though there is no unanimity in the quantitative evidence over whether they play a role in attracting foreign investment (Franck, 2007; Sauvant, 2009; Spess, 2005; Yackee, 2006).[19] Nonetheless, a panoply of states across the world pursue them in the name of protecting and securing capital and investment flows. Many Southern states retain the belief that every possible tool must be used to create a good investment image. Regular poverty reduction strategy papers, developed by these governments in conjunction with the World Bank and donors, usually list foreign direct investment as a key pillar of domestic economic policy (Anderson, 2008). UNCTAD in its country reviews of the investment environment usually recommends the adoption or improvement of bilateral investment treaties (see UNCTAD, 2010).

Moreover, it is arguable that the growing use of arbitration reveals that many corporations prefer this method of adjudication once disputes become intractable. As Figure 9.1 indicates, dozens of disputes are filed each year and the total number is trending upwards, with 57 per cent filed in the last five years (UNCTAD, 2009: 2). Some adjudicators have of course been more willing to entertain public interest arguments from states[20] and investors do not consistently

18 *Banco Nacional de Cuba v Sabbatino* 376 U.S. 398, at 428 (1964), quoted in Lowenfeld (2008: 467).

19 Note that mining and oil companies often claim the treaties are important in protecting large upfront investment costs. The same argument is used in the energy sector: Inadomi (2010).

20 See *Compañía de Aguas del Aconquija S.A. and Vivendi Universal v Argentine Republic* (ICSID Case No. ARB/97/3), Award of 20 August 2007 and *Biwater Gauff (Tanzania) Ltd v United Republic of Tanzania* (ICSID Case No. ARB/05/22), Award of 24 July 2008.

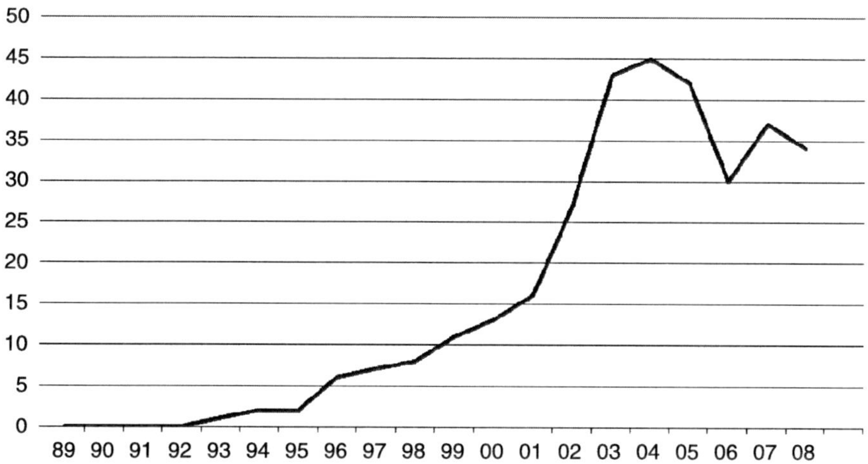

Figure 9.1 New cases: 1989–2008.
Source: UNCTAD (2009: 3)

find success. States have won 38 per cent of 164 concluded cases, with 29 per cent being won by investors and 34 per cent settled. Nonetheless, the jurisprudence gives investors a high degree of comfort. As the lawyer for the mining investors in *Foresti v South Africa* candidly stated to the *Financial Mail*:

> how much you respect the independence of the SA courts, the fact is [claims for alleged expropriation] will end up in the Constitutional Court, which will have to consider the impact of a finding that there has been a generalized expropriation of mineral rights with compensation running into billions of Rand. An international arbitration tribunal will not have those implications in mind.[21]

Of more relevance, the mere existence of arbitration adds to the armoury of corporations in policy and contractual negotiations with domestic government. The threat of litigation can cast a regulatory chill over government initiatives. One notable example is Indonesia's ban on open-mining in 1999. It was rescinded after multinationals indicated they would turn to international arbitration (Suda, 2006: 100). As Morgan (2006) notes, multinational water companies have a preference for national standard setting and international dispute resolution, which fits well the pattern of the BITs regime. BITs are thus a sword for influencing domestic policy and an international shield in case of disagreement with a host state.

The second lesson to be drawn from the post-MAI experience is the *unintended consequences* of 'successful solutions'. Specifically, the civil society campaign

21 *Financial Mail*, 26 January 2007.

that took the MAI off the multilateral negotiating table has done little to affect the actual practice of international investment law. It can be argued that developing states were empowered during this process: they have subsequently kept MAI-copycats off further trade negotiation rounds. But is this Southern stance a smokescreen? With the use of quantitative analysis, Elkins, Guzman and Simmons (2006) suggest that less developed countries conclude BITs due to a prisoners' dilemma: it is strategically better for such states to oppose the development of a global regime and then 'defect' and sign the BITs individually with other states in the *hope* of preferential treatment by foreign investors. The authors concede there are other significant explanatory variables, such as *uncertain legal regimes* vis-à-vis property rights (China being the classic case which has signed numerous treaties while Western countries have signed few between themselves) and *Washington-based coercion* (e.g., there is a high correlation between signing of BITs and countries classified as highly indebted and reliant on IMF loan re-financing). But they conclude that the main driver for less developed countries is to gain or maintain a competitive advantage with states also competing for foreign investment in the same sectors.

The third lesson to be learned is that the simple political cartography that drove the for-and-against positions over the MAI has disappeared in the last decade. The MAI was a clear product of the OECD, an organization founded like the World Bank on the premise of supporting foreign investment while the developing states attained the title of 'victims' of such an agreement. 'Villains' and 'victims' are not so clear ten years later. The global financial crisis has partly weakened the role of Western capital. Simultaneously, China, Arab states and a range of other emerging economies from the Czech Republic to Malaysia to Chile are beginning to invest outwards. We are now seeing the emergence of numerous South-South bilateral investment treaty agreements that are not being 'engineered' by Northern states or international organizations, as they were from 1960 to 2000.[22] This lack of attention to new empires of capital is evident in Douzinas (2007). His focus on American military decisions and leadership in economic globalization obscures the fact that the current hegemony is being accompanied by new empires.

Paul Collier (2009) classifies the emerging multi-polar world from a largely economic perspective, and his form of taxonomy sheds light on what we already seeing in the field of BITs ratification as well as emerging alternatives and lines of resistance. He breaks up the twenty-first century into three Gs: G5 (USA, India, China, Japan and the EU), the G60 (bottom 60 countries which account for around 1 per cent of economic growth) and the in-between and diverse 'sack of potatoes'

22 The South African Department of Trade and Industry (2009), which has suspended the negotiation of further BITS pending a current inquiry, noted that it was under significant pressure from its embassies in many Middle Eastern states which were anxious to sign such treaties with their hosts.

G103. According to Collier, the G5 will be bullies but will be, like the US today, under constant pressure to behave responsibly and make others do so. Using this framework, we might expect that BITs will continue to be promoted by many of the G5, although scepticism may increase in the US and some European Union states if capital inflows begin to outweigh capital outflows.[23] Given the economic desperation of the bottom 'G60', many of these states will be under considerable self- and externally-imposed pressure to continue within and join the regime.

We can however expect diverse reactions from the middle group of G103 countries, a phenomenon that is already manifest. A number of defendant states in investment arbitration, such as Czech Republic and South Africa, have initiated internal policy reviews to reconsider their overall membership in the system, while Bolivia and Venezuela with starker leftist governments announced their intention to withdraw from all such treaties. In recent negotiations over a free trade deal with the United States, Australia simply refused to include a chapter in the agreement allowing international investment arbitration, arguing its courts were sufficient for such purposes. Countries are being urged forward in this regard by bodies such as the UN Committee on Economic, Social and Cultural Rights. After considering evidence of conflict between the protections of investor rights under NAFTA and the provisions of the International Covenant on Economic, Social and Cultural Rights (ICESCR), they recommended that Canada 'consider ways in which the primacy of Covenant rights may be ensured in trade and investment agreements, and in particular in the adjudication of investor-state disputes under Chapter XI of NAFTA'.[24] At the same time, countries with increasing capital reserves and multinationals, such as the Arab states and Norway, have become particular interested in BITs, while many remain particularly anxious to increase their shares of inward foreign investment. All this to say that contemporary political economy complicates binary responses to bilateral investment treaties.[25] The empire of investment is hydra-headed and its subjects unruly and unpredictable.

9.5 THEOLOGY AND POLITICAL ECONOMY

In moving beyond 'neo-liberal capitalism and human-rights-for-export', Douzinas (2007: 293) draws on theology in a sketching out an alternative vision, his

23 The scuttling by the US Congress of Cnooc's (China National Offshore Oil Corporation) attempt to purchase controlling shares in Unocal (Pottinger, 2005) indicates their discomfort with their own investment medicine.

24 UN Committee on Economic, Social and Cultural Rights, *Concluding Observations on Canada* (May, 2006) E/C.12/CAN/CO/5 para. 48.

25 One can disaggregate even further. If the domestic level, one witnesses conflicts over BITs between competing ministries and constituencies.

'cosmopolitanism to come'. It is Derrida's 'democracy to come' practised by Ackerman's (1994) 'rooted cosmopolitans'. To categorize and summarize crudely, Douzinas seems to posit four theologies: resistance, liberation, presence and event. The theology of *resistance* means for him that 'human rights can reclaim their redemptive role in the hands and imagination of those who return them to the tradition of resistance and struggle against the advice of the preachers of moralism, suffering humanity and humanitarian philanthropy' (ibid). It evokes a certain Judeo-Christian practice of looking to those who are 'outside the camp', 'outside the city'.

Such resistance is shaped by the sacredness of the individual which provides the departure point for all action according to Douzinas. This *liberational* perspective is captured by his axiom of cosmopolitan justice, which is respect for the 'singularity of the other' and an individual's 'bare sovereignty'. Thus, cosmopolitanism to come 'extends beyond nations and states' and it is here that human rights is summoned, as a way to 'attack the omnipotence of the sovereign, humanitarianism, the brutality and excess of its unlimited power' (2007: 245).

This liberation is multi-relational and Douzinas invokes the religious traditions of *presence*, but in a somewhat excessively Christian/Islamic manner, states that the 'other comes first'.[26] Quoting Jean-Luc Nancy, one exists through relating to the 'existence of others, to other existences, and to the otherness of existence'. This form of encounter is thoroughly within the present and includes the task of resistance:

> Dissatisfaction with nation, state, the international comes from a bond between singularities. What binds me to an Iraqi or a Palestinian is not membership of humanity, citizenship of the world or of a community but a protest against citizenship, against nationality and thick community. This bond cannot be contained in traditional concepts of community and cosmos or of polis and state. What binds my world to that of others is our absolute singularity and total responsibility beyond citizen and human, beyond national and international. The cosmos to come is the world of each unique one, of whoever, or anyone; the polis, the infinite number of encounters of singularities.
>
> (Douzinas, 2007: 295)

Lastly, Douzinas evokes what some call a theology of *event* in order to avoid the overemphasis on abstract utopianism of the Diogenes' and Zeno's Greek Stoicism, Pauline Christianity (and much Marxism and neoclassical economics)

26 I would though prefer Martin Buber (1937) on this score. He begins with the individual first who then moves with his whole being toward the other: the thou of others and nature and the eternal Thou. But we have the same idea, that it is the encounter with the other in the present that we must strive, encounters that transform how we use and are used by power.

and foregrounds the role of history and relationship. Thus, 'the past is the most important normative source for the promise of the future' and that this 'memory of the future must by complemented by the image of the past' (2007: 295). The dialectic of the cosmopolis is built by the groundings of the past in the relationships of the present. As another theologian and philosopher, Martin Buber (2002: Sermon VI), puts it:

> Most of us achieve only at rare moments a clear realization of the fact that they have never tasted the fulfillment of existence, that their life does not participate in true, fulfilled existence, that, as it were, it passes true existence by. We nevertheless feel the deficiency at every moment, and in some measure strive to find — somewhere — what we are seeking. Somewhere, in some province of the world or of the mind, except where we stand, where we have been set — but it is there and nowhere else that the treasure can be found.

How do we assess all of this? On one hand, I very much welcome Douzinas' invocation of theology over terms such as philosophy, ideology or even religion. In understanding patterns of large-scale social change one constantly finds a strong theological dimension within particular struggles – the mere overcoming of oppressive structures has required a sustainability that demands some form of 'spiritual stance', which not only draws on notions of some higher power, morality and idea but some form of personal response and responsibility. While these theological modes of mobilization may be tactical at times, it is impossible not to observe the religious-tinged nature of many movements in their discourse

On the other hand, one cannot help feel overwhelmed by the power of the polis, and in this case study the global polis of the international investment regime. Moreover, even when resistance attains great heights, such as in the campaign against the MAI, it seems poorly equipped to deal with the ongoing political economy, the core of the polis. Tarrow's (2005: 219) survey of globalized civil society ends with a modest conclusion: 'transnational activism does not resemble a swelling tide of history but it more like a series of waves that lap on an international beach, retreating repeatedly into domestic seas but leaving incremental changes on the shore'.

In hindsight, one wonders whether engagement with that polis in 1999, in order to secure a slightly tamed multilateral investment arrangement, might have been more strategic and possibly more consistent with the principles of cosmopolitan justice as Wai suggests.[27] Indeed, when France first withdrew from leading the initiative in 1997 within the OECD they warned that their strategy was not temporally bound (Lalumière, 1998). Indeed, Martin Buber remained always cautious to how much and how fast one can move from a from *I-It* relationship (the polis) to an *I-Thou* relationship with others (cosmos).

27 See preceding chapter.

Douzinas is alive to the limits of raging against the dying of the light and the many inherent contradictions of attacking sovereignty and supra-sovereignty:

> What must be attacked is the theological mask of sovereignty, represented today by the hegemonic power rather than its pale homonymic imitations ... we must be aware that we cannot fight sovereignty and the nation-state in general without risking giving up the principles of equality and self-determination to the emerging super-sovereign. These principles were inaugurated by, with and against national sovereignty. They are today an indispensable barrier against ideological, religious, ethnic or capitalist hegemonies which masquerading as universalism or cosmopolitanism, claim the dignity of the cosmos that is nothing more than a marketplace or the moral rationalization of particular interests. When a hegemon attacks the weakened sovereigns around the world, resistance may demand supporting the local against the global.

Thus he reserves a role for political economy as well as sovereignty in informing the *tactics* to guide those who resist. The question is whether greater attention to the power of the polis, its structures and its weaknesses, can complement the more theological standpoint of those who work for a genuine cosmopolitan order? Or, are the possible gains outweighed by the compromises therein?

9.6 ROADS TO REFORM

We now turn to four possible roads for reform that allow for some alternative and *systematic* reform of the investment regime. I do not include amongst them options that call for a *multilateral* investment treaty or a mere *model* agreement that may or not be adopted in the future by a country or many countries.

9.6.1 Domestic supremacy and neo-calvoism

Douzinas' concession to state sovereignty, to support the 'local against the global', provides one possible road to reform; to simply halt and withdraw from the bilateral regime. It was the nationalist humiliation of extra-territorial capitulations that sparked their demise in Turkey and various Asiatic states a century ago and it is international commercial arbitration that is now triggering similar domestic responses, whether withdrawals, moratoriums or internal reviews. Indeed, the consultation paper distributed by the Government of South Africa in 2009 is recommended reading for its collective *mea culpa* for the lack of an overarching policy towards BITs negotiation, its risible anger at the humiliations of arbitration and its forthright articulation of human rights and environmental concerns.[28] This stands out in a country where the bedrock of foreign and trade policy has been the avoidance of any destabilization of international investment and capital stability.

There are two potential options if 'domestic supremacy' is to be pursued. The first is to emulate Brazil's approach and desist from ratifying any bilateral investment treaties at all. Many have pointed out that, from an instrumental perspective, the level of foreign investment into Brazil has not been affected by the decision not to join the regime. Brazil is consistently amongst the top three developing country recipients of foreign investment (Gallagher, 2006). However, poor developed countries risk signalling disinterest in investment by following this strategy (Gallagher, 2006).

The second approach is to continue with investment agreements but remove the option of investor-state arbitration in the manner that Australia has done. As has been noted by one government:

> There is no compelling reason why review of an investor's claims against a state cannot be undertaken by the institutions of the state in question—provided these are independent of the public authority that is in dispute and they discharge their duties in accordance with basic principles of good governance, including an independent judiciary.

Thus the invocation of *sovereignty* and national humiliation may be one discursive path forward. One of the key advantages of this approach is it does away with two of the most problematic aspects of international arbitration, that foreign investors may receive greater protections than local citizens/investors, both procedurally and substantively, and that closeted and unpredictable arbitration is abandoned in favour of the more unitarian and transparent domestic adjudication system. One might argue that turning to domestic courts would ensure corporations and the World Bank place more emphasis on improving domestic rule of law; and it is perhaps no surprise the latter has numerous programmes to this end, although few are concerned with the rule of law for the poor.

Indeed, the importance of domestic, particularly constitutional, review, has been underlined by the gruelling *Solange* litigation in Germany. In *Solange I* (1974),[29] the Federal Constitutional Court, refused to cede its authority over constitutional rights to the European Court of Justice over matters of European Community law. While European law was not under its jurisdiction, the Court maintained its responsibility to measure it against the norms on fundamental rights in the Constitution. As time progressed, ECJ jurisprudence and Community Law evolved to allow for sufficient protection of fundamental human rights, in the view of the Constitutional Court.[30] In *Solange II*, the Court retreated and

28 Bilateral Investment Treaty Policy Framework Review, Government Position Paper, June 2009, Department of Trade and Industry, Pretoria.

29 BVerfGE 37, 371 (1974), [1974] CMLR 540 [*Solange I*].

30 BVerfGE 73, 339 2 BvR 197/83 *Solange II* decision, at 342.

relinquished its supervisory power, subject to European Community law continuing to protect fundamental rights.[31]

Such an approach could be adopted by constitutional courts elsewhere. The Colombian Constitutional Court has followed a similar approach in reviewing the draft Colombia-US free trade deal.[32] However, many courts are likely to be uncomfortable with adopting such a role, given the clear provisions of much domestic arbitration legislation that entrenches the role of international arbitrators. Thus, for countries without bolder apex courts, a more radical step would be required, such as halting or withdrawing from treaties.

But there are risks and dangers of this clear embrace of the polis. The first, like in the field of trade, is that one needs to be careful that the international 'constitutionalism' of human rights is not lost in the process of reasserting sovereignty. Does the praise of sovereignty risk the same fate for international human rights?

The second is that the solution doesn't necessarily deal with the economics. Where countries have strong outward flows of investment, pressure from finance ministries, home multinationals and embassies abroad is overwhelming. International investment agreements provide more of a quid pro quo for states with internal and external capital interests, particularly when countries have no strong historical or legal system ties, as Australia and the US have. Linked to this problem are the perceptions generated by withdrawal, which may send a signal of high risk to investors, particularly if a country is put in the same camp as Venezuela, which has been vocally pursuing this policy.

The third problem is that some countries simply can't guarantee the rule of law to any foreigners, let alone their own citizens. Who would trust Robert Mugabe with a few or many dollars? In Russia, foreign investors sometimes find themselves in the same threatened position as NGOs (Peterson and Gallus, 2008). Courts in Latin America also face accusations of succumbing to political influence and corruption at times. It is pertinent to note that even NGOs and victims of multinational abuses in South Africa in *Lubbe and Others v Cape (Plc)*,[33] amongst other cases, argued for the case to be heard by the UK's courts against the parent multinational, on the basis of the lack of experience by South Africa courts with such complex cases; a position supported by the South African Government (Meeran, 2006). That was ten years ago, but when human rights NGOs and states themselves make these sorts of arguments, the challenge is readily apparent.

A fourth problem is the unintended consequences. Will the lack of the option of international commercial arbitration prompt foreign investors to secure other forms of protection, e.g. particular concessions for a particular company, a

31 Ibid at 343, see fn 7.

32 *Comunicado de Sentencias* C-750 y C-751 de 24–07-2008, available at http://actualicese.com/normatividad/2008/07/24/comunicado-de-sentencias-c-750-y-c-751-de-24-07-2008/.

33 *Lubbe and Others v Cape (Plc)* [2000] UKHL 41; [2000] 4 All ER 268; [2000] 1 WLR 1545 (20 July 2000), www.bailii.org/uk/cases/UKHL/2000/41.html.

company–state agreement for arbitration, monetary or other legal benefits etc? Inadomi (2010) demonstrates how investors in the energy sector seek significantly greater concessions from developing country governments due to the perceived lack of protection of BITs for large up-front investments. One possible response to this scenario is the proposal by Schneiderman (2008). He champions the removal of BITs and proffers the alternatives of anti-discrimination laws that provide clear protection to all, including corporations and their shareholders, and 'foreign investment insurance programs, both public and private', particularly in those countries with a weak rule of law. David Collier (2009: 232), however, dismisses the possibility of the latter on the grounds that:

> [S]urely the cost of funding insurance against damaging host state intervention in large scale investment projects will be passed on to vulnerable consumers or else it will render such projects prohibitively expensive. Insurance against the risk of regulatory expropriation will be priced according to the ability of host states to intervene lawfully…

Therefore, unscrambling the egg may simply not be possible. The best such a global movement could hope for is a slogan of 'no more BITs'. But even this is problematic. The current web of treaties largely favours Northern countries, and the prisoners' dilemma for developing countries once again appears with even more force.

9.6.2 Domestic 'lite' – exhaustion of domestic remedies

These challenges suggest a second possible option: introducing domestic exhaustion of remedies into existing and future investment agreements. Such a procedure would bring investment agreements into line with general international law, particularly human rights. The ILC's Articles on the Responsibility of States For International Wrongful Wrongs provide, with regard to the admissibility of international claims, that the, 'responsibility of a State may not be invoked if … the claim is one to which the rule of exhaustion of local remedies applies and any available and effective local remedy has not been exhausted'.[34] While this position seemingly confines the rule to the substance of the particular treaty, the commentary by the ILC on Article 44 is revealing. Douglas (2003: 191) notes that the Commentary 'makes it clear' that the principle of exhaustion of local remedies has a 'fundamental character' – it contains the 'conditions for invoking the responsibility of a State in the first place'. Article 15(3) of the draft Norwegian Model Agreement seeks to do precisely this. International arbitration is only

34 See Art. 44, ILC's Articles on Responsibility fo States for Internationally Wrongful Acts (2001) located at http://untreaty.un.org/ilc/texts/instruments/english/draft%20articles/9_6_2001.pdf.

permitted if 'agreement cannot be reached between the parties to this dispute within 36 months from its submission to a local court' or 'there are no reasonably available local remedies'.

There are two clear advantages to this proposal. The first is that the obnoxious elements of opaque and distant arbitration are partly removed. The litigation must occur in the full glare of a domestic audience while there is also pressure on the state to provide a fair and efficient court hearing. The second is that the procedural nature of the reform makes it amenable to universalization. For instance, it is possible for all states to conclude a simple treaty, within or outside the ICSID/UNICTRAL framework, with provisions to the effect that all investment arbitration must undertake this domestic exhaustion route. Of course the disadvantage is that the substantive rights remain largely preserved in the treaties and a period of three years does not apply in similar human rights treaties.

9.6.3 International integrationism within human rights or 'neutral' adjudication

However, Road 2 should not automatically presume that ad hoc international investment arbitration is the preferable route for investor-state dispute resolution, even after the domestic exhaustion of remedies. Other permanent fora already exist for review of many of these disputes.

One possibility is regional human rights courts. The European Court of Human Rights is currently used by companies, including for foreign investment claims (Emberland, 2006). The Inter-American Court of Human Rights has heard claims from shareholders on the right to property since its rules do not permit 'legal persons' such as companies to submit claims (Cassel, 2008). The potential benefits of this route can be seen in the jurisprudence of these courts. Emberland (2006) points out that the margin of appreciation applied to property rights cases by the European Court of Human Rights is particularly wide; the Court has striven to give states sufficient regulatory space, for example to restrict rent levels to protect tenants. Indeed, Norway's draft model BIT, launched for discussion in 2008, sought to explicitly link the expropriation standard to the jurisprudence of the European Court of Human Rights.[35] The Inter-American Court of Human Rights has also addressed the relationship between BITs and human rights. In *Sawhoyamaxa v Paraguay*, indigenous groups challenged Paraguay's reliance on a BIT with Germany as a ground for its refusal to return land owned by a German national to an indigenous community. The Court held that human rights (in this case, a collective right to property under the Inter-American Convention) have supremacy in such circumstances:

35 See discussion in letter from Norwegian Centre for Human Rights to Business and Industry Department, 15 April 2008, available at http://www.humanrights.uio.no/nasjonal-institusjon/overvakning/horinger/2008/investeringer.pdf.

> [T]he application of bilateral commercial agreements do not provide a justification for the breach of states obligations emanating from the American Human Rights Convention; on the contrary, their application must always be compatible with the American Convention.[36]

However, there is considerable discomfort amongst many human rights lawyers and activists over companies availing themselves of human rights courts. There may be significant resistance to further embracing companies within the individual singular theology of liberation.[37]

An alternative is fused international jurisdiction where courts possess broader powers to adjudicate on all aspects of relevant international law. For instance, the Court of First Instance (CFI) of the European communities, indirectly reviewed the legality of Security Council (SC) anti-terror resolutions against the background of human rights peremptory norms. It held that it was:

> [E]mpowered to check, indirectly, the lawfulness of the resolutions of the SC (imposing financial sanctions on individuals and entities allegedly affiliated with the Al Qaeda network) in question with regard to ius cogens, understood as a body of higher rules of public international law binding on all subjects of international law, including the bodies of the United Nations, and from which no derogation is possible.[38]

In *Stauder*,[39] the European Court of Justice (ECJ) stated that the Court should ensure respect for fundamental human rights, while in *Hauer*[40] it stated that fundamental rights, including those in international treaties, 'form an integral part of the general principles of law' and European community law. In the case of the Southern Africa Development Community (SADC), its Tribunal has addressed human rights and expropriation simultaneously. In *Campbell v Zimbabwe*,[41] the Tribunal held that: 'SADC as a collectivity and as individual member states are under a legal obligation to respect and protect human rights of SADC citizens. They also have to ensure that there is democracy and the rule of law within the region'.[42] The Tribunal went on to find that the right to property and other human rights were violated in the expropriation of the farmer's land.

36 Corte Interamericana de Derechos Humanos *Caso comunidad indígena Sawhoyamaxa v Paraguay*, Sentencia de 29 de Marzo de 2006.

37 See Emberland's (2006) discussion of the competing literature.

38 Case T-315/01, *Yassin Abdullah Kadi v Council of the European Union and Commission of the European Communities*, Judgement of the CFI, 21 Sept. 2005 at para. 226 cited in n. 1 above, p. 498.

39 *Erich Stauder v City of Ulm* (1969) E.C.R. 419 at 425.

40 Case 44/79 *Liselotte Haeur v Land Rhineland-Pfalz* (1979) E.C.R. 3727.

41 *Mike Campbell (Pvt) Ltd et al. v Republic of Zimbabwe*, SADC (T) Case No. 2/2007.

42 Ibid.

Promoting a fused agenda in practice is not particularly straightforward. It would require amendment to the provisions of some regional arrangements (e.g. the Americas), creation of new regional systems which are still nascent (e.g. Asia) and significant support for some that already exist to deal with the influx of cases (e.g. the European Court of Human Rights and SADC Tribunal). Moreover, consideration would need to be given as to whether jurisdictional opportunities under BITs would need to be curtailed; a move that is likely to be resisted by investors.

9.6.4 Integrationism within investment arbitration

A fourth approach is to ensure that, at the very least, investment arbitrators integrate human rights principles in their decision-making. It is a strategy being pursued by legally-oriented NGOs and some social movements, which Peterson (2009) has characterized as the clearest acknowledgement that the investment treaty 'genie is out of the bottle'. All one can do is begin to claw back some of the lost ground. Ernst-Ulrich Petersmann (2009: 4), asks:

> Why do national and international courts, investor-state arbitral tribunals and alternative jurisdictions for the settlement of transnational investment disputes and other economic disputes, in their judicial review of treaty claims and related contract claims (for example, regarding alleged government interferences into property rights), refer so rarely to the customary law requirement of settling 'disputes concerning treaties, like other international disputes ... in conformity with the principles of justice and international law', including 'universal respect for, and observance of, human rights and fundamental freedoms for all', as codified in the Vienna Convention on the Law of Treaties?

This call for substantive legal positivism has been embraced by some arbitral panels. The ICSID tribunal's statement in the early case of *Asian Agricultural Products Ltd v Republic of Sri Lanka* is commonly cited in this regard:

> [An investment treaty is not] a self-contained closed legal system limited to provide for substantive material rules of direct applicability, but it has to be envisaged within a wider juridical context in which rules from other sources are integrated through implied incorporation methods, or by direct reference to certain supplementary rules, whether of international law character or of domestic law nature.[43]

43 *Asian Agricultural Products Ltd v Rep. of Sri Lanka (Award)* 1990, 4 ICSID Rep. 245.

Some ICSID Tribunals have taken into account a host state's other international obligations (Mann, 2008: 25–9). In *SPP v Egypt*, the tribunal considered the argument that a host state's failure to interfere to protect the investor might have led it to violate its international obligations under the UNESCO Convention on the protection of cultural antiques.[44] Although the argument was found to be factually irrelevant in that case, it 'nevertheless signalled that ICSID Tribunals may take account of a state's broader international law commitments' (Peterson and Gray, 2006: 29).

The invocation of human rights and environment treaties in defendant and *amicus curiae* submissions has accelerated in recent years. In 2002, Argentinian organizations gained the right to intervene in ICSID arbitral proceedings,[45] while in 2009 in *Foresti v South Africa*, the amicus organizations additionally secured the right to access to redacted pleadings and evidence in the arbitration.[46] In the former, case, the tribunal held that, water and sanitation systems 'provide basic public services to millions of people and as a result may raise a variety of complex public and international law questions, including human rights considerations'.[47] In its Award eight years later, the Tribunal affirmed that the Argentina must comply with its obligations under human rights treaties. However, it was clear that human rights do not trump investment obligations, and 'Argentina's human rights obligations and its investment treaty obligations are not inconsistent, contradictory, or mutually exclusive'.[48] The Tribunal avoided expressing itself on what happens when there is a direct conflict, but it implicitly suggested that the test is whether Argentina had other alternatives to avoid violations of its human rights obligations. In this case, the majority found that the state could have used other means to respect the right to water without imposing a freeze on water prices. And this is the rub. It is the particular jurisprudential doctrines and their application that is crucial, rather than the broad questions of applicable law. The key legal question for such cases is what sort of proportionality and reasonableness test should be applied when evaluating state conduct, and what level of deference is to be accorded. If human rights are to be relevant, they must connect with these underlying jurisprudential markers and lead to the sort of conclusions articulated by the tribunal in *Methanex v United States*:

44 See Award in *Southern Pacific Properties (Middle East) Ltd v Arab Republic of Egypt*, 32 International Legal Materials, No. 4 (1993) para. 154.

45 *Aguas Argentinas, S.A., Suez, Sociedad General de Aguas de Barcelona, S.A. and Vivendi Universal, S.A. v Argentine Republic* (Case No. ARB/03/19). This right of amicus was subsequently granted in *Biwater v Tanzania* to a similarly constituted group of interveners. *Biwater Gauff (Tanzania) Ltd v United Republic of Tanzania* (ICSID Case No. ARB/05/22), Award of 24 July 2008. While the NGO submission was welcomed by the tribunal in this case, it was not substantively taken into account in the decision.

46 Letter from ICSID Tribunal Secretary to Legal Resources Centre and the International Commission of Jurists, 5 October 2009.

47 The Centre for Legal and Social Studies et al. (Press release, 28 June 2005).

48 *Suez and Vivendi v The Argentine Republic* (n. 18 above), para. 262.

> [A]s a matter of general international law, a non discriminatory regulation for a public purpose, which is enacted in accordance with due process and, which affects inter alios, a foreign investor or investment is not deemed expropriatory and compensable unless specific commitments had been given by the regulatory government to the then putative investor contemplating investment that the government would refrain from such regulations.[49]

However, there are a myriad of other problems with this approach since the interpretive space remains defined by the architecture of investment treaties and arbitration. There also remain serious questions as to the competence and authority of *ad hoc* arbitral panels to adjudicate on matters of fundamental rights – even as limitations on investors' rights. The remedial powers of these tribunals, though significant, are restricted to compensating investors for violations of the terms of investment treaties; they cannot make orders with respect to violations of fundamental human rights.

The danger of skewed appropriation of human rights remains patently clear. Philip Alston has lacerated Ernst-Ulrich Petersmann for the way in which he earlier called for human rights to be addressed within the WTO:

> [D]espite his consistent invocation of the discourse of human rights – and contrary to the reader's first impressions as well as to Petersmann's own perception of his work – his approach is at best difficult to reconcile with international human rights law and at worst it would undermine it dramatically. In essence, the result of following the approach set out would be to hijack, or more appropriately to Hayek, international human rights law in a way which would fundamentally redefine its contours and make it subject to the libertarian principles expounded by writers such as Friedrich Hayek, Richard Pipes and Randy Barnett.
>
> (Alston, 2002: 816)

This threat of appropriationism should give one pause, when Petersmann now advances the argument for the incorporation of human rights within the investment regime.

9.7 CONCLUSION

The seemingly unstoppable and spinning spider's web of investment treaties presents a clear challenge; not only for lawyers concerned over the fragmentation of international law, but in the commandeering of international law for largely private

49 *Methanex Co-operation v United States*, Final Award, 3 August 2005, p. 278, part 4, Chapter D, para. 7.

commercial purposes. Despite mounting what seemed to be the archetypal transnational campaign to limit its expansion, the breaking of the web in one place has done little to stop it growing elsewhere. Douzinas' invocation of various theologies are important for adopting a clear stance in relation to thinking about the reform of the system, lest international human rights lawyers simply lead the movement down the path that makes the international human rights subject to that of stronger international constitutional order grounded only on investor property rights.

However, the choices are difficult. Resistance is easy to mobilize when investment litigation directly threatens access to a particular right, such as water or electricity or indigenous peoples' access to land. But where the possible impact on citizens is more diffuse, such as the Italian company's challenge to South Africa's mineral legislation, civil society organizations have struggled to incite mobilization. And, in most instances, the real effect of the BIT remains hidden, silently affecting government decisions when threats are made by companies to litigate.

This post-MAI scenario reveals the limits of the 'cosmpolitanism to come' and the inherent weakness of its adherents. It is difficult to expect that the investment regime will soon collapse under the weights of its internal contradictions. Some engagement will be needed with the rapidly changing political economy of BITs in order to move towards a more fair and just solution; moving beyond 'oppose' to 'propose'. This will mean sometimes cooperating and with and against different parts of the national and international polis and making principled compromises.

In doing this, one might think about a theology of political economy that informs the types of choices that are made in such process and, critically, who makes these choices. It might mean forming a clearer economic version that not only allows the post-development rejectionist alternative to economic capitalism but may also seek to simply tame capitalism as advocated by Wai. It might require a greater engagement with political parties and the difficult task of constituency-building.

In the country where I write from, Norway, the social democratic order is largely the product of the use and alliances of power from below. But at the same time, the country's international investment profile – which includes hosting a large number of unregulated multinationals, buying weapons from corporations with stained human rights records and administering a massive pension fund that invests in what one commentator has called a 'dirty list of the world's worst corporations' (Curtis, 2009) – reveals that the international polis requires its own sustained counter-politic.

Bibliography

Ackerman, B. (1994) 'Rooted Cosmopolitanism', *Ethics* 104: 516–35.

Alston, P. (2002) 'Resisting the Merger and Acquisition of Human Rights by Trade Law: A Reply to Petersmann', *European Journal of International Law* 13(4): 815–44.

Alvarez, J. (2009) 'Contemporary International Law: An "Empire of Law" or the "Law of Empire" ', *American University International Law Review* 24: 811–42.
Anderson, E. and McKay, A. (2008) *Human Rights, the MDG Income Poverty Target, and Economic Growth*, Geneva: UN OHCHR.
Buber, M. (2002) *The Way of Man: According to the teaching of Hasidim*, London: Routledge.
Cassel, D. 'Defending Against Expropriation in Latin America' (updated 2008), http://www.robertamsterdam.com/2008/03/defending_against_expropriatio.htm.
Ciblis, A. (2003) 'Argentina's IMF Agreement: The Dawn of a New Era?', *Foreign Policy in Focus*.
Cohn, T. H. (2005) *Global Political Economy Theory and Practice*, New York: Pearson Longman.
Collier, D. (2009) Book Review: *Constitutionalizing Economic Globalization: Investment Rules and Democracy's Promise* by David Schneiderman, *Cambridge Law Journal* 68(1): 231–3.
Collier, P. (2009) 'Rich bullies, we need you', *The Guardian Weekly*, 25 September.
Curtis, M. (2009) 'Norway's dirty little secrets: Norway is no ethical leader – its pension fund, oil policy, environmental record and arms exports give the lie to its image', *The Guardian Weekly*, 24 September.
Douglas, Z. (2003) 'The Hybrid Foundations of Investment Treaty Arbitration', *BYIL*, 151–219.
Douzinas, C. (2007) *Human Rights and Empire: The Political Philosophy of Cosmopolitanism*, London: Routledge.
Dupuy, P-M., Francioni, F. and Petersman, E-U. (eds) (2009) *Human Rights in International Investment Law and Arbitration*, Oxford: Oxford University Press.
Elkins, Z., Guzman, A. and Simmons, B. (2006) 'Competing for Capital: The Diffusion of Bilateral Investment Treaties, 1960–2000', *International Organization* 60(Fall): 811–46.
Emberland, M. (2006) *The Human Rights of Companies: Exploring the Structure of ECHR Protection*, Oxford: Oxford University Press.
Fairstein, C. (2006) 'Legal Strategies and the Right to Water in Argentina', in E. Riedel and P. Rothen (eds), *The Human Right to Water*, Berlin: Berliner WissenschaftsVerlag.
Franck, S. (2007) 'Foreign Direct Investment, Investment Treaty Arbitration, and the Rule of Law', *Pac McGeorge Global Bus. and Dev L.J.* 19: 348–53.
Fry, J. D. (2007) 'International Human Rights Law in Investment Arbitration: Evidence of International Law's Unity', *Duke Journal of International and Comparative Law* 77–149.
Gallagher, K. and Zarsky, L. (2006) 'Rethinking Foreign Investment for Development', *Post-Autistic Economic Review* 37: 10–32.
Inadomi, H. (2010) *Independent Power Projects in Developing Countries*, Amsterdam: Wolters Kluwer.
Kennedy, D. (2001) 'The International Human Rights Movement: Part of the Problem?', *Harvard Human Rights Journal* 15: 99–126.
Lalumière, J-P. and Landau, C. (1998) 'Report on the Multilateral Agreement on Investment, Intermediary Report'.
Leubuscher, S. (2003) 'The Privatisation of Justice: International Commercial Arbitration and the Redefinition of the State', Conference presentation (MRes Birkbeck College, 2 June).

Lowenfeld, A. (2008) *International Economic Law* (2nd edn), Oxford: Oxford University Press.

Mango, A. (1999) *Atatürk*, London: John Murray.

Mann, H. (2008) *International Investment Agreements, Business and Human Rights: Key issues and opportunities*, International Institute for Sustainable Development.

Marchi, S. (2007) 'The MAI Debate: YES: Canada Needs Clear Investment Rules', *Montreal Gazette*, 10 November.

Meeran, R. (2006) 'Multinational Litigation as a Weapon in Protecting Economic and Social Rights', in M. Langford and B. T. J. Squires (eds), *The Road to a Remedy*, Sydney: UNSW Press.

Morgan, B. (2006) 'Turning off the Tap: Urban Water Services Delivery and the Social construction of Global Administrative Law', *The European Journal of International Law* 17(1): 215–46.

Petersmann, E-U. (2009) 'Introduction and Summary', in P-M. Dupuy, F. Francioni and E.-U. Petersmann (eds), *Human Rights in International Investment Law and Arbitration*, Oxford: Oxford University Press.

Peterson, L. (2009) *Human Rights and Bilateral Investment Treaties: Mapping the role of human rights law within investor–state arbitration*, Montreal: Rights and Democracy.

—— (2011) 'Bilateral Investment Treaties and Investment Arbitration', in M. and A. R. Langford (eds), *The Right to Water: Theory, practice and prospects*, Cambridge: Cambridge University Press.

Peterson, L. and Gray, K. (2006) 'International Human Rights in Bilateral Investment Treaties and in Investment Treaty Arbitration', Research Paper prepared by the International Institute for Sustainable Development (IISD) for the Swiss Department of Foreign Affairs.

Peterson, L. and Gallus, N. (2008) 'International Investment Treaty Protection of Not-for-Profit Organizations', International Centre for not-for-Profit Law Working Paper.

Pottinger, M., Gold, R., Phillips, M. M. and Linebaugh, K. (2005) 'Oil Politics: Cnooc Drops Offer for Unocal, Exposing U.S.-Chinese Tensions', *Wall Street Journal*, 3 August.

Sauvant, K. and Sachs, L. (eds) (2009) *The Effects of Treaties on Foreign Direct Investment: Bilateral Investment Treaties, Double Taxation Treaties and Investment Treaties*, Oxford: Oxford University Press.

Schneiderman, D. (2008) *Constitutionalizing Economic Globalization: Investment rules and democracy's promise*, Cambridge: Cambridge University Press.

Schwebel, S. (2009) 'The United States 2004 Model Bilateral Investment Treaty and Denial of Justice in International Law', in C. Binder, U. Kriebaum, A. Reinisch and S. Wittich (eds), *International Investment Law for the 21st Century: Essays in honour of Christop Schreuer*, Oxford: Oxford University Press.

Spess, L. and Neumayer, E. (2005) 'Do Bilateral Investment Treaties Increase Foreign Direct Investment to Developing Countries?', *World Development* 33: 1567–85.

Suda, R. (2006) 'The Effect of Bilateral Investment Treaties on Human Rights', in O. de Schutter (ed.), *Transnational Corporations and Human Rights*, Oxford: Hart.

Tarrow, S. (2005) *The New Transnational Activism*, Cambridge: Cambridge University Press.

UNCTAD (2007) *Investor–State Dispute Settlement and Impact on Investment Rulemaking*, New York: United Nations.

—— (2009) 'Recent Developments in International Investment Agreements (2008–June 2009)', *IIA Monitor* 3.

—— (2010) *Investment Policy Review – Sierra Leone*, New York: United Nations.

Vallianatos, M. (1997) 'Multilateral Agreement on Investment', *Foreign Policy in Focus* 2(39): 1–4.

Vandevelde, K. J. (1998) 'The Political Economy of a Bilateral Investment Treaty', *American Journal of Internaitonal Law*, 92: 621–41.

Waincymer, J. (2009) 'Balancing Property Rights and Human Rights in Expropriation', in P-M. Dupuy, F. Francioni and E-U. Petersmann (eds), *Human Rights in International Investment Law and Arbitration*, Oxford: Oxford University Press.

Yackee, J. W. (2006) 'Sacrificing Sovereignty: Bilateral Investment Treaties, International Arbitration, and the Quest for Capital', USC Center in Law, Economics and Organization Research Paper No. C06–15.

Chapter 10

Cosmopolitianism in practice?

The case of the Norwegian Government Pension Fund

Andreas Føllesdal

Globalization – the increasing territorial reach of the impact of a wide range of actors – fuels various calls for a Cosmopolitan Justice.[1] One area where calls for reform of global regimes and of the actors within them are very vocal and visible concerns the responsibilities of corporations and investors. The normative constraints on the investments of the Norwegian Government Pension Fund may be explained and assessed by such trends and standards.

The following reflections first comment on globalization and moral cosmopolitanism. This chapter then lays out a 'standard' case for why corporations may legitimately restrict their objectives to value creation for their owners – within domestic settings – and why this argument fails to hold under circumstances of globalization, before presenting some of the most salient normative objectives and standards for investors, concerning shareholder activism and exclusion. The paper then presents the Norwegian Pension Fund Global and how its Council on Ethics brings certain normative standards to bear, and then considers potential conflicts and benefits of coordination between two activities: those of shareholder activism and exclusion, arguing for certain ways to address the conflicts from a cosmopolitan perspective. The chapter concludes by drawing some lessons from this case.

10.1 GLOBALIZATION AND COSMOPOLITAN JUSTICE

International corporations and those who invest in them have a large impact across state borders. This impact, combined with other factors, has reduced the capacity of governments and civil society. In earlier times sovereign states could

1 The present chapter benefited from discussions at the conference on Cosmopolitan Justice, 16 October 2009, and at a conference hosted by the Norwegian Ministry of Finance: 'Investing for the Future', 16 January 2008. I am grateful to the editors for comments. The chapter in part draws together arguments from Føllesdal (2004, 2007) as noted.

respond to global economic liberalization by a domestic 'grand social bargain' to avoid dismantling their social protection schemes. They could 'embed' economic liberalism by buffering the adjustment costs of liberalization by taxation, tariffs and non-tariff trade barriers, exchange rates and other means (Ruggie, 1982).

The new forms of economic globalization have rendered developed states less able to protect their citizens – not to mention the governments of developing countries. Many states have shifted from being policy-makers to being policy-peddlers, partly because they have chosen to refrain from some of the instruments of yore, such as reduction of tariffs and exchange rate flexibility (Ruggie, 2003). Multinational corporations are visible and powerful policy 'shoppers' in the global competition for capital and corporations. Some argue that the shift of power is not as stark as critics paint the picture – at least regarding developed welfare states (Pierson, 2001). But economically weaker states often face several new challenges under these forms of globalization. Sometimes conventions or regional cooperation help states maintain control, but many poor or weak states may be unable to uphold strict labour and human rights standards against corporations – especially multinationals who can credibly threaten to move to other, more friendly jurisdictions.

The normative worries are particularly obvious for 'cosmopolitan' or 'global' theories of ethics or of justice. Following John Rawls (1971), I am concerned here with considerations of justice for the moral assessment of social rules – laws, social conventions, institutions and the like, rather than to assess individual's or collective agents' actions. The concepts of 'cosmopolitan' or 'global justice' challenges received distinctions between intranational and international relations, and instead extends considerations of justice across these institutions. Central to this framework is one assumption of globalization, namely that the causal impact of the design of the global institutional order has both direct and indirect causal impact on the living conditions of human beings worldwide (Føllesdal and Pogge, 2005: 1–11).

A central normative premise of such cosmopolitan or global theories of justice is that all human beings are subjects of equal moral worth. One might explicate this commitment in a 'contractualist' vein familiar from John Locke, Immanuel Kant and more recently John Rawls: justification of shared practices and institutions is owed to every person as moral equals, that is as parties worthy of equal concern and respect.

Note that this premise is independent of substantive claims about what institutional designs are least objectionable or most justifiable. Thus whether there are good reasons in favour of 'Institutional Cosmopolitanism' is a quite different issue – that is, whether the world order should be one of a universal republic.

Indeed, the role of a global or cosmopolitan theory of justice is to assist us in the normative assessment of alternative allocations of responsibility among states, corporations and intergovernmental bodies – such as a universal republic, a world federation, a modified system of states, etc. – also when the traditional distinctions between domestic and international relations and justice are blurred.

Space and format does not allow an elaborate justification of some normative implications of the premise of equal moral worth, but I submit that at least four requirements of normative principles follow, for an acceptable global basic structure as a whole:

- *Respect vital interests*: no one must damage the vital interests of others.
- *Protect vital interests*: the vital interests of all must be protected against threats by third parties.
- *Secure important 'public goods'*: institutions should be in place to help individuals create valued benefits that benefit all, yet cannot easily be obtained due to coordination problems. Such goods may include those central to markets: the enforcement of contracts, etc.
- *Distribute and redistribute benefits and burdens fairly* by means of taxation, tariffs.

10.2 WHY THE BUSINESS OF BUSINESS IS BUSINESS – THE 'STANDARD CASE'

Milton Friedman is among the theorists frequently cited in support of the claim that close to unbridled pursuit of profit by corporations and their investors might be justifiable – ignoring almost all normative claims of other affected parties. He held that:

> A corporate executive is an employee of the owners of the business. He has direct responsibility to his employers. That responsibility is to conduct the business in accordance with their desires, which generally will be to make as much money as possible while conforming to the basic rules of the society, both those embodied in law and those embodied in ethical custom.
>
> (Friedman, 1970)

Such a defence might find its most convincing elaboration by Adam Smith, who argued that – at least under certain conditions – even self-motivated market agents would exchange goods in Pareto-improving ways – that is, so that some will be better off without rendering anyone worse off. This provides one normative defence of allowing self-interested actors to operate in markets: voluntary exchange helps individuals secure their own vital interests.

But we should note that this defence relies on an elaborate distribution of social responsibility between corporations, government, and what we would think of as NGOs, and civil society. Adam Smith argued for several constraints on the market, even beyond those needed to correct 'imperfections' (Føllesdal, 2004; Satz, 2007), consistent with the four norms of cosmopolitan justice mentioned above. Governments must regulate the market and correct market failures – thus provide certain 'public goods', but must also take on further tasks.

The government should tax luxury items to benefit the poor, schools should socialize all to full citizenship, and bodies must scrutinize governments and corporations. Elaborating, we might say that corporations are permitted to focus on value creation for their owners, but only when other bodies secure background conditions that ensure a just distributive outcome overall, – thus promoting and protecting the vital interests of all. It is within such a complex division of moral labour and responsibility that Milton Friedman's claims might be justifiable.

This justificatory strategy for the unbridled pursuit of profit by corporations and their investors fails under globalization as we know it today. International commerce benefits very many participants, but the distribution of moral responsibility fails some third parties abysmally. Many are detrimentally affected: obligations to protect workers' rights and other human rights are not honoured, nor are educational obligations, partly due to governments' inability or unwillingness to tax.

One central reason is that the opportunity space for different actors has shifted, particularly strikingly and urgent in the case of multinational corporations – which themselves are part of the reason why many governments are sapped of opportunities to protect and promote their citizens' basic interests and human rights. Governments appear unable to secure a decent economic floor and a safe working environment for workers in the global economy, from fear that such requirements will lead multinationals to exit.

Economic and financial globalization reduces many states' ability to protect and promote citizens' social, economic, civil and political interests, when they come into conflict with corporations' interests. Governments compete for mobile capital, possibly in a race to the bottom as regards wages, labour rights, or environmental and safety standards. These changes affect the moral justification of a distribution of responsibilities between states and corporations.

Under such conditions, we must reconsider whether corporations and investors should still be excused from all other moral obligations than the pursuit of their economic self interest. The changes in the options and capacities of corporations and domestic governments threaten and sometimes demolish plausible defences of corporations and their investors' licence to pursue profits unbridled by concerns to respect and protect vital interests of others, or to secure a fair distribution of benefits. If global markets and their major players are to be normatively justified, they may have to shoulder the responsibility to distribute benefits and to prevent harms, together with states, international civil society and consumers – insofar as this is possible under other institutional arrangements. – at least corporations and their investors have to take on these responsibilities in the medium range, until such times that states, or a coalition of states act to close this 'governance gap' (Ruggie, 2007: §82).

I submit that norms that prohibit individual corporations from moral complicity in human rights violations, and other norms of socially responsible investing (SRI) may be interpreted as a central part of such requirements of global or cosmopolitan justice.

For our purposes, we may rely on the definition of SRI offered by Kinder, Lydenberg and Domini:

> An investment that combines an investors financial objectives with his or her commitment to social concerns, such as peace, social justice, economic development, or a healthy environment; an investment, which may or may not have economic return as its principal goal, made with an intent to take into account the impact of the investment on the society in which the investment is made.
>
> (Kinder, Lydenberg, and Domini, 1992: 852, as quoted in Vallentin, 2003: 114)

When sound SRI norms are established and generally complied with, the 'global basic structure' as a whole may be closer to satisfy the normative requirement of respecting and protecting the vital interests of all, and to ensure a fair distribution of the benefits – even under economic and financial globalization where legitimate political structures of governance are not yet in place.

I submit that SRI and corporate social responsibility norms may be interpreted and assessed in this light.

10.3 THREE NORMATIVELY VALUABLE OBJECTIVES AND STANDARDS FOR INVESTORS

I here lay out what I regard as three normative objectives that responsible investment practices must handle in defensible ways, to be consistent with cosmopolitan justice under present conditions of globalization. In no particular order, and most decisively not in order of moral priority, these three are:

1. To secure returns – indeed, possibly to *maximize* returns for shareholders, – but constrained or combined with the two other normative objectives. These further concerns seek to respect the fundamental interests of all parties affected by the investment, in two distinct ways.
2. To improve on the wrongs in the world, including those perpetrated by corporations within the global economy. One central means is by *active shareholder engagement*, aimed in part directly at preventing wrongs from occurring, by seeking to change unacceptable practices in each corporation and to overcome collective actions concerning such issues as environmental problems, fundamental ownership rights, etc. Selection of corporations for such engagement should be according to where the expected marginal impact of a particular shareholder's involvement will be largest – both directly on management and on the willingness of other shareholders, to prevent the most outrageous wrongs.

   Thus shareholder engagement *cannot* justifiably be limited to those issues that maximize return in the long run.

3 To avoid moral complicity in the wrong acts that nevertheless do occur. The main mechanism of concern here is to divest from certain corporations, especially where gross violations of certain fundamental norms must be expected to continue – e.g. where the violations are part of the business strategy and essential to give the corporation a comparative advantage.

Of course, we should not forget that such divestment still leaves other investors to continue to urge change from within, and those parties who divest are free to pursue *other* means to influence those businesses – e.g. by changing the regime: the rules and practices they operate within. We see these possibilities already in what was arguably the first-ever case of socially responsible investing. In 1696 a Quaker community decided to not invest in some of the earliest multinationals – the companies that owned slave ships (Føllesdal, 2007; 2010). The Quakers continued to lobby other important actors, so that eventually the British Parliament eventually outlawed the slave trade.

The Norwegian Government Pension Fund Global provides one interesting case of implementing socially responsible investment norms.

10.4 THE NORWEGIAN GOVERNMENT PENSION FUND – GLOBAL

The investment practices of the Norwegian Government Pension Fund draw international attention, partly due to its mechanisms for socially responsible investing.[2]

The Fund is meant to help shoulder the future economic burden invoked by demographic changes combined with declining oil revenues for Norway. The Ministry of Finance has delegated responsibility for the operational management of the Fund's international assets to Norges Bank Investment Management – NBIM. NBIM achieves an impressive return, in fulfilment of its obligation to secure that a portion of Norway's petroleum wealth also benefits future generations of Norwegians. The market value of the Government Pension Fund – Global at 30 December 2009 was 2,640 billion kroner (approximately US$446 billion or €330 billion). In 2009 it yielded a total return of 25.6 per cent (Norges Bank Investment Management, 2010).

The Norwegian Parliament has also sought to ensure that the Fund does not contribute to unethical acts or omissions, such as violations of fundamental humanitarian principles, serious violations of human rights, gross corruption or

2 The Norwegian Ministry of Finance revised these guidelines during 2009–10; the presentation concerns the practices and guidelines in place until 2009.

severe environmental damage. It has established two main mechanisms to avoid such complicity. These mechanisms ensure that the Fund is involved in SRI of two distinct kinds (Vallentin, 2003: 117): an activist approach and a negative approach.

The Fund must exercise its ownership rights to reflect the UN's Global Compact and the OECD's principles of corporate governance and guidelines for multinational companies.

In addition, Parliament established a Council on Ethics to assist the Ministry of Finance and the Fund, so as to avoid the risk of moral complicity in particularly problematic cases. The Council may recommend that the Minister of Finance exclude certain corporations from the portfolio of the Fund. By the end of 2009, 48 companies had been excluded (Etikkrådet, 2010: 6). In the following we consider some details of how these filters are operationalized.

10.5 HOW THE COUNCIL ON ETHICS IMPLEMENTS SRI STANDARDS

The Fund shall not invest in certain corporations, as identified by the Council on Ethics. The mandate of the Council specifies two central tasks. It shall first screen companies that produce weapons that violate fundamental humanitarian principles. Secondly, it shall recommend exclusion of companies that, through acts or omissions, entail an unacceptable risk that the Fund contributes to certain unethical acts:

- Serious or systematic human rights violations, such as murder, torture, deprivation of liberty, forced labour, the worst forms of child labour and other forms of child exploitation.
- Serious violations of individuals' rights in situations of war or conflict.
- Severe environmental damage.
- Gross corruption.
- Other particularly serious violations of fundamental ethical norms.

The Council may act on its own initiative or as requested by the Ministry of Finance.

Assisted by a Secretariat, the Council gathers information as it sees fit, to document claims made for and against the corporation in question. A wide range of sources have been exploited: companies' own websites, the Norwegian People's Aid landmine division, Human Rights Watch's Arms Division, Jane's Information Group, the International Campaign to Ban Landmines (ICBL), and the Norwegian Ministry of Foreign Affairs.

The procedure also includes an adversarial arrangement, so that companies seriously considered for exclusion are invited to comment and challenge the proposed recommendation before the Council makes its final recommendation.

Recommendations are submitted to the Ministry of Finance, which may heed the advice and instruct the Norwegian Central Bank to exclude the company. The Bank usually has a window of two months to sell its shares, before the Ministry makes its decision public. Important for assessing the impact of such recommendations is that the mandate, the recommendations and their grounds are publicly available in Norwegian and English at the Council website http://www.etikkradet.no.

To give some indications of the workload of the Council, every month various searches reveal approximately 30 companies as possible violators of the guidelines. Of these, two to four are considered with greater care by the secretariat and Council. In 2009, sixteen recommendations for exclusion were made public by the Ministry by the year's end.

To implement the guidelines the Council must interpret and operationalize them in ways that merit some comments.

With regard to the negative screening of companies that produce weapons that violate fundamental humanitarian principles, the debate in Parliament made clear that companies should be excluded that 'develop and produce key components to nuclear weapons'. This goes beyond the production of nuclear warheads, to include the missiles that carry these warheads, and to testing and maintaining them.

Parliament also made clear that companies that contribute to cluster weapons are to be excluded. The Council interpreted this to include companies that produce key components, such as the canisters and guidance mechanisms, and the 'bomblets' themselves. Similar considerations lay behind the exclusion of companies involved in the production of some other weapons, such as anti-personnel mines.

The Council has laid out several conditions that must be satisfied, for a company to be held morally complicit in present human rights violations:

- There must be a linkage between the company's activities and the relevant human rights violations.
- The violations must be perpetrated in order to secure the company's interests.
- The company must have contributed to the violations, or be aware of the violations yet have refrained from attempts to prevent them.
- The violations must be ongoing, or there must be an unacceptable risk that they will occur in the future, as for instance established by past conduct.

In 2005 the Council recommended excluding Kerr-McGee Corporation due to its contract with the Moroccan state oil company ONAREP exploring oil offshore Western Sahara. The concern was whether investment in the company would put the Fund at risk, to contribute to future acts or omissions that would violate fundamental ethical norms. The Moroccan authorities claim sovereignty over the area, while the UN established Western Sahara as a Non-Self-Governing Territory under the UN Charter in 1963. The Norwegian official position is to not prejudice peace efforts by the UN. The Council found that Kerr-McGee contributed to the aim of Morocco. When Kerr-McGee later ceased this activity, the company was re-introduced into the investment universe.

In comparison, the Council did not find that the Fund's investments in Total violated the guidelines, even though Total operated in Myanmar (Burma). Total was accused of complicity in past human rights violations, and ongoing complicity, since Total continued to generate revenue for the Myanmar regime. But since only risk of *future* guideline violations merits exclusion, *past* violations are insufficient except as indication of future breaches. The Council considered it unlikely that Total would start projects that would involve similar human rights violations. This was partly because of the very negative reputation wrought by such past allegations.

Among important issues to be resolved is the relevant kind of moral complicity in human rights violations. Some of the relevant sources is international case law on companies' complicity in war crimes, including the Nuremberg tribunal that sentenced senior executives of companies producing Zyklon B gas for the Nazi regime.

John Ruggie, UN Special Representative of the Secretary-General on the issue of human rights and transnational corporations and other business enterprises, notes that:

> A company trying in good faith to avoid involvement in human rights abuses might have difficulty knowing what counts as moral support for legal purposes. Mere presence in a country and paying taxes are unlikely to create liability. But deriving indirect economic benefit from the wrongful conduct of others may do so, …, it will not be absolved of liability if it knew, or should have known, that it was providing assistance, and that the assistance would contribute to the commission of a crime.
>
> (Ruggie, 2007: § 42)

A few comments may indicate the complexity and special features of these assessments. First, we must distinguish between a risk assessment and what actually ends up occurring. Whether the assessment procedure is sound can best be determined by considering far more cases. Second, for some decisions it is more important to avoid 'false positives', than 'false negatives'. That is, it might be better to exclude too many corporations rather than too few – but sometimes the other way around. In the judicial system it is thus better to err in favour of the guilty. However, for exclusion by the Norwegian Pension Fund, arguments may be stronger for a risk assessment that is as accurate as possible: Moral obligations are in favour both of maximizing yield and to avoid complicity in wrongdoing.

Finally, the Council can decide to reverse its recommendations – either to start divesting, or to re-include particular companies in the investment universe again. Changes may be due to changes of substance – as with Kerr-McGee. But indications of risks of future human rights violations may also change.

10.6 ENGAGEMENT OR DIVESTMENT: POTENTIAL CONFLICTS AND OPPORTUNITIES

Engagement through exercise of ownership rights and divestment, as done by the Norwegian Government Pension Fund Global, may sometimes conflict.

In some cases, long-term financial self-interest may go hand in hand with promoting normative objectives. Some such cases may be activism to promote corporate governance issues, e.g. to secure some of the public goods that governments should provide. But if engagement is limited to such issues, important normative concerns may be ignored. Cases may include some of the worst forms of child labour or violations of labour rights. These may be sustainable by some corporations, and even crucial for their maximal yield, even over time. In these cases, we might expect that engagement aimed to maximize yield will not be pursued. Indeed, we cannot expect engagement to change business procedures toward normative standards that will reduce returns. Moreover, bodies that only engage in shareholder activism in order to promote long-term profit alone may want to prevent all divestment from morally objectionable corporations that maximize investments, since such divestment will tend to reduce profits, however slightly.

A related conflict arises if involvement is focused not on those corporations where activism is most likely to reduce evil in the world, but instead mainly to prevent divestment. There is then a high risk that the investor remains morally complicit in wrongdoing, and that ills in the world remain that otherwise might have been addressed by active engagement.

Thirdly, there are tensions if divestment – or even the mere possibility thereof – reduces the impact of involvement. This might happen in at least two ways. The managers of morally objectionable corporations may decide to ignore activist calls to change their ways, in the hope that noisy and 'hypersensitive' investors will pull out. This strategy may be less attractive if the future divestment will occur with enough bad publicity to damage the company reputation and share price. The managers may also find the criteria for divestment so blurry that managers will ignore its repercussions. They may prefer to stick to their previous policies regardless of engagement, since no strategy will avoid the bad press wrought by divestment.

We then consider some opportunities to enhance the effects of shareholder activism and exclusion.

Divestment may boost the objective and impact of shareholder engagement, to promote cosmopolitan justice. I submit that a real, predictable threat of divestment can increase the influence of shareholder engagement, even more so if decisions about divestment are taken by another body than those involved in the dialogues with management. Such a division of labour – as in the Norwegian case – can:

- boost the credibility of warnings of divestment by those engaged with management;

- increase the quality of information from management, and reduce the likelihood of cooptation by those engaged in activism, since lies or distortions are more likely to be detected by an independent body;
- reduce public suspicion that there has been an unacceptable sacrifice that entails moral complicity, to achieve some marginal changes in the corporation – or even in order to not reduce profits.[3]

Such opportunities for mutual enhancement may arise under certain conditions:

(a) When divestment imposes high reputational costs. This is not always the case: some funds, such as the Vice Fund (VICEX) may regard exclusion as a 'buy' signal. Reputational costs may also vary across sectors, and depends crucially on whether the normative triggers are broadly shared. This is a reason to use divestment only for certain violations that are likely to command broad agreement, and which have well argued reasons.
(b) Publicity about reasoned divestment. Publicity and argued decisions are necessary to maximize shaming effects, to facilitate copying by other investors, to strengthen NGOs and other concerned parties, and to facilitate the corporation's strategies for improvement.
(c) Trustworthy and predictable threats. The divestment threat must be credible. This requires publicity about past cases, and about the consequences of failed attempts at shareholder involvement.
(d) Procedures for re-inclusion in the investment universe. Once excluded, there should be real, predictable prospects of lifting a divestment decision, to increase the corporation's willingness to engage in dialogues with 'future shareholders'.
(e) Procedures for dialogue with excluded companies. There should be ways to engage with the corporation to prompt their speedy re-inclusion into the investment universe.

A second way that the two mechanisms enhance each others' objectives is that shareholder engagement may boost the objectives of divestment.

Recall that the objective of divestment mechanisms – such as that addressed by the Council on Ethics – is to avoid risks of moral complicity in violations of certain norms. The aim is *not* to maximize the number of divested companies. Rather: if corporations can credibly commit to internal changes to avoid risks of future complicity, this is a way to avoid having to divest. Shareholder engagement may contribute to such changes.

3 For similar criticism raised against UN Special Rapporteurs on human rights, cf. Americas Watch (1986) *Four failures: A Report on the U.N. Special Rapporteurs on Human Rights in Chile, Guatemala, Iran and Poland*, New York.

But recall that there is sometimes a risk that such changes reduce the profitability and the comparative advantages of the corporation. If so, the investor may nevertheless move its investments elsewhere anyway – but for financial reasons.

Several conditions make activism more conducive to the objectives of the divestment strategy:

(a) Visible and credible changes. The changes must be visible for those deciding on divestment. However, it is not necessary that these changes are seen as the result of, or admitted to result from, the engagement process itself. That may be too difficult to discern, and would not be necessary to avoid complicity.
(b) The corporation's changes must be done with all due speed. Otherwise, the morally best strategy may be to divest, and let other investors be involved in bringing the corporation around. Investments may again be permitted if the risks have been reduced.

10.7 LESSONS/IMPLICATIONS

In conclusion, I summarize some of the central implications for the Norwegian system of socially responsible investing, in light of the normative perspective of global or cosmopolitan justice.

10.7.1 The role of transparency

I have argued that many of the processes should be as transparent as possible, both for reasons of fiduciary responsibility, and to maximize learning among corporations. This case is even stronger in circumstances such as the Norwegian Pension Fund Global, which manages public funds. This adds an argument of democratic accountability to these mechanisms.

10.7.2 Clear standards and indicators

The normative standards and indicators must be as clear as possible, when it comes to measuring shareholder impact, to determine when exclusion should occur, and standards for re-inclusion. These standards should be informed by considerations of global justice, with due attention to the challenges of corporations whose competitors may not abide by the same rules. The fact of frequent 'partial compliance' does not yield the conclusion that corporations should not be bound by any norms, but the norms may reasonably be different. And the damages wrought by these 'governance gaps' that allows corporations to continue to violate the basic interests of individuals, lend further support to the calls for more just structures of global governance.

I have argued that globalization – the cross-border impact of a wide range of actors – increases the need for a Cosmopolitan Justice that can address the obligations of non-state actors. One important such issue area concerns the responsibilities of corporations and investors. We have considered some of the normative constraints on the investments of the Norwegian Government Pension Fund in light of cosmopolitan justice, and explored how these norms are brought to bear on investment strategies by means of ownership rights and divestment. I have suggested some lessons with regard to clarity of rules and transparency, drawing on normative perspectives of cosmopolitan justice that seek to ensure that all affected parties are treated as moral and political equals.

Bibliography

Etikkrådet (2010) Årsrapport 2009, http://www.regjeringen.no/pages/1957930/Etikkradet_N2009.pdf.

Føllesdal, A. (2004) 'Political Consumerism as Chance and Challenge', in M. Micheletti, A. Føllesdal and D. Stolle (eds), *Politics, Products and Markets: Exploring political consumerism past and present*, New Brunswick, NJ: Transaction Press.

—— (2007) Ethical Investment and Human Rights: A Norwegian Case, *Nordic Journal on Human Rights* 25: 420–33.

—— (2010) 'Liberal Contractualism – Partial and Particularist, Impartial and Cosmopolitan', in S. Caney, and P. Lehning (eds), *International Distributive Justice: Cosmopolitanism and its critics*, London: Routledge.

Føllesdal, A. and T. Pogge (eds) (2005) *Real World Justice: Grounds, principles, human rights, and social institutions*, Doordrecht: Springer.

Friedman, M. (1970) 'The Social Responsibility of Business is to Increase its Profits', in Beauchamp, T. L. and Bowie, N. E. (eds), *Ethical Theory in Business*, Englewood Cliffs, NJ: Prentice-Hall.

Norges Bank Investment Management (2010) Annual Report of the Norwegian Government Pension Fund Global 2009, http://www.nbim.no/Global/Reports/2009/NBIM_annual report09.pdf.

Rawls, J. (1971) *A Theory of Justice*, Cambridge, MA: Harvard University Press.

Satz, D. (2007) 'Liberalism, economic freedom, and the limits of markets', *Social Philosophy and Policy*.

Epilogue

Frictions of hospitality and the possibilities of cosmopolitan justice in everyday life

Thomas Hylland Eriksen

The term 'justice' can be an everyday concept, or a lofty and formal one. Cosmopolitan justice can refer to a particular kind of rule of law whereby universal rights and entitlements trump parochial identities and selective distribution of rights: a condition where the ideal is to treat all humans equally; where rights reside in our shared humanity and not in the colour of the passport or a person's skin.

Yet cosmopolitanism cannot refer merely to a formal arrangement of jurisdiction and politics where it is sought, at the large-scale level of state affairs, to transcend the limitations of ethnicity and territorial boundaries. Charity begins at home, and in a cosmopolitan society, everyday practices and interpersonal relations strive to fulfil the requirements of cosmopolitanism: a practical humanism where the respect for difference is balanced with the conviction that humans are equally valuable. Cosmopolitanism in practice, or everyday cosmopolitanism, tends to be intuitive rather than theoretical in its motivation; it is implicit where theoretical cosmopolitanism spells everything out; it takes place in the small situations of everyday life – greetings on the street, cups of tea, civility on the bus – and forms the glue, the substratum of civil society that is necessary for cosmopolitan law to be possible at a higher level of systemic integration. In the context of migration and cultural diversity characteristic of North Atlantic societies today, many of the frictions and tensions involving majorities and minorities can be traced to a lack of everyday cosmopolitanism. Notwithstanding variations and fluctuations in immigration regimes and integration policies aimed at immigrants, the main evidence of a functioning society lies in interpersonal relations. A key term to be explored in this regard is hospitality, a universal sign of openness and respect, a relationship which places a burden not only on the host but also on the guest, and which can easily turn awry when the parties either do not understand or do not respect each other.

In an analysis of everyday life in a small hamlet on the southern seaboard of Norway, Døving (2001, 2003) develops some subtle insights into the dynamics of hospitality, a foundational practice of all human societies and a precondition for practical cosmopolitanism. Describing the conventions of social visits in the community, he asks what the reaction would be if a guest insisted on being served nothing but a glass of water. Convention dictates that tea or coffee be served on such visits, usually along with a slice of cake or some biscuits.

In Norway, 'a glass of water' usually means tap water, which is, in effect, tantamount to nothing. 'Water', Døving notes (2003: 30), 'is something one tends to think of as free. It is categorised as an unlimited good.' Referring to the Biblical myth in which Jesus transformed water into wine, Døving notes that water was not seen as fit for wedding guests in ancient Galilee either.

By refusing to imbibe anything but water, the guest refuses to accept the host's offer of reciprocity. In effect, s/he rejects an offer of engaging in a relationship of mutual moral commitment. This is the reason why the host has a culturally sanctioned right to feel offended. (Now, as an experiment of thought, project this generic situation onto a global canvas involving minority rights claims, international academic collaboration, development aid or simply diplomacy, and you see why I think the example is significant in the present context.)

My friend Eduardo Archetti, an Argentine anthropologist who settled in Norway from the early 1970s until his death in 2005, often commented upon the inclination towards balanced reciprocity characteristic of civil society in Norway. If he bought a colleague a cup of coffee in the canteen, he said, the colleague would immediately pay him for the coffee. Rather than entering into a long-term relationship of small gift exchanges, the colleague would 'settle his debt' here and now. This prevented, in Archetti's interpretation, the glue of civil society from thickening.

By refusing to accept a gift, one effectively says: I refuse your friendship. In Marcel Mauss's seminal treatment of the gift (Mauss 1995 [1924]), the institution of gift exchange (which can be material or immaterial) consists of three elements: the obligation to give, the obligation to receive, and the obligation to offer a return gift. The fulfilment of these three elements ensures that respect is confirmed and trust can develop.

One can be a disgraceful guest by demanding too much or too little of the host. But one can also be a disgraceful host, by not showing any interest in one's guests. A host can serve the most sumptuous dishes, but little is gained if he declines to listen to the guest's conversation or refuses to accept an offer of a return visit. In such a situation, the guest is left humiliated.

Many refugees and immigrants in rich countries feel this way about their relationship to the host society. The refugees have been offered shelter and food, for which they are grateful, and they now wish to reciprocate by doing something in return. They are often denied the right to do so. Nationalist populists of every political shade (in Norway, incidentally, represented not just in the traditional populist party but also in the Labour Party) sometimes argue the need to 'place demands on immigrants'. This kind of formulation turns the problem on its head and reveals a poor understanding of the dynamics of reciprocity. In fact, there is nothing immigrants want more than to have demands placed upon them, which would indicate that they are needed, that someone out there needs their contribution to society. I have met asylum-seekers at detention centres who have spent months waiting for a decision. They are grateful to Norwegian society for having given them protection, but they have one big wish: to be allowed to do something useful.

King Carl XIV Johan of Sweden and Norway (1763–1844) was an immigrant from France. Born Jean-Baptiste Bernadotte, he never learnt to speak Swedish, but his motto is telling of the aspirations of many immigrants – *Folkets kärlek, min belöning*: 'The love of the people – my reward'. Carl Johan struggled hard to gain the love of his people, and in spite of some controversial attempts to increase his power in Norway, he succeeded well enough for the prestige street of Christiania (now Oslo) still to be named after him, more than 100 years after the dissolution of the Swedish–Norwegian union.

Immigration policies in Europe tend to be based on suspicion and indifference, immigration generally being seen as a problem rather than an opportunity. A truly hospitable attitude would encourage a situation where minorities were able to gain the love of the people. This demands of the majority that they do not insist on 'just a glass of water' when offered something from the minorities. A lack of interest in one's guests may in fact be a more serious impediment to integration than is commonly assumed. It creates asymmetrical relationships, where humiliation may take over from gratitude, contempt from pity.

Add to this the situation in Afghanistan, where the soldiers of the occupying forces are advised not to accept food offered by Afghans, nor even to buy fruit in the market, to the considerable annoyment of locals. Instructed to take such precautions, troops from the rich countries bring their own pre-packaged food. One is reminded of the story about Bill Clinton and his staff who, when paying Bangladesh a twelve-hour visit in 2000, were said to have brought everything, including washing water and instant coffee, from home. Being a disgraceful guest is scarcely more productive of mutual trust and respect than being a disgraceful host.

Hospitality, in other words, relies on the observance of the simple rules of reciprocity, which, when followed, engender trust and respect. Yet, giving and receiving in a mutually bonding fashion, so crucial both in social and intercultural relationships, presuppose a social ontology where difference is not seen as a threat, and where the world is acknowledged to be a complex web of interlocking cultural spheres. To this issue I now turn – the problem of cosmopolitanism, its pernicious cousin, identity politics, and its opposite, imperialism.

* * *

Asked, doubtless by an adoring disciple, about the nature of truth, the German polymath and iconoclast Rudolf Steiner reacted by asking a counter-question: 'What is the truth about a mountain?' Responding to his own question, the great man said that one could approach the mountain from the north, from the south, from the east and from the west – and, indeed, from above – and one would see different things. And, one might add: one could approach the mountain with the mind of a mountaineer, a geologist, a skier, a landscape painter … so what is truth? Perhaps the most sacred contribution of European thought to world culture is the insight that all these views of the mountain are equally true and that we need a world where all the perspectives have a rightful place. As Goethe famously said: 'He who speaks no foreign language knows nothing of his own.' This openness is a prerequisite for a cosmopolitan attitude, seeing the world's inhabitants as equals, not as friends and enemies.

Tzvetan Todorov, in his memoir from the twentieth century, *Mémoire du mal, tentation du bien* (Todorov, 2000), describes three dangers facing the post-totalitarian world. One is instrumentalization of social relations – typically expressed as unfettered market liberalism, or rather, a loss of the social principles of solidarity and decency, which prevented markets from expanding outside the economy, strictly speaking, and which also curtailed the power of state bureaucracies in liberal societies. In passing, it may be mentioned that these anxieties are neither uncommon nor new. Similar concerns with bureaucracies were expressed by the inventor of the theory of modern bureaucracy, Max Weber, and anxieties about market expansion were voiced by Habermas in the 1960s, Lukács in the 1920s, and Marx in the 1850s. The second danger is moral correctness – sanctimonious and authoritarian conformism, in European countries typically expressed through the recently implemented bans on smoking in public places. The third danger identified by Todorov is the main topic to be explored here: fragmenting identity politics, where universal values are bracketed in the name of group self-determination, where commitment to shared societal projects is weakened, and where open conflict between identity-based groups may easily flare up – not so much because they are culturally different, but because they have few interests in common. This is a vision of a classic plural society without a colonial ruling class.

I share all his anxieties, although I might have wanted to add one or two myself. Yet there can be no easy way out. The only credible responses to the challenges facing humanity have to be ambivalent, doubtful, cautious, with instincts favouring pluralism and a multiplicity of voices, rather than universal recipes for happiness. It is, in other words, the openmindedness of the Renaissance and the optimistic view of human nature of the Enlightenment that we should carry with us in this new, old world, as the convenor of this conference has reminded us. It is an ironic fact – given that neither the USA of the Bush II era (2001–2008) nor its adversaries, real as well as imagined, are easily given to ambivalence – that the two perhaps most influential ideological thinkers of the American right are both partly correct, although they are wrong in crucial respects. Both are authors of widely distributed books about the 'new world order', and both are listened to keenly in circles near the White House. However, they seem to be saying opposite things. Francis Fukuyama (1992) has argued that Western democracy is the only game in town worthy of the name, and that global politics nowadays simply consists in attempts, by the less unfortunate nations, to achieve the same levels of consumption and liberal rights as those enjoyed by Americans. In this context, he also argues that the quest for recognition is fundamental and accounts for various forms of identity politics. The late Samuel Huntington (1996), on the other hand, has argued that current and future conflicts take place not between ideologies, but between 'civilizations', that is related clusters of cultures, such as the West, Islam, Hinduism and Eastern Christianity. Both Fukuyama and Huntington have been severely criticized by academics and other intellectuals, and this is not the place to repeat all the criticisms. On the contrary, I would argue that they are both partly right. Fukuyama is right to assume that recognition by others is a notoriously scarce resource in the contemporary world, but he is wrong in believing that recognition can only be achieved through the successful adoption of Western values and ways of life. Huntington is correct in saying that cultural differences are important, but he is hopelessly off the mark when he tries to map out those differences – his concept of civilizations is theoretically inconsistent and empirically misleading – and there is also no reason to assume that such differences necessarily lead to conflict. In fact, it has been shown that *none* of the armed conflicts of the 1990s were in line with Huntington's predictions (Fox, 2000).

We must nonetheless concede that these conservative American thinkers correctly argue that recognition and respect are important, and that cultural differences matter in politics. Now, where does this lead us?

The above reasoning appears to lead us in the general direction of postcolonial theory. According to writers like Frantz Fanon, Ngugi wa Thiong'o and Edward Said, the most difficult form of decolonization consists in decolonizing the mind (Ngugi, 1985); in developing a self, and an identity, and a self-consciousness which is not based on the categories of the colonizers. In giving the people of the world the choice of being either with the US or with the terrorists, Bush II infamously refused to acknowledge any position which is developed out of other concerns than the US–Al-Qaeda axis.

In the context of the twenty-first century global security crisis involving US global military hegemony and violent reactions often based on the politics of identity, this starting point implies certain preliminary conclusions: Effective human rights activism requires at least a minimal knowledge about local contexts and, particularly, about local conflicts. For poor countries to give wholehearted support to notions of the inalienable rights of the individual, more is required than decisions to cut aid to countries which are not yet committed to a free press and multi-party parliamentary democracy. What is needed are social reforms which give people increased control over their own existence – land reforms, job opportunities, accountable state institutions and so on. As an implication, a global policy is needed where both big power (state, geopolitics) and small power (family, community) are more equitably distributed. This struggle, moreover, is as much about the means of communication as about the means of production. As the late Algerian author Rachid Mimouni put it, what ought to be required of the Europeans is 'an attempt to understand rather than material aid. What can democracy mean in a country like Ethiopia, where dozens die of starvation every day?' (Mimouni, 1992: 156). There are, in other words, serious problems which are not solved by a formulaic introduction of human rights, and there are people who for perfectly understandable reasons see talk about the freedom of expression as a diversion from the real issues. One may by all means argue that Muslim men should give their wives the same rights and opportunities as, say, Scandinavian women have (opinions are free), but it would be silly to assume that they think in the same way as we do. If one does so – promoting human rights with the subtlety of a bulldozer – one implicitly says, as missionaries and foreign aid aristocrats have done for years, that the experiences of others have no value, and that the others had better become like ourselves before we bother to listen to them. One actually says that they *do not exist* until they have become similar to ourselves. Respecting other life-worlds is, it must be emphasized, not the same as ethical relativism, but on the contrary a recognition of the need for a dialogue to go both ways, since the alternative is monologue or worse: the sound from one hand clapping.

The very conceptual pair 'The West' and 'Islam' is deeply problematic. 'The West' is a vague, relational, pseudo-geographic term, which includes the EU, the USA and their richest satellites (Canada, Norway etc.), as well as two of the easternmost countries in the world, Australia and New Zealand. Islam is a universalistic religion with adherents in every country, including all the Western ones. Could 'The West and the East' have been used instead, as a more consistent dichotomy; or perhaps 'Christianity and Islam', as in the old days? Hardly. All such dichotomies are Trojan horses concealing the hidden agenda of overstating the importance of one particular boundary at the expense of neglecting all the others.

There is little to indicate that religion as such can be a source of conflict. A Christian fundamentalist has more in common with a Muslim fundamentalist, at the level of basic values, than each of them has with non-religious persons. The forms of religiosity and the expressions of respect for al-Lah (or God, as we say in English), are similar in both cases. Many European Muslims have discovered this and have joined Christian Democratic parties. Moreover, there are important ecumenical dialogues taking place across 'religious divides' in many places, including a major Islamic conference in Cairo in 1995, where central Muslim leaders condemned all forms of terrorism on Islamic grounds, calling for extensive dialogue with the other monotheistic religions from West Asia. At a more everyday level, it is easy to see that folk religiosity on either side of the Mediterranean, for example, has many similarities – saints, prayers, beliefs in the evil eye, and so on. One should also keep in mind that, following the attacks of 11 September 2001, all Muslim heads of state except for Saddam Hussain and the Taliban condemned the mass murder. On the very evening that the towers fell to the ground, the *Tehran Times* stated that Islam forbids suicide, and that the murder of an innocent, according to the Koran, is tantamount to the murder of all humanity.

Malaysia's then prime minister Mahathir offered to negotiate between the USA and its adversaries in the autumn of 2001, and this might have been a fruitful move: Malaysia is an overwhelmingly Muslim country, but it is also committed to Western notions of modernity. The USA did not take up the offer, and during a visit a month after the bombing, I heard of no Malays who defended the terrorist attacks, though a lot of them seemed to admire Osama for his courage.

If Malaysia's 'moderate Islam' (which has, admittedly, in some ways turned less 'moderate' more recently) had been granted its place in the sun, fewer Malays would have looked up to Osama bin Laden, and more Westerners would have discovered the similarities between the three great West Asian religions. Seen from a Hindu or East Asian point of view, the three religions appear virtually identical. Even from the inside, the parallels are striking. The Muslims who have joined Christian Democratic parties in European countries have done so because Christians and Muslims have shared interests in fighting phenomena such as religious slackness, secularization, birth control and divorces. During another Cairo conference, in the autumn of 1994, the Catholic Church and Muslim clerics joined forces to make a joint statement condemning abortion. Moreover, many – anthropologists, journalists and others – relentlessly show the absurdity of lumping together Indonesian rice farmers with Turkish merchants under the umbrella of 'Islam'; just as intellectuals in Muslim countries are perfectly well aware that 'the West' contains something close to a billion individuals with a variety of values, societies and ways of life.

The current trend is nonetheless one of growing polarization. The relationship between the West and Islam, as it has developed since the Gulf War, is beginning to resemble the armaments race between the USA and the Soviet Union. In the end, both superpowers had enough nuclear weapons to annihilate humanity many times over. These days, self-proclaimed representatives of both Islam and the West compete – not over the number of warheads, but over the souls of unattached individuals, in rhetorical attacks on each other. In research on ethnic relations, this kind of mechanism can be called *contrasting*, that is the mutual defining of the other as the opposite of oneself – as that which one does not want to be (Eriksen, 2010). Enemy images always depend on this or a similar kind of simplistic, stereotypical depictions of the other. Realistic, nuanced descriptions contain too many shades of grey and too much complexity to be of ideological use in creating hatred and implacability. Seen from the north-west, Muslims, or 'Islam', may thus appear as undemocratic, sexist, illiberal, underdeveloped, brutal and culturally stagnated. The enemy image, incidentally, is adjusted as the relationship changes historically. While the generalized Muslim woman today is depicted as an oppressed, intimidated and powerless person, it was common in Victorian times to depict her as a profoundly erotic, mystical and seductive character.

Seen from the south-east, the Europeans, or the people of the West, may appear as cold individualists, as normless, immoral, arrogant, brutal, decadent and insensitive. These dichotomizations owe little to objective differences between Islam and Christianity, but to power relations feeding into assumptions about cultural differences. Roughly the same stereotypes that are now commonly used about Muslims have been used variously to describe South Europeans, North Norwegians, blacks and 'Hindoos' in the past. They are responses to a need in the population where the stereotypes are formed, rather than expressions of characteristics in the stereotyped population.

Muslim stereotypes of 'the West' would themselves have been worthy of a book-length treatment; suffice it here to say that they are no less simplistic and no less antithetical to openness and dialogue than the eastern images of Islam and Muslims. For a recent example, it has been shown how the Pakistani press, in the months following the attacks, contributed to strengthening mutual stereotyping through portraying the 'clash of civilizations' perspective as the only Western view of the matter.

Beyond cultural stereotypes is the language of undiluted bigotry and chauvinism, as in certain forms of war reporting. During the Gulf War, the Western press wrote of the US-led forces as 'lionhearts, professional, heroes, daring, loyal, resolute, brave', while Iraqi soldiers were described as 'brainwashed, paper tigers, cowardlike, desperate, the bastards from Baghdad, mad dogs, unscrupulous, fanatical'. Some years later, Bush II spoke of the suicide pilots of 11 September notoriety as 'cowards'. As Susan Sontag pointed out shortly afterwards, many strong words may be used to describe these madmen (such as, for example, brainwashed or psychotic), but cowards they were definitely not. Similarly, it is difficult to defend the view that the US pilots, who dropped their cluster bombs on Afghanistan from a comfortable height before returning for breakfast, were exceptionally courageous.

In Gregory Bateson's original model of schismogenesis, elaborated in his seminal *Steps to an Ecology of Mind* (Bateson, 1972), the only way the self-reinforcing circuits could be changed, would be through the interference of a third agent (or network node) leading to a new framing of the issue. Translated into poststructuralist language, the discursive hegemony pitting 'the West' against 'Islam' in a deadly embrace can only be broken through the intrusion of one or several counter-discourses framing the world in different terms. These counter-discourses were abundantly available both before and after 11 September. However, politicians and a majority of influential media commentators seem to accept that the conflict has something to do with the West and Islam, even if they usually concede that Islam is complex and that most Muslims are naturally peaceful. In the Muslim part of the world, where the media are less liberal and the political leadership by and large less attuned to the population, the situation has been different. While the political leaders have supported the US against the Taliban/Al-Qaeda, the media have generally not offered a very nuanced picture of the West, portraying the 'clash of civilizations' view as representative of 'Westerners'. In spite of important cracks in the mutual enemy images, therefore, there are clear indications that they have been strengthened after 11 September. The anti-immigrant new right in the politics of several European countries experienced a healthy growth after the attacks, and in countries like the Netherlands and Denmark, they currently have considerable political power. Public debates about minorities in several European countries have been redefined from a dominant focus on discrimination and labour market issues to a less charitable focus on enforced marriages, sexual mutilation and most recently *hijabs*. Condolezza Rice is on record as having explained to a concerned citizen that the reason 'they' hate 'us' so much, is that 'we elect our leaders' and that 'you and I [meaning women] are allowed to work'. Travelling in Muslim countries in the months following the attacks, the French Islam scholar Gilles Kepel (2002) met religious leaders who worry that the attacks have led to a deep setback in the ongoing, and in many ways progressing intellectual dialogue between Muslims and Westerners.

There are some exceptions. A few influential commentators and politicians saw the terrorist attacks and the retaliation of the USA in the same light. In an address to the summit of the Organization of Islamic Countries in February 2002, Malaysia's then prime minister Mahathir defined a terrorist as 'someone who attacks civilians', thereby seeing the 11 September suicide pilots and the US Air Force over Afghanistan as the same kind of agents.

At this point, some personal reflections of a general character may be appropriate, which have nothing to do with the current impasse in global communication as such, but which concern the role of 'the West', or the North Atlantic, and particularly the USA, in world society. Europeans and North Americans of predominantly European origin have now dominated the world for more than 500 years. It may perhaps be about time that this long hegemony comes to an end, whether it happens indirectly through migration, violently through self-destructive entrenchment against a foe which is generated from within (terrorism), or simply through shifts in the dynamics of the global economy. One may only hope, if this happens in the new century, that the new hegemons will continue to absorb, renew and develop the genuine contributions of European and North American society to global civilization, such as the respect (at least in principle) for human life and integrity, impartial bureaucracy and, especially, the capacity for doubt and ambivalence which has been a trademark quality of European culture (if not of European power politics) since the Renaissance, and where the new American president takes a very different position from his predecessor. It may also be hoped that the new hegemons are able to learn the right lessons from the mistakes of Europe and the West: the fanatical technological optimism, the lack of community and solidarity, the class divisions and indifference, the fundamentalist arrogance in relation to others, the stressful way of life under careerist regimes of work, growing street crime, racism and discrimination, the lack of consideration for the environment ... Looking back on the last centuries – let us say the period that began with Columbus' landing on 12 October 1492 and the subsequent expulsion of Muslims and Jews from Spain a few weeks later – the chances are good that the networked, decentralized world which may now be emerging, can turn out to be more humane than 500 years of European hegemony have been. It will not happen with the help of Osama bin Laden and Taliban-like networks, but it won't happen with the help of American bomber planes either. One would have to be blind and deaf in order to believe that this is the 'best of all possible worlds', a world where every person has the same values and where opportunities are equally distributed. The currencies of the global society are dollars and bombs, and this society speaks business English with an American accent. Nobody ought to be surprised if some of those who are overwhelmed, or overrun, by this power react like greenhouse plants are proverbially supposed to react to heavy metal rock: by rolling up into small, hard balls.

No matter where power and dominance may be concentrated – now and in twenty years – the early twenty-first century appears to be a good period for a renewal of world-views. The old, dominant world-view presented a hierarchical world composed of peoples, civilizations and nations that were clearly delineated in relation to each other, geographically and culturally speaking; they had their own history, their own values and their own customs, as it were. Europe and the West, according to this view, represented reason and progress, even if others had also contributed bits and pieces. This image is now about to be replaced by a world characterized by exile, flows, intensified contacts, creolization, hybridization and all forms of mixing; where no boundaries are absolute, notwithstanding attempts to build ever taller walls; but where people continue to have different experiences because they live under varying circumstances. Territorial power is faltering and is being challenged everywhere – Microsoft to Al-Qaeda – by the more flexible power of networks. If the demands for justice, respect and recognition from Muslims and others are not now met by another response than condescending arrogance, this world will almost certainly catch fire. In the old world, injustice and rage could be 'contained'. Not so in the network world.

This is a world of impurities, fuzzy frontier zones, uncertainties and ambiguities, where the belief in progress is being replaced by ambivalence, where self-confidence is being replaced by anxiety, where trust is threatened by suspicion, and where the ability to listen has become a more important faculty than ever before in history.

However, a mere plea for dialogue and mutual understanding will not do. Nor will it be sufficient, even if it is necessary, to follow Amin Maalouf (2001) and many other subtle and wise intellectuals in showing that each of us has many potential identities, and that it is our duty to resist attempts to classify us as incumbents of only one – be it national, as in this country, or religious, as among many Jews, Hindus and Muslims. This is necessary, I stress, but not sufficient. In order to break out of the vicious circle of identity politics, we need to build structures which immunize politics from their takeover. It is a human right to belong, to feel the security of group membership and the intimate warmth of cultural familiarity – and, of course, conversely, to leave that group or to invent one's own hybrid identity. Making ironic comments about neo-tribalism, as Western liberals routinely do, fails to take the need for security and belonging into account, and it also underestimates the real and perfectly understandable sense of humiliation that is the basis of mobilization for various politics of identity. Instead, impersonal structures must be put into place that prevent legitimate personal and collective identities from degenerating into political mass movements. Nobody has anything to gain from the politicization of religious and ethnic categories. The complaints from the non-North Atlantic world are legitimate, but if they end up crystallizing in secterian religious or ethnic movements, that is an indication that they have been sent to the wrong address. It is our duty to understand how this can happen, and it may often be our duty to engage in earnest dialogue with identity politicians, but it is also our duty to point out that if the human world is going to come to terms with itself, it needs not only economic redistribution and a global dialogic democracy, but it is also going to need universal values and a proper separation of culture, including religion, and politics. But, I have tried to argue, the universalism of the twenty-first century has to be more accommodating and wide-angled than former, unilateral universalisms; it has to make some detours and to acknowledge that the universal is always particular as well. It has to approach the proverbial mountain from all four sides, morning, afternoon and evening.

In a characteristically ambivalent review of Kwame Anthony Appiah's *Cosmopolitanism* (Appiah, 2006), John Gray states that 'As a position in ethical theory, cosmopolitanism is distinct from relativism and universalism. It affirms the possibility of mutual understanding between adherents to different moralities but without holding out the promise of any ultimate consensus' (Gray, 2006).

In other words, fervent missionary activity is not, according to this view, compatible with cosmopolitanism, nor is an ethical position which assumes that there is but one good life. The question asked by liberals may be why they should tolerate intolerance; the answer is that they are not asked to do so. They are only asked to coexist with, and collaborate with people of different persuasions when the need arises. Most of the tensions conflicts involving immigrants in Oslo, where I live, are of a practical nature: Why do the parents of immigrant children active in sports so rarely take part in the community work – organizing flea-markets, selling hot dogs on match days and so on – which is essential to raise money for the children? Why do immigrant parents let their children play noisily outside late in the evening? Why do Norwegians never invite their immigrant neighbours for a cup of tea? It is this kind of everyday problem that creates coldness and distance between natives and newcomers – I have yet to hear of a single conflict between ethnic Norwegians and immigrants that directly involved differences in religious beliefs. The main flaw, therefore, in most theoretical accounts of cosmopolitanism consists in their reliance on dialogue, verbal exchange, mutual cognitive understanding and so on. Most of us don't really care which political party the neighbour votes for, and we may not know whether they have any religious beliefs or if they love European classical music as much as we do, nor do we care, as long as they take their turn shovelling snow in our common courtyard during the cold and dark winter months.

Cosmopolitanism may degenerate into missionary liberalism, but it may also degenerate into indifference. As long as there are practical tasks at hand, which need to be handled collectively, this is not a danger. If anything, it is the lack of such tasks that prevent cosmopolitanism in North Atlantic societies, not the lack of things to disagree or agree about in the media or in theoretical analyses. This brings us back to the topic with which I began this chapter: the obligation to give, the obligation to receive, and the obligation to offer a return gift. Everyday cosmopolitanism, cosmopolitanism in practice, is as simple as this. And as difficult.

Bibliography

Appiah, K. A. (2006) *Cosmopolitanism: Ethics in a world of strangers*, New York: Norton.

Bateson, G. (1972) *Steps to an Ecology of Mind*, New York: Bantam.

Døving, R. (2001) 'Vaffelhjertets makt – en analyse av norske kvinners hushold' ('The Power of the Waffleheart – An Analysis of the Households of Norwegian Women') in S. Meyer and E. D. Holm (eds), *Varene tar makten*, Oslo: Ad Notam Gyldendal.

—— (2003) *Rype med lettøl. En etnografi fra Norge* ('Grouse with Non-alcoholic Beer. An Ethnography from Norway'), Oslo: Pax.

Eriksen, T. H. (2001) *Bak fiendebildet: Politisk islam og verden etter 11. September* ('Behind the Enemy Image: Political Islam and the World after 9–11'), Oslo: Cappelen.

—— (2010) *Ethnicity and Nationalism: Anthropological Perspectives* (3rd edn), London: Pluto.

Fox, J. (2000) 'Clash of Civilizations or Clash of Religions: Which is a More Important Determinant of Ethnic Conflict?', *Ethnicities* 1(3): 295–366.

Fukuyama, F. (1992) *The End of History and the Last Man*, New York: Avon.

Gray, J. (2006) 'Easier Said Than Done', *The Nation*, 30 January 2006.

Huntington, S. (1996) *The Clash of Civilizations and the Remaking of a World Order*, New York: Simon & Schuster.

Kepel, G. (2002) *Chronique d'une guerre d'orient*, Paris: Gallimard.

Maalouf, A. (2001) *Les identités meurtrières*, Paris: Livres de poche.

Mimouni, R. (1992) *De la barbarie en général et de l'intégrisme en particulier*, Paris: Le pré aux clercs.

Ngugi wa Thiong'o (1986) *Decolonizing the Mind: The Politics of Language in African Literature*, London: Heinemann.

Todorov, T. (2000) *Mémoire du mal, tentation du bien*, Paris: Robert Laffont.

Index